Beautiful Built-Ins

Connie Edwards

McGRAW-HILL

New York   Chicago   San Francisco   Lisbon   London   Madrid
Mexico City   Milan   New Delhi   San Juan   Seoul
Singapore   Sydney   Toronto

McGraw-Hill

A Division of The **McGraw·Hill** Companies

Cataloging-in-Publication Data is on file with the Library of Congress

34567890 DOC/DOC 09876543

ISBN 0-07-137796-4

The sponsoring editor for this book was Shelley Carr, the editing liaison was Steven Melvin, and the production supervisor was Pamela Pelton. It was set in Century Schoolbook by Pro-Image Corporation.

RR Donnelley was printer and binder.

McGraw-Hill books are available at special quantity discounts to use as premiums and sales promotions, or for use in corporate training programs. For more information, please write to the Director of Special Sales, McGraw-Hill, 2 Penn Plaza, New York, NY 10121-2298. Or contact your local bookstore.

 This book is printed on recycled, acid-free paper containing a minimum of 50% recycled, de-inked fiber.

Dedication

To Wendy,
my daughter and best friend
and to the kitchen and bath industry
that I have enjoyed for so many years.

Table of Contents

Introduction: Kitchen Cabinets . . . Where?

I started designing built-ins for other rooms from manufactured kitchen cabinetry many years ago after a bedroom furniture-shopping foray. Finding a headboard that suited me turned out to be relatively easy. It was a beautiful Windsor-style with a warm oak finish. But the casework that went with it, while pretty on the outside, didn't meet my storage needs and offered me no options.

A short time at the drafting board (well, it would be an even shorter time at the computer these days) produced the answer to my dilemma, a chest-of-drawers. As luck would have it, the cabinet company offered a standard color that matched my headboard. The order was placed and several weeks later, the cabinets arrived. Installation went quickly because the cabinets were fully assembled and factory finished. All that had to be done was assemble the base, wood top, upper chest section, apply the crown molding and install the decorative hardware. It was a snap for my professional installer, and the piece still sits in my guestroom today. But bedrooms are not the only place that can benefit from built-in cabinets.

Nearly every room in the house can enjoy the benefits of more storage. And it has a lot to do with the fact that today's lifestyles are increasingly complicated. Our homes have had to evolve to meet our needs. Both parents often work full time and children are involved in a host of after school activities. Evening time has become the only time the family can come together. This lifestyle of the 2000s has caused the open floor plan to be the number one request for new home construction. Even remodeling projects often call for removing the walls between the kitchen and the family room so that everyone can interact during meal preparation and evening activities. Making the cabinets in the adjacent room, whether it is a great room or dining room, match or blend with those in the kitchen makes a lot of sense.

A side benefit of building-in entertainment centers, bookcases, or other cabinets is that the costs can be rolled up into a mortgage or in most cases, home improvement loans. Try doing that with new family room furniture.

No matter what the style of the home or the theme of the interior decorating, the cabinetry can be given a complementary look. Country French calls for arches, wood aprons, and flowing details. Traditional homes often favor cherry cabinetry with mullion doors, deep crown molding, and polished brass hardware. Contemporary calls for simple clean lines, stainless steel decorative hardware, and is often asymmetrical in design.

Country styling may mean different things to different people. Is it a farmhouse, cottage, Southwest, or Shaker look? No matter, there are certain things that all these country styles have in common. Country is always casual, reminiscent of another time and usually features open shelving for collectibles.

Now let's talk about the cabinetry available in the market today. Manufactured cabinets are broken down into three categories, custom, semi-custom, and stock. Custom cabinets are completely made to your order. The quality is usually high and so is the price. But if you are willing to spend the money, you can have an almost unlimited choice of finishes, door styles, and other options. Semi-custom cabinets offer fewer choices in door styles, finishes, and features, but are more affordable. The third category, and the object of this book, is stock cabinets.

The term stock cabinets used to mean that cabinets were made in advance and were sitting (in stock) in a warehouse somewhere. Generally, that is no longer true. New manufacturing processes have made short production times possible today. Each order is made for one customer at a time at even the largest companies. While your choices in finishes are limited (don't look for antiqued lavender cabinets here), they are based on the most popular choices in the marketplace. Door style selections will also be limited, but choices are getting broader every day. You will find an array of flat and raised panel door styles in square and cathedral shapes as well Shaker and Thermofoil offerings. Most will be available in both standard and full overlay construction.

Surprisingly, stock cabinets now come with many features that used to be part of the offering of higher priced cabinetry. Dovetail drawers, optional plywood construction, and an array of moldings and interior accessories are now available. Features like these are what make built-ins from stock cabinetry beautiful both inside and out.

Beautiful Built-Ins can be used as a source book for builders to improve their house plans and offer upgrade options to their clients. It can be a great idea book for remodelers, interior designers, or homeowners. Each of these designs can be adapted to different spaces or decorating styles. Most importantly the book will help you with all aspects of your project. You will discover ideas for every room in the house, walk through the installation of an entertainment center project in Chapter 1, and take a look at a home in Chapter 10 that in filled to the roof with creative built-in storage and work areas.

As you will see, built-ins made from stock kitchen cabinetry don't have to *look* like they were made from kitchen cabinets. Throughout the book there are designs for every room in the home that look like high-priced custom built-ins. It is all a matter of design, proportion, and finish details. In the last two chapters of the book, we will pay special attention to just how to use these elements to create the rooms you want.

Acknowledgments

I thank my past clients, the builders, and magazine editors who have given me many opportunities to create whole house built-ins throughout the country. From those experiences I have learned a great deal of what works and what doesn't.

In addition, I have long admired the works of Frank Lloyd Wright. His use of built-ins as important elements of the whole house has been an inspiration.

In the actual making of this book, I want to thank the staff of McGraw-Hill. No project of this size and duration can be completed without the encouragement, and the assistance and prodding of many people. To all my family and friends, who have borne with me during this process, my sincere appreciation.

A very special thanks to American Woodmark Corporation who very kindly supplied the photographs throughout the book.

CHAPTER 1

Assembly Tips and Tricks: How to Put It All Together

Most stock cabinetry comes fully assembled, so the difficult part of these projects has already been done for you. Do-it-yourselfers can fabricate many of these designs, but nothing beats a qualified cabinet installer for getting the entire job done right. A flawless installation requires careful planning. That flawless installation begins with careful measurement of the space. Measure the height, width, and depth of the space to the nearest 1/8″ inch to be sure that the unit will fit. An old adage says, "You can't put ten pounds of flour in a five pound sack." Likewise, you can't put a 72″-wide hutch on a wall that is 69″ wide. However, most of the plans in this book can be adjusted to fit job-site conditions. It might be as simple as downsizing one or two cabinets while maintaining the overall integrity of the design, so don't give up too easily. Chapter 12, *Striking Out on Your Own,* will give you some additional information on adjusting the designs to fit job-site conditions.

The plans in this book should be re-drawn to scale on paper or with computer-aided design software. Not all manufacturers offer the same exact cabinets, moldings, or panels. For example, some stock manufacturers offer reduced depths and matching interior options, and others do not. So work out the design, in the brand and style of cabinets that you will be using, before proceeding.

Once the plans reflect the desired finished product, the order must be placed, cabinets made, shipped, and delivered. Some cabinets may be in inventory at your local distributor or home center. At the same time, order any specialty materials such as door inserts or hardware, so that everything will be on hand when the installation begins. If countertops are part of your plan, you will find that many fabricators prefer to measure the installed cabinets and make a template for 100% accuracy. So factor extra time for that into your plan. After you have the cabinets at the site and have checked them against the order to make sure that everything is present and accounted for, then the real fun begins.

Standard Overlay versus Full Overlay Cabinet Installation. Full overlay cabinetry (see glossary) requires a few more installation considerations than those using standard overlay cabinetry. For one thing, full overlay cabinets placed against a wall must have a *minimum* one-inch of filler material to allow doors and drawers to open freely. More filler material may be needed if there are window or door casings nearby. Another consideration is top and light rail molding installation. Both must be installed with blocking so that they don't interfere with the opening of cabinet doors. The designs in this book have taken basic full overlay requirements into consideration.

Tools. Most units in this book can be assembled with little more than assorted hand tools, a drill, and a saw. A circular saw will work for many installations, but a table saw is really more useful. If you are creating a unit from white cabinetry, it is best to keep the design simple. White cabinetry tends to show even the most minor installation error. It is also wise to use a brand-new, small-toothed saw blade to reduce chipping of the painted surface.

Room Preparation. If the built-in is to be installed in a new house under construction, baseboard, flooring, and mechanical needs can be accommodated from the very beginning. Remodeling jobs will probably require changes in electricity and plumbing. Certainly you will have to deal with how the new cabinets will affect the flooring and baseboards. You may even have to alter crown molding at the ceiling in some cases. Whether new construction or a remodeling project, be sure to use qualified professionals and follow all building codes and licensing requirements.

Like most cabinet installations, begin by finding the high spot in the floor, shim and level the cabinets to this point. Most installations will begin with corner base cabinets and work outwards. A straight run will usually begin with the middle cabinet and work outwards.

Pre-Assembly. Often there is work that can be done before the cabinets are actually installed in their final location. If there are stacked wall cabinets, such as the Break-front Design on page 411, vertical sections can be fitted together ahead of time. The exposed sides of stacked cabinets can be finished with paneling (also called skins) applied to cover the joints well ahead of time.

Often wall cabinets are used as base cabinets as in the Corner Hutch on page 415. When this application is used, a platform is built from dimensional lumber to support the cabinet at the right height off the floor.

This work too can be done ahead of time. Partial assembly of these various components will reduce the time and mess during the final installation.

General Tips. Despite the fact that many of these pieces look like furniture, they are actually built-in cabinetry. Every one must be screwed to the wall for stability and support. Use panhead screws specifically designed for cabinet installation to attach the cabinets to the walls. Panhead screws are preferable to screws with tapered heads that might permit the cabinets to be easily pulled off the wall. Remember, safety first.

To join the cabinet frames together, tapered-head screws are just fine. These screws can often be concealed behind hinge plates. To do this, remove the hinges, pre-drill and countersink the screws first. Then, re-install the hinges. This makes a very clean, professional installation.

Some of the designs in this book require stacking cabinetry. While most stock cabinets are made with pre-finished sides, applying paneling (skins) to conceal the joint is necessary in all but the most utilitarian projects. It is good practice to then skin every exposed side on the unit for continuity of design.

The finishing touch of any built-in is often the molding. High-quality carpentry standards call for careful mitering of corners and staining or painting the raw edges before applying to the cabinetry. All nails used in molding installation should be countersunk and the holes puttied. If the molding application is longer than eight feet, use a scarf joint (see glossary) rather than a butt joint for the least noticeable seam. If the molding treatment consists of several layers, stagger the joints so that they don't all fall in the same line.

Doors and drawers can become misaligned during shipping and handling. One of the last steps in the installation is to adjust all the doors and drawers for proper alignment followed by the installation of the decorative hardware.

Every built-in project is different. Some are simple and some more complex. Let's take a look at the assembly of a three-section television cabinet with side bookcases. The techniques required for the assembly of this somewhat complicated unit are essentially the same for many of the built-ins featured in this book.

Assembly of a Three-Section Entertainment Center

Step 1. Carefully remove the toe kick of the utility cabinet. The cabinet will be inverted for the middle part of the entertainment center.

Step 2. Raise the television floor by blocking and installing a false bottom. Cover the bottom with paneling.

Step 3. If desired, panel the entire upper section. Apply paneling to both exterior

sides of the center unit. Note: for this unit we ordered and installed 170°-opening hinges typically used on lazy susan cabinets. This allows the doors to open fully for television viewing.

Step 4. Clamp and join the wall cabinets used as base cabinets to the bookcase units. Countersink the screws.

Step 5. Trim the skin to fit, and apply to the exterior sides of both the combined cabinets to conceal the joints.

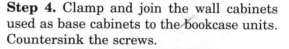

Step 6. Build a 3 1/2″-high platform for the entire unit from dimensional lumber. The platform supports the inverted utility cabinet as well as the wall cabinets used as base cabinets.

Step 7. Securely screw the cabinets to the wall, platform, and each other.

Step 8. Install the rollout shelves in the lower section of the middle cabinet.

Step 9. Install the furniture base consisting of filler material and inside corner molding.

Step 10. Install blocking material at the top of the cabinet to support crown molding.

Step 11. To install the crown, cut to fit, miter, and pre-drill the molding. Install with 4d finishing nails, countersink nails, and putty the holes. The final step is to adjust the doors and drawers for proper alignment and the installation of the decorative hardware.

Even though this installation is one of the more complex in the book, a professional installer will make quick work of this project. A skilled do-it-yourselfer should be able to assemble this unit in a weekend. And look at the results!

Reading the Plans in this Book

Cabinet types and sizes are shown in two ways:

First, the Cabinet Lists show general descriptions and dimensions. A cabinet may be described as a 36″×30″ wall cabinet. Or a base cabinet might be called out as a 15″ drawer base.

Second, the floor plans show generic industry abbreviations for cabinets:

- *Wall cabinets* are shortened to "W" followed by the cabinet dimensions shown width first, and then height. For example, a W1830 is a wall cabinet 18″ wide and 30″ high. The cabinet depth is indicated only when it varies from the standard 12″.

- *Base cabinets* are abbreviated to "B" plus the width since standard kitchen base cabinets are 24″ deep. A B15 is a base cabinet that is 15″ wide.
- *Drawer Bases* are shown as "DB" plus the width. A DB18 is an 18″ drawer base.
- *Utility cabinets* are shown as "UT" plus the width, depth AND height. A UT3024×96 is a tall utility cabinet that is 30″ wide by 24″ deep by 96″ high.

While this book shows some variations, such as a bookcase, a kitchen file base or a vanity cabinet, the same general rules apply. The cabinet is abbreviated to three letters or less followed by the width and then the depth.

CHAPTER 2

Bedrooms, Bathrooms, and Exercise Areas

Bedrooms, bathrooms, and exercise areas are the very private places in our home. We retreat there to relax and unwind. With the frenetic pace we live, no other place in the home deserves as much extra special attention. In this chapter we will look at various ways to make these areas functional and beautiful.

To begin with, today's health and fitness craze has brought an increased interest in home exercise rooms and even spas. Whirlpool and soaking tubs have almost become commonplace in bathrooms, but how about a massage room next door? Check out page 34. Recycling an unused bedroom or dedicating 100 to 200 square feet in a new home to an exercise room is a good investment.

Bedrooms also offer many opportunities to enhance creature comfort. Bedroom furniture sets come with a limited number of options for the casework. And if the standard offering doesn't meet individual needs, well, so much for that. With built-ins, the space can be personalized for function and beauty. Some projects are relatively simple like a bench for the foot of the bed. Others are more complicated such as the bedroom storage wall, which includes space for sophisticated audio-visual equipment. So, whether it is a wall-to-wall dresser or a large make-up area, bedrooms can become the haven that today's consumers are truly looking for. Also check out Chapter 8 for lots of creative ideas for children's bedrooms and bathrooms, too.

Upscale homes, with luxurious master bath suites, call for expanded vanities, often with separate his and her vanity cabinetry. However, well-designed vanity and storage areas can improve bathrooms of every size and style. So, whether the need is for a taller height vanity, extra towel storage, or vanity arrangements with some real style, there are ways to accomplish the task.

Look for innovative ways to use standard components, like a headboard made from replacement cabinet doors or appliance garages and standard wall cabinets called into duty as medicine cabinets. So if the bedroom, bathroom, or exercise area are your focus, stock cabinets make it possible and economical at the same time.

Banjo Vanity

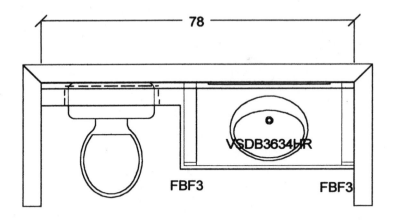

Cabinet List:

1 36″×34 1/2″ high combination vanity
2 base fluted fillers
1 sink front return
4 rosettes
1 8'-0″ base toe material
1 toe kick cap cover
3 knobs or pulls
1 pint stain
1 putty stick

Additional Materials Needed:

- Miscellaneous fasteners and adhesives
- Banjo countertop with access panel
- Dimensional lumber
- Mirror
- Lav and faucet
- Toilet

Required:

- Block and install sink front return behind left fluted filler as a return
- Cleat countertop over toilet

Variations:

- Skin exposed side and apply decorator matching door
- Add valet cabinet over toilet for additional storage

Small bathrooms are often short on counterspace. This arrangement with a countertop extension over the toilet is called a banjo top because of its shape. The real secret here is to have an access panel designed into the extension over the toilet, so that it can be serviced, should the need arise. The access can be hinged or set in place depending on the type of countertop material selected.

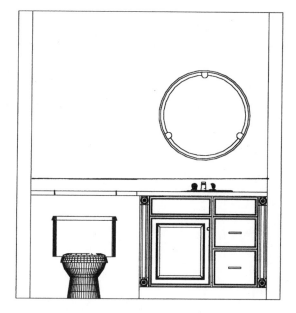

Bedroom Bench

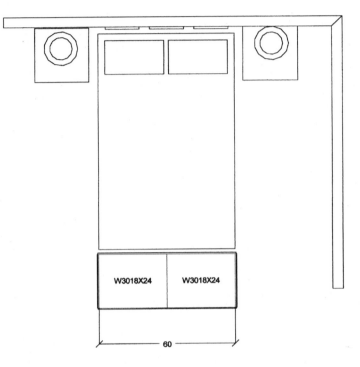

Cabinet List:

2 30"×18"×24" wall cabinets
2 base skins
2 8'-0" countertop edge molding
2 8'-0" scribe molding
4 decorator matching doors
4 knobs or pulls
1 pint stain
1 putty stick

Additional Materials Needed:

- Miscellaneous fasteners and adhesives
- Plywood
- Matching wood countertop
- Cushion

Required:

- Make a top for the bench with plywood and finish the edge with scribe molding
- Install countertop edge molding as 3/4" thick base on bench

Variations:

- Reduce cabinet depth to 18" if space is limited
- Finish back of bench with paneling

A bench at the foot of the bed makes a comfortable place to sit down to put on socks and shoes. It is also a great place to store out of season clothing. Finished skins and decorator matching doors add a dressy look to the bench.

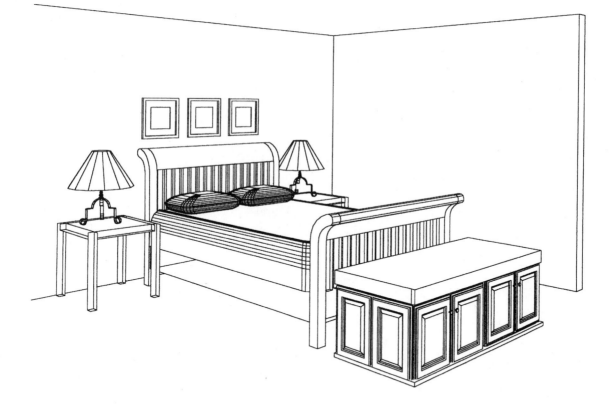

Bedroom Storage Wall

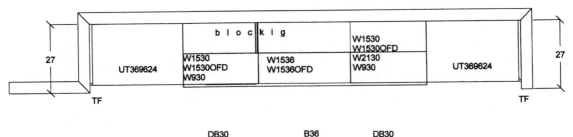

Cabinet List:

2 36″×96″×24″ utility cabinets
16 utility shelves
1 tall filler (split)
2 15″×30″ wall cabinets
1 15″×36″ wall cabinet
2 15″×30″ wall cabinets with open-frame doors
1 15″×36″ wall cabinet with open-frame doors
2 9″×30″ wall cabinets
1 21″×30″ wall cabinet
1 3/4″ tall return
1 48″×34 1/2″ paneling
2 8′-0″ inside corner molding
2 base toe material
33 knobs or pulls
1 pint stain
1 putty stick

Additional Materials Needed:

- Miscellaneous fasteners and adhesives
- Dimensional lumber to block wall cabinets forward
- Matching wood countertop
- Speaker cloth
- Racking system to fit cabinet opening

Required:

- Recess with a minimum 27″ deep return walls
- 10′-0″ high ceiling with 9″ high × 27″ deep floating soffit
- All specifications on audio-visual equipment
- Minimum 1″ filler at each wall
- Block all wall cabinets forward 12″
- Trim 3/4″ return as partitions for television opening
- Panel wall behind television
- Inside corner molding between top of wall cabinets and the bottom of the soffit

Variations:

- Change utility shelves to full width slide-out trays

With tall utility cabinets on each end of this storage wall, there is a great deal of room to store bedding and off-season clothing. The upper center section is devoted to entertainment equipment. Wall cabinets with open-frame doors are fitted with speaker cloth to house speakers.

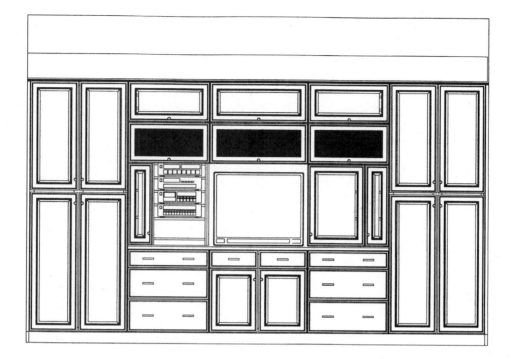

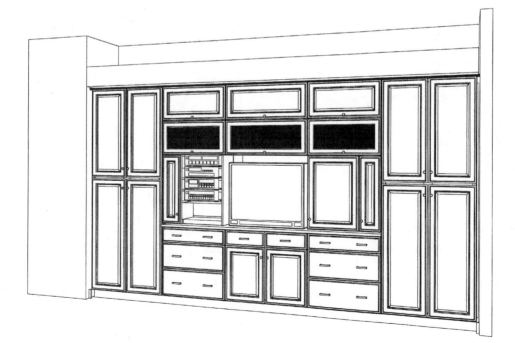

Built-in Dresser

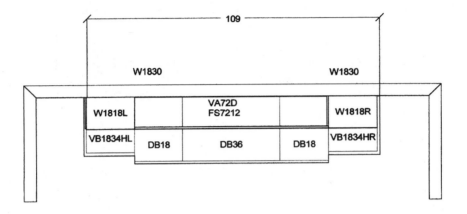

Cabinet List:

2 18″×18″ wall cabinets in square door style
2 18″×30″ cathedral wall cabinets
2 tall skins (split)
2 18″×34 1/2″ high vanity base cabinets
2 base skins (split)
2 18″ drawer bases
1 36″ drawer base
1 72″ shelf
1 72″ decorative valance
2 8′-0″ crown molding
2 8′-0″ base toe material
20 knobs or pulls
1 pint stain
1 putty stick

Additional Materials Needed

• Miscellaneous fasteners and adhesives
• Mirror
• Matching wood countertop

Required:

• Trim finished shelf and install behind valance as soffit board
• Split base skin for the vanity and the exposed sides on the 18″ drawer bases
• Split the tall skins to finish the exposed sides of the wall cabinet stacks

Variations:

• Use all square wall cabinets
• Add open-frame doors and tempered glass or fabric inserts in wall cabinets
• Use fluted fillers to frame the mirror
• Add lighting behind the valance

Vanity depth cabinets flank a 72″ section of drawers in the bedroom built-in. The stacked wall cabinets can hold folded sweaters, jewelry boxes, and even baskets of socks. A matching wood countertop finishes off the look.

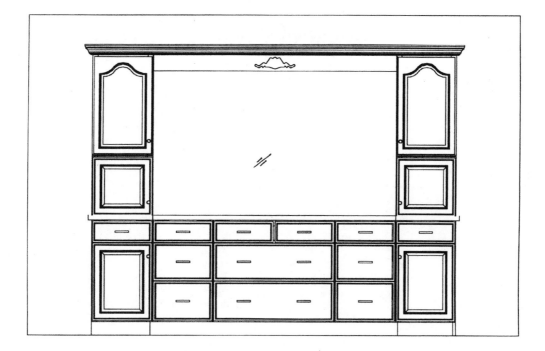

Chest of Drawers

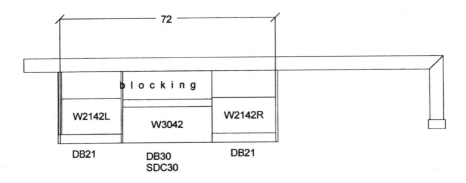

Cabinet List:

2 21″×42″ wall cabinets
2 21″×42″ replacement doors as decorator matching doors
1 30″×42″ wall cabinet
1 30″ spice drawer unit with matching wood knobs
2 tall skins (split)
2 21″ drawer bases
1 30″ drawer base
2 base skins
2 base decorator matching doors
2 8′-0″ crown molding
1 base toe material
2 toe kick cap covers
16 knobs or pulls
1 pint stain
1 putty stick

Additional Materials Needed

• Miscellaneous fasteners and adhesives
• Substrate
• Dimensional lumber
• Matching wood countertop

Required:

• Pull forward to 21″ and block W2142s
• Trim skins, apply to substrate as returns
• Pull and block middle wall cabinet and spice drawers to 24″; skin sides
• Skin exposed sides of base cabinets and apply decorator matching doors

Variations:

• Add fluted filler accents
• Adjust cabinet sizes to fit available space

Create a chest of drawers by stacking wall cabinets on the base cabinets. A matching wood countertop pulls the unit together. Give the chest a more formal look by adding layers of additional decorative top molding or making the unit in cherry wood.

Contemporary Vanity

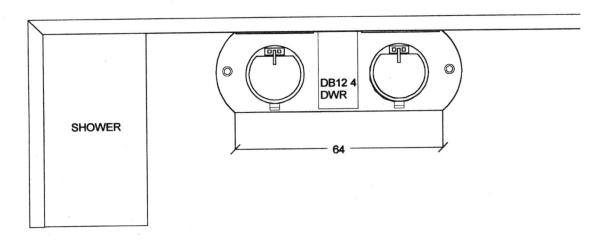

Cabinet List:

1 12″ four-drawer base
1 6″ wall filler
4 knobs or pulls
1 pint stain
1 putty stick
1 sealer

Additional Materials Needed

- Miscellaneous fasteners and adhesives
- Dimensional lumber
- 2 mirrors
- 3 hanging light fixtures
- 2 decorative contemporary support legs
- Countertop designed to accommodate an unsupported span
- 2 lavs and faucets
- Drain and supply lines in finish of choice

Required:

- Cleat countertop at wall for additional support
- Trim filler as toe material; sand, stain, and seal exposed ends

Variations:

- Use a standard vanity base for a shorter and more shallow vanity

The sleek lines of this dual vanity look best without a backsplash. So the countertop should be made from a nonporous material such as stone or solid surface products. Even covering the wall in a nonporous material is a great idea. Be sure to order all the exposed plumbing in a decorative finish to match the faucets, since they will be exposed.

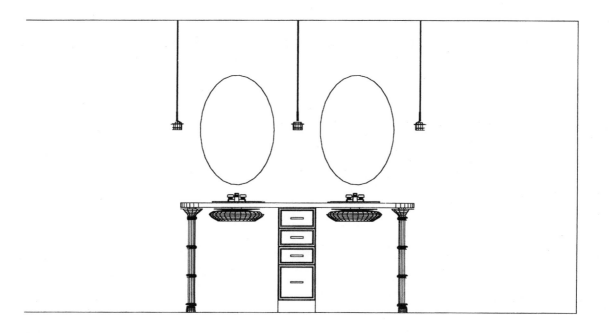

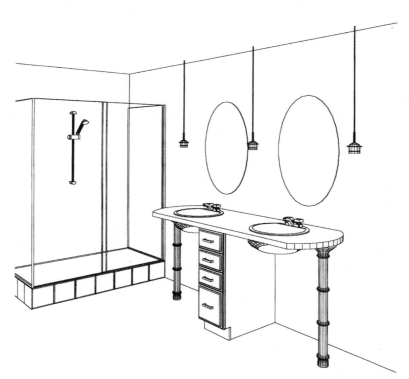

Double Floating Vanities

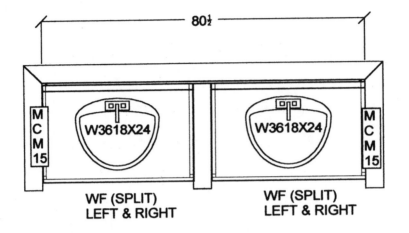

Cabinet List:

2 36″×18″×24″ wall cabinets
2 wall fillers (split)
2 30″×30″ recessed medicine cabinets
1 8′-0″ light rail molding
4 knobs or pulls
1 pint stain
1 putty stick

Additional Materials Needed

- Miscellaneous fasteners and adhesives
- Undercabinet lighting
- 2 basins and faucets
- 2 countertops made for 24″ deep cabinets
- Mirror

Required:

- Install cabinets at 33″ above finished floor
- Minimum 1″ filler at each wall
- Through-the-wall plumbing for the lavs
- Return walls and 39″ high separating wall
- Cut basins into the top of the wall cabinets
- Install undercabinet lighting behind the light rail

Variations:

- Adjust installation height to suit individual needs
- Reduce wall cabinet depth to 21″ to use standard depth vanity countertops

These dual floating vanity cabinets are made from 24″ deep wall cabinets, typically used over refrigerators. The extra countertop depth is always welcome especially in a small space like this. Undercabinet lighting installed behind the light rail, serves as a nightlight.

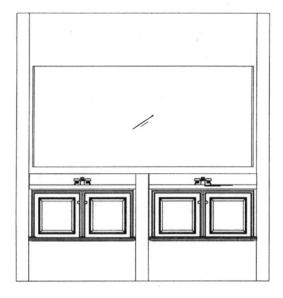

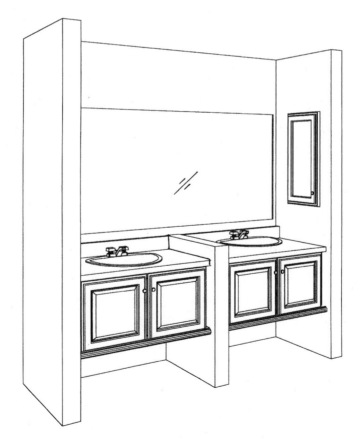

Dressing Room

Cabinet List:

2 30″×42″ wall cabinets with mullion doors and matching interiors

1 15″×42″ wall cabinet with mullion doors and matching interiors

5 tempered glass inserts

1 42″ wall filler

1 base filler

3 30″ drawer base cabinets

1 36″ lazy susan

2 18″×21″ deep desk drawer bases

1 trimmable 36″ kneehole drawer

2 30″×12″×24″ wall cabinets reduced to 15″ deep

1 8′-0″ countertop edge moldings

1 30″ wall filler (split)

2 30″×30″ wall cabinets

1 piece of paneling: 60″×18″

1 8′-0″ crown molding

1 8′-0″ outside corner molding

4 8′-0″ base toe material

3 toe kick cap covers

37 knobs or pulls

1 pint stain

1 putty stick

Additional Materials Needed

- Miscellaneous fasteners and adhesives
- Dimensional lumber
- Plywood

- Three countertop sections
- Bench cushion

Required:

- Minimum 1″ filler at each wall
- Construct a 4″ platform for the bench
- Create deck for bench with plywood edged with countertop edge molding.
- Panel rear of W3030s and finish raw corner with outside corner molding

Variations:

- Install shirred fabric behind the mullion doors for more hidden storage
- Rather than using reduced depth cabinets for the bench, pull standard depth wall cabinets forward to 15″ and skin the end

As part of a brand-new master suite or converted from an extra bedroom, a dressing room is a wonderful addition to any upscale home. Twelve-inch high wall cabinets are built on a platform and backed up to taller wall cabinets for a seating area and additional storage. Three wide drawer bases, counterspace, and a sit-down makeup area complete the area.

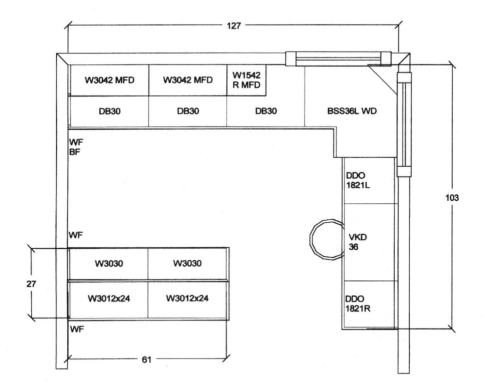

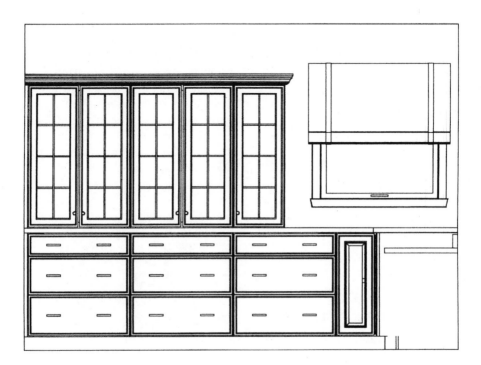

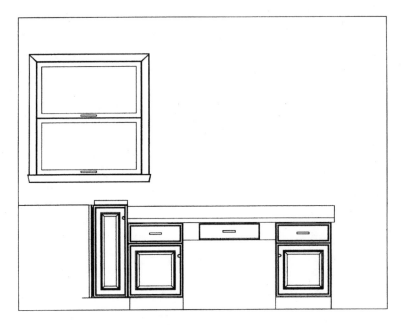

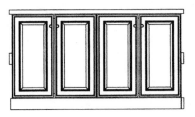

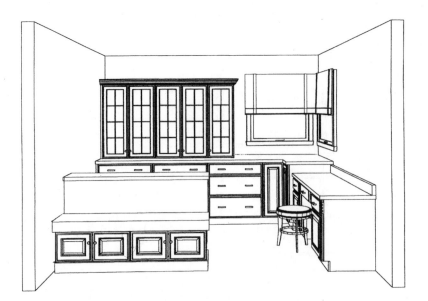

Dual Vanities with Stacked Storage

Cabinet List:

4 15″ vanity bases
1 30″ vanity sink base
1 48″×96″ plain paneling (split)
1 vanity filler (split)
1 trimmable 36″ kneehole drawer
2 48″ finished shelves
1 72″ finished shelf
1 24″ appliance garage
1 24″ frieze valance
1 8′-0″ base toe kick material
4 toe kick cap covers
1 8-0″ crown molding
11 knobs or pulls
1 pint stain
1 putty stick

Additional Materials Needed:

• Miscellaneous fasteners and adhesives
• Dimensional lumber
• 2 mirrors
• Lav and faucet
• 2 sidelights
• 1 matching bar light
• 2 countertop sections

Required:

• Pull vanity base cabinets in the makeup area to 25 1/2″
• Use 48″ finished shelves as wall storage vertical members
• Cut 72″ shelf into three 24″ sections: one above and one below the appliance garage and one behind the valance
• Cut paneling into skins for exposed ends of vanity base cabinets and open area above and below tambour

Variations:

• Add decorator matching doors to exposed ends

Vanity and makeup areas are installed at right angles to each other in this gracious bathroom. The wall storage stack made of finished shelves, valance, and a tambour provides both open and closed storage. By pulling the makeup area base cabinets forward to 25 1/2″, a standard 24″ wide appliance garage can be accommodated.

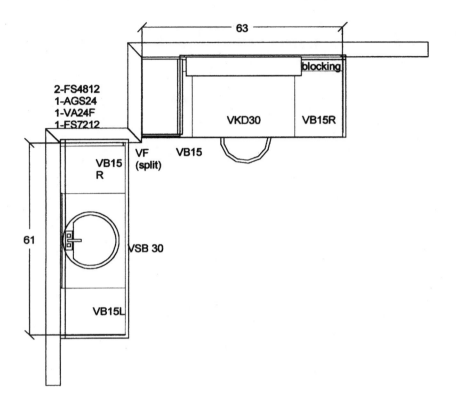

2-FS4812
1-AGS24
1-VA24F
1-FS7212

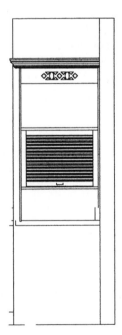

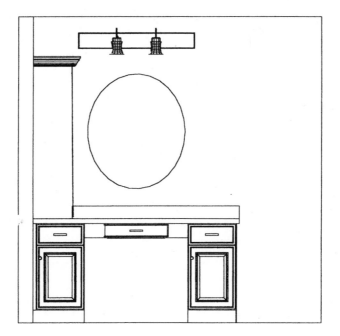

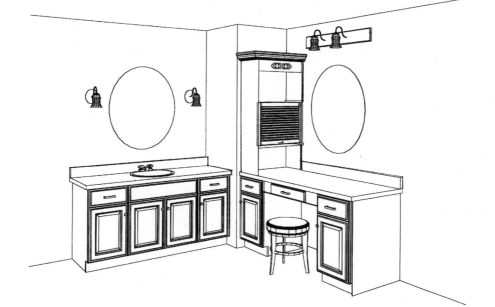

Exercise Area with Television Niche

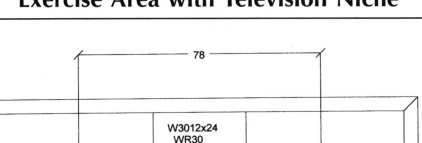

Cabinet List:

2 24″×24″×84″ utility cabinets
12 utility shelves
1 30″×12″×24″ wall cabinet
1 base skin
1 two-piece wine bottle holder
1 30″ base cabinet
1 8′-0″ base toe material
2 toe kick cap covers
2 8′-0″ crown molding
1 8′-0″ light rail molding
14 knobs or pulls
1 pint stain
1 putty stick

Additional Materials Needed:

• Miscellaneous fasteners and adhesives
• Substrate
• Countertop
• Television/VCR or DVD combination

Required:

• Specifications for television/VCR or DVD unit
• Electrical/cable hookups

• Adjust wine rack spacing to hold hand weights
• Trim base skin and apply to substrate to finish bottom of the 12″ high wall cabinet
• Finish raw edge of substrate and paneling with light rail molding

Variations:

• Adjust cabinetry to fit television requirements
• Add skins and decorator matching doors to exposed cabinet sides
• Add rollout shelves in place of standard utility shelves
• Panel wall behind television

A home exercise space can be made from an unused bedroom, basement, or created in a dedicated room in a new home. Two utility cabinets hold towels, videos, DVDs, and exercise clothing. Two tall cabinets flank a space for a television/VCR or DVD so that the user can watch exercise videos. Wine bottle holders are installed close together to hold hand weights.

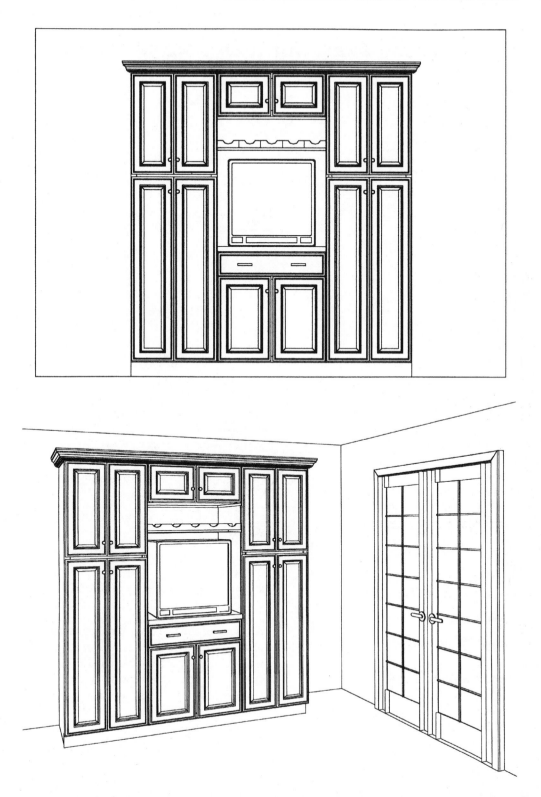

Headboard for a Double Bed

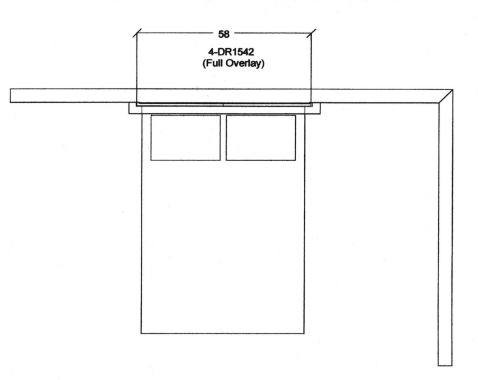

Cabinet List:

4 15″×42″ replacement doors
1 6″ tall filler
1 8′-0″ crown molding
1 pint stain
1 putty stick
1 sealer

Additional Materials Needed:

- Miscellaneous fasteners and adhesives
- Double bed

Required:

- Attach replacement doors directly to wall at approximately 48″ AFF
- Trim filler to width; sand, stain, and seal the ends
- Install filler on top of doors, top with crown molding

Variations:

- Adjust door sizes to fit bed size

This headboard has a rich paneled look that will match the other bedroom built-ins in this book. By attaching the doors directly to the wall, the room's baseboard is not disturbed. A tall filler installed horizontally and topped with crown molding gives the finished look.

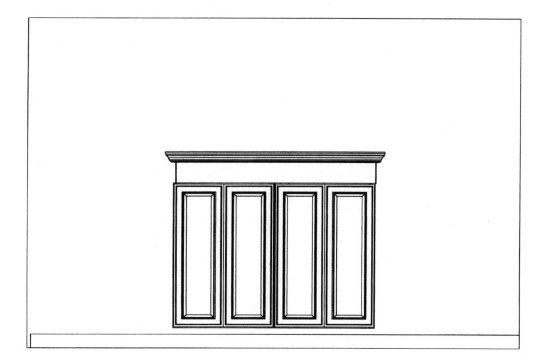

High-Low Vanities

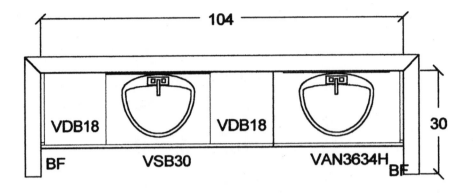

Cabinet List:

1 base filler (split)
2 18″ vanity drawer bases
1 30″ vanity sink base
1 34 1/2″ high 36″ vanity combination base
2 8′-0″ base toe material
12 knobs or pulls
1 pint stain
1 putty stick

Additional Materials Needed:

- Miscellaneous fasteners and adhesives
- 2 basins and faucets
- 2 mirrors
- Countertop
- Tile backsplash

Required:

- Minimum 1″ filler at each wall

Variations:

- Adjust widths of each cabinet area to job-site conditions

These high-low vanities accommodate family members of two different heights. Because of the varying countertop levels, the backsplash works best when made of a continuous line of ceramic tile. The tile is installed at the appropriate level for the tallest vanity, carried across in one straight line and tiled down to the lower level.

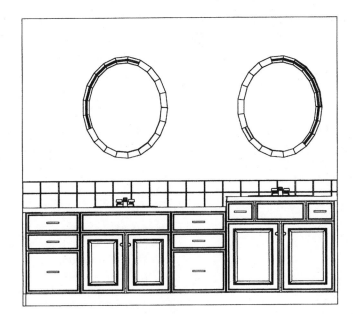

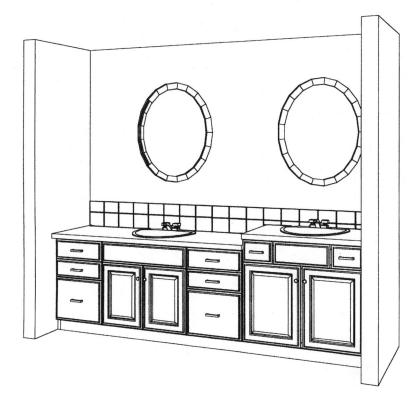

Home Spa

Cabinet List:

2 36″×18″×24″ wall cabinets
1 18″×48″ bookcase cabinet
3 30″×30″ wall cabinets
1 24″×24″×36″ corner wall cabinet
1 corner appliance garage
2 tall skins
1 18″×24″×90″ utility cabinet
6 utility shelves
1 30″ drawer base
1 21″ base cabinet
1 hamper insert
1 36″ base lazy susan
1 15″ base cabinet
3 8′-0″ base toe kick material
1 toe kick cap cover
3 8′-0″ crown molding
2 8′-0″ scribe molding
24 knobs or pulls
1 pint stain
1 putty stick

Additional Materials Needed:

• Miscellaneous fasteners and adhesives
• Plywood
• Dimensional lumber

• Robe hooks
• Cushion
• Massage table
• Countertop
• Undercounter refrigerator

Required:

• Build a platform for 24″ wall cabinets, used as a bench
• Make deck for bench from plywood edged with scribe molding
• Pull and block corner wall cabinet to 27″ and install appliance garage below
• Trim tall skins and finish the sides of corner wall cabinet stack

Variations:

• Add skins and decorator matching doors to all exposed ends

This home spa has everything! The open bookcase holds oils and creams, and the utility cabinet has plenty of room for linens. A hamper insert keeps the area tidy. The undercounter refrigerator is for storing bottled water and there is even a bench for relaxing.

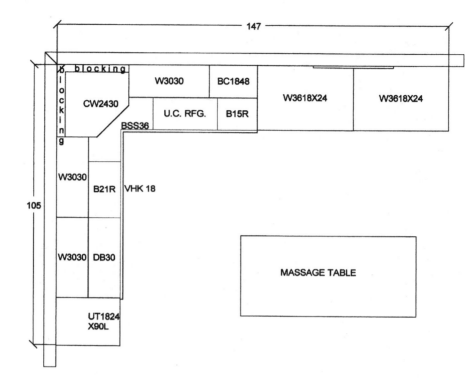

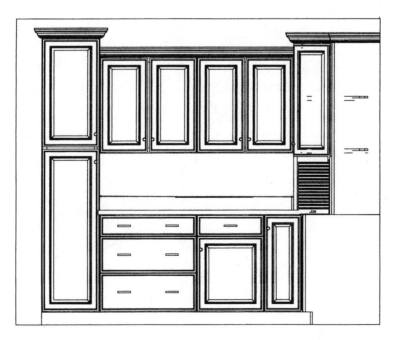

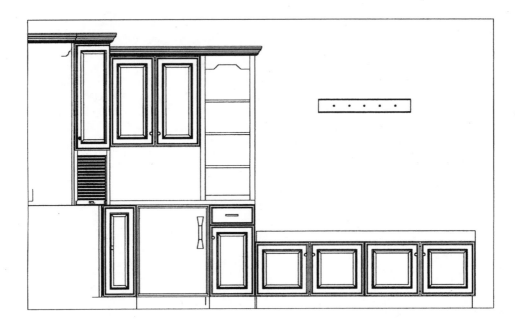

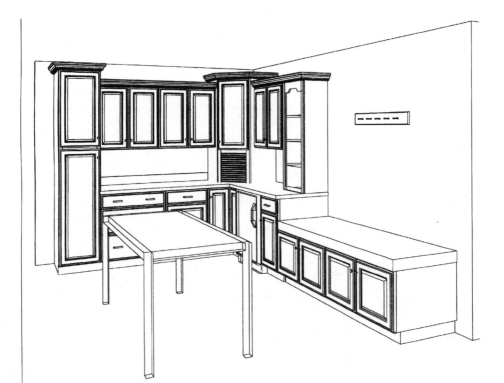

Layered Countertop Vanity

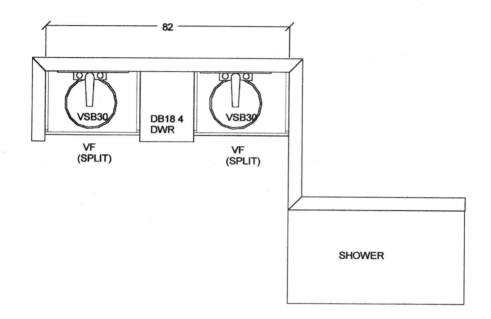

Cabinet List:

2 vanity fillers (split)
2 30″ vanity sink bases
1 18″ kitchen drawer base
2 96″ tall filers
1 8′-0″ base toe material
2 toe kick cap covers
8 knobs or pulls
1 pint stain
1 putty stick

Additional Materials Needed:

- Miscellaneous fasteners and adhesives
- 3 countertops, 3/4″ thick, with matching cleat material
- 2 mirrors
- 2 raised-style lavs and faucets

Required:

- Minimum 1″ filler at walls and at deeper drawer base

- Cut fillers to make two stair-step decorative layers on top of drawer base
- Cleat higher countertop with matching material
- Finished plumbing lines

Variations:

- Add decorative solid surface or metal posts between the countertops
- Adjust width to fit job-site conditions
- The stair-step treatment can also be made from countertop material

Bowl or raised-style basins offer many design options. Here is one idea that features two layers of countertops. Approximately 4″ is allowed between the countertop levels so that rolled-up hand towels can be stored there, and it makes the area easy to clean.

Master Closet

Cabinet List:

6 30″ drawer bases
1 base filler (split)
2 30″ base cabinets with full-width slide-out trays
2 30″ drawer bases reduced to 21″
1 48″×96″ paneling (split)
1 39″×15″×24″ wall cabinet reduced to 15″ deep
1 base skin (split)
2 decorator matching doors
1 6″ tall filler
1 8′-0″ inside corner molding
1 8′-0″ scribe molding
4 8′-0″ base toe material
6 toe kick cap covers
58 knobs or pulls
1 pint stain
1 putty stick

Additional Materials Needed:

- Miscellaneous fasteners and adhesives
- Dimensional lumber
- Plywood
- Closet rods and supports
- 3 countertop sections
- Cushion

Required:

- Minimum 1″ filler at each wall
- Build a 4″ high platform for base of seat
- Cut paneling into skins for the back to back island cabinets
- Cut base end panel into two skins for the sides of the seat and apply decorator matching doors
- Create deck for bench from plywood and cover edge with scribe molding
- Cover front of platform with furniture toe treatment consisting of tall filler material topped with inside corner molding

Variations:

- Adjust cabinets to fit job-site conditions

For the upscale home, a custom-designed master bedroom closet features rods for both long and short garments. The center island provides counterspace and a built-in bench. The drawers provide storage for polo shirts, socks, and undergarments, so that the entire day's wardrobe can be coordinated in the master closet. Great lighting is essential to this room.

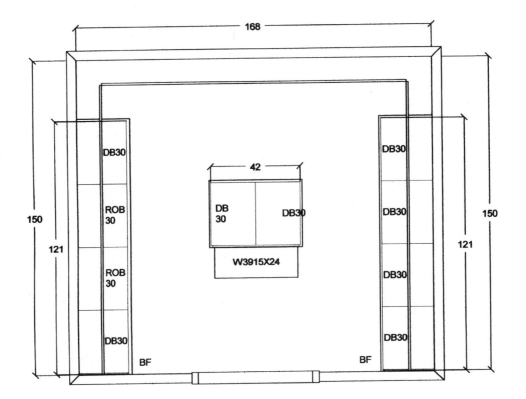

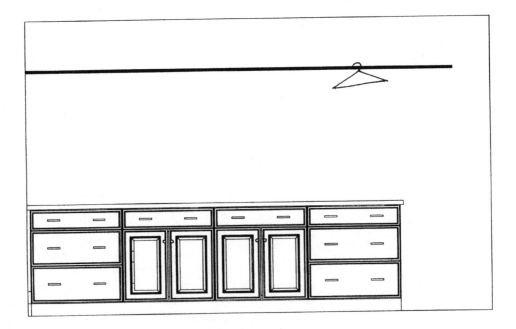

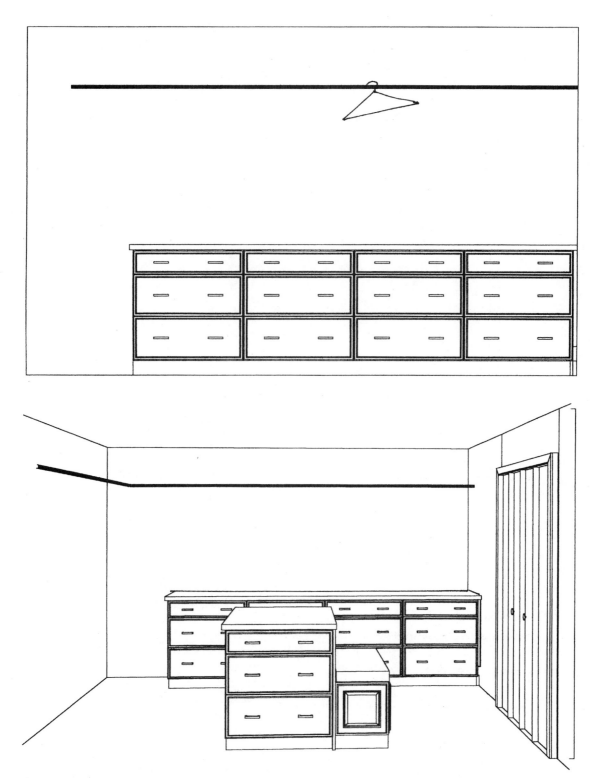

Matching Vanities with Slatted Shelves and Tank Topper

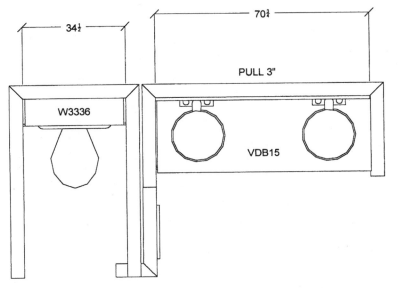

Cabinet List:

1 33"×36" wall cabinet reduced to 9" deep
1 wall filler (split)
1 8'-0" crown molding
1 15" vanity drawer base
2 6"×30" wall fillers
5 84" tall fillers (trimmed)
1 15" piece base toe material
2 toe kick cap covers
5 knobs or pulls
1 pint stain
1 putty stick

Additional Materials Needed:

- Miscellaneous fasteners and adhesives
- Mirror
- 2 raised-bowl style lavs and 2 faucets
- Toilet

Required:

- Minimum of 1" filler at each wall for the cabinet over the toilet

- Install 6" wall fillers as countertop aprons below each sink
- Trim fillers and cleat in place as slatted shelves
- Through-the-wall installation for supply and discharge lines
- Supply lines, traps, etc., finished to match faucets

Variations:

- Adjust to fit wall dimensions
- Skin exposed sides of drawer base

Raised-bowl style lavs are skirted with fillers, giving a contemporary look. Fillers trimmed to fit and installed as a slatted shelf provide great towel storage. The reduced depth wall cabinet, that is installed over the toilet, provides storage for cleaning supplies and other bathroom necessities.

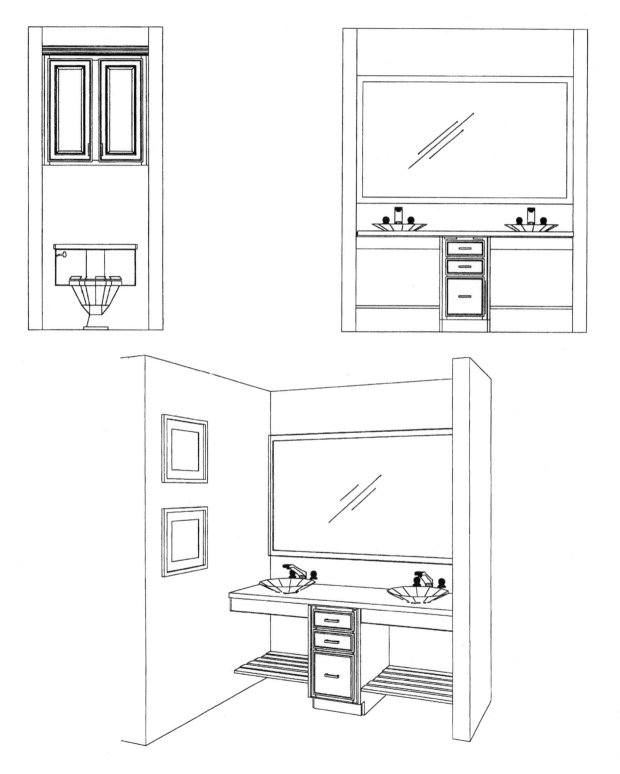

Separated Double Vanities

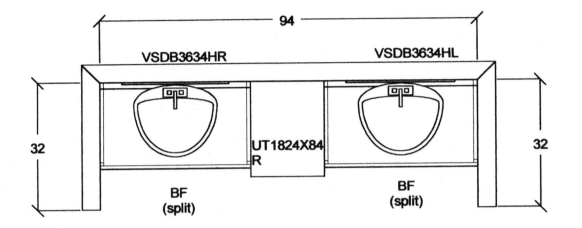

Cabinet List:

2 base fillers (split)
1 36″×34 1/2″ combination vanity with drawers right
1 36″×34 1/2″ combination vanity with drawers left
1 18″×84″×24″ utility cabinet
6 utility shelves
2 48″ finished shelves
2 8'-0″ crown molding
1 8'-0″ base toe material
2 toe kick cap covers
8 knobs or pulls
1 pint stain
1 putty stick

Additional Materials Needed:

- Miscellaneous fasteners and adhesives
- 2 countertops with side- and back-splashes
- 2 lavs and faucets
- 2 mirrors
- 4 recessed mini lights

Required:

- Minimum 1″ base filler at walls and at utility cabinet
- Trim and install finished shelving flush with top of utility cabinet as soffit boards
- Install recessed mini lights in soffit board

Variations:

- Adjust to fit job-site conditions
- Add rollout shelves or wire hampers to bottom of utility cabinet

Even a master suite with double bowls can have a little privacy for each user. The utility cabinet separates the two vanities and gives the necessary storage for toiletries and linens. The vanities each have two working drawers, adding even more storage. Countertops should have side-splashes to protect the walls and cabinetry.

Surround for a Pedestal Lav

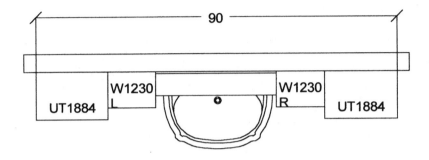

Cabinet List:

2 18″×12″×84″ utility cabinets
12 utility shelves
2 12″×30″ wall cabinets reduced to 9″ deep
2 8′-0″ crown molding
1 8′-0″ base toe material
4 toe kick cap covers
6 knobs or pulls
1 pint stain
1 putty stick

Additional Materials Needed:

- Miscellaneous fasteners and adhesives
- Mirror
- 6″ deep shelf with supports
- 2 towel rings

Required:

- Install wall cabinets 6″ below utility cabinets

Variations:

- Add a soffit board, valance, and lighting between wall cabinets

Pedestal lavs are long on style but short on storage and counterspace. This surround features both tall and standard wall cabinets to store everything from towels and toiletries to bathroom cleaning supplies. A 6″ deep shelf spans the space between the tall cabinets for efficient landing space.

Tall Bedroom Storage Unit

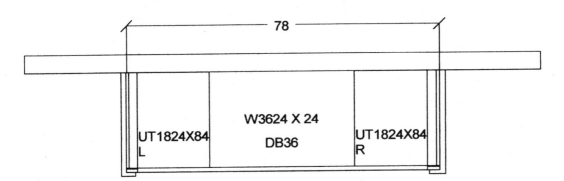

Cabinet List:

2 tall fillers
2 tall fluted fillers
2 3/4″ tall end panels
2 18″×24″×84″ utility cabinets
4 utility shelves
8 pull-out shelf trays
2 36″×24″×24″ deep wall cabinets
1 36″ drawer base
1 8′-0″ countertop edge molding
2 6″ tall fillers
2 8′-0″ inside corner molding
14 knobs or pulls
1 pint stain
1 putty stick

Additional Materials Needed:

• Miscellaneous fasteners and adhesives
• Dimensional lumber

Required:

• Install center cabinets at 84″ and cover any void with countertop edge molding
• Layer fluted fillers over plain fillers
• Block behind fluted fillers and install 3/4″ tall end panels
• Install furniture toe of tall filler and inside corner molding around base

Variations:

• Adjust cabinets to fit available wall space
• Add decorator matching doors on both exposed ends

Twenty-four inch deep wall cabinets that are commonly used over a refrigerator are combined to form the center section of this bedroom storage unit. Tall utility cabinets are framed with layered tall fillers that create a pilaster detail on both ends.

Tank Topper with Positive and Negative Design

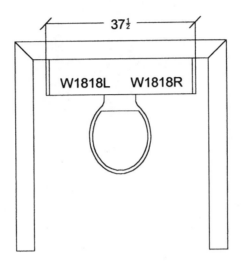

Cabinet List:

2 18″×18″ wall cabinets reduced to 9″ deep
1 72″ finished shelf (trimmed and split)
3 48″ finished shelves (trimmed and split)
1 8′-0″ crown molding
2 knobs or pulls
1 pint stain
1 putty stick

Additional Materials Needed:

• Miscellaneous fasteners and adhesives

Required:

• Reduced depth wall cabinets
• Cut 72″ shelf into left and right verticals

• Cut 48″ shelves into three horizontal shelves

Variations:

• Panel back wall of open spaces with matching paneling

Segregating the water closet to its own private space is popular especially in new construction. However, storage for this area is often overlooked. Necessities like cleaning supplies and spare rolls of tissue need to be conveniently located. This combination of open and closed (positive and negative) storage was designed to meet these needs. Yet at just 9″ deep, this storage unit doesn't become a "head-banger."

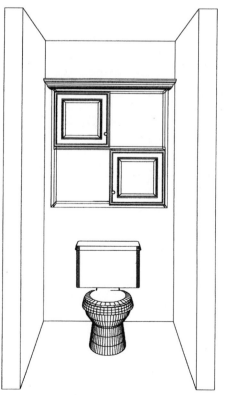

Tub Surround

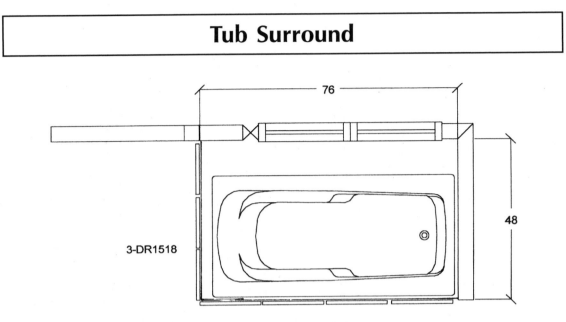

3-DR1518

4-DR1818

Cabinet List:

4 18″×18″ replacement doors
3 15″×18″ replacement doors
2 tall skins
1 8′-0″ outside corner molding
1 pint stain
1 putty stick

Additional Materials Needed:

- Miscellaneous fasteners and adhesives
- Dimensional lumber
- Substrate material
- Tub with fittings
- Tub deck

Required:

- Tub specifications
- Framed box covered with substrate to support tub
- Tub deck with a minimum 1 1/2″ overhang on two sides

- Panel vertical sides of tub deck with trimmed tall skins
- Apply replacement doors
- Cover paneling corner with outside corner molding

Variations:

- Use front frame and doors in place of replacement doors if access to the tub plumbing is required.
- Use paneling in place of tall skins if vertical grain is preferred
- Adjust door sizes to fit tub and deck dimensions

Paneling and replacement doors are combined to cover the sides of the deck of this soaking tub. While this application is not suitable for a child's bathroom, where there is a lot of splashing, it adds an elegant look for a master bathroom.

Two-Level Vanity with Lowered Angled Front

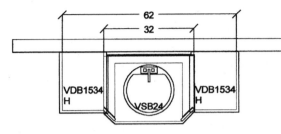

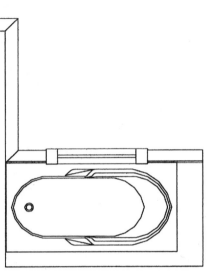

Cabinet List:

2 15″ vanity drawer bases that are 34 1/2″ high
2 6″ vanity fillers
1 24″ standard height vanity sink base
1 8′-0″ base toe material
4 toe kick cap covers
8 knobs or pulls
1 pint stain
1 putty stick

Additional Materials Needed:

- Miscellaneous fasteners and adhesives
- Two countertop sections
- Lav and faucet
- 2 wall sconces
- Mirror

Required:

- Pull vanity sink base 4″ from wall and each adjacent drawer base
- Trim 6″ vanity fillers, bevel long sides and install at a 45° angle

Variations:

- Apply fluted fillers on angle fillers as overlays
- Add skins and decorator matching doors to exposed ends

Even a moderate-size vanity area will have lots of style if it is treated to two different levels and an angled front. The lower vanity requires side and backsplashes on three sides. The upper countertop is U-shaped and extends over the splashes. The upper countertop does not require a backsplash, although one may be added, if desired.

Ultimate Makeup Area

Cabinet List:

1 30″×24″×84″ utility cabinet
3 tall skins
2 utility shelves
4 full-width rollout shelves
1 24″×18″ wall cabinet
1 24″×36″ wall cabinet with mullion doors
  and matching interiors
2 tempered glass inserts
2 desk drawer bases
1 36″ trimmable kneehole drawer
1 6″ wall filler
1 24″×24″ desk base cabinet
3 base skins
2 8′-0″ base toe material
2 8′-0″ crown molding
4 toe kick cap covers
17 knobs or pulls
1 pint stain
1 putty stick

Additional Materials Needed:

- Miscellaneous fasteners and adhesives
- Dimensional lumber
- 2 wall sconces
- Recessed can lights
- Lav and faucet
- Countertop
- Towel bar
- Vanity bench and tabletop mirror

Required:

- Recess kneehole drawer and trim 6″ filler
  as two side extensions
- Block countertop in corner
- Skin all exposed sides
- "Dummy" drawer in 24″ desk base to ac-
  cept lav
- Split one tall skin for sides of wall cabinet
  stack

Variations:

- For a space without windows, install full-
  width mirrors in the corner
- Add decorator matching doors to exposed
  sides

End bathroom competition by adding a makeup area in the master bedroom that includes a built-in lav. Because this unit is made with desk cabinets, remove the top-drawer body of the cabinet to be used for the vanity sink base. The utility cabinet is the perfect place for folded garments, shoes, or handbags.

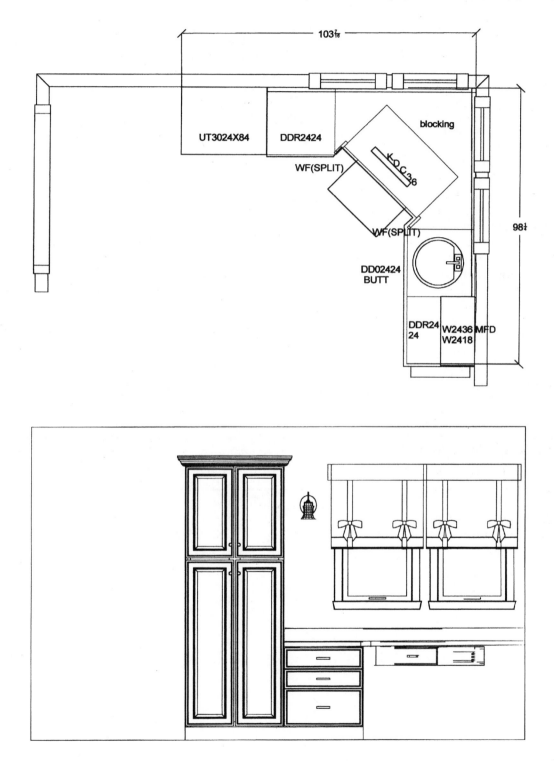

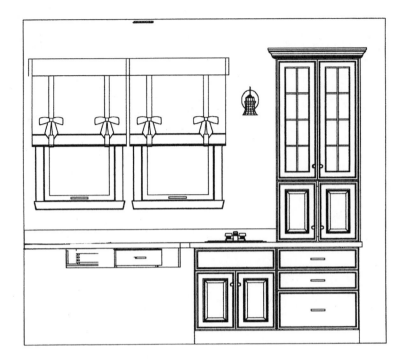

Valet with Frieze Top Molding Treatment

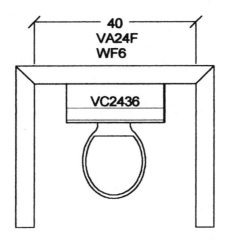

Cabinet List:

1 24″×36″ valet cabinet
1 24″ frieze valance
1 6″×30″ wall filler
1 8′-0″ crown molding
2 knobs or pulls
1 pint stain
1 putty stick

Additional Materials Needed:

- Miscellaneous fasteners and adhesives
- Dimensional lumber

Required:

- Block frieze valance in place and make returns from trimmed 6″ filler

Variations:

- Adjust installation height to suit homeowners
- Opt for a simpler top molding treatment
- Create a false top for the molding treatment if plants or other decorative items will be placed on top of the unit

Every water closet niche requires storage. Here a standard valet cabinet is dressed up with a tall top molding treatment that incorporates a valance, filler returns, and crown molding.

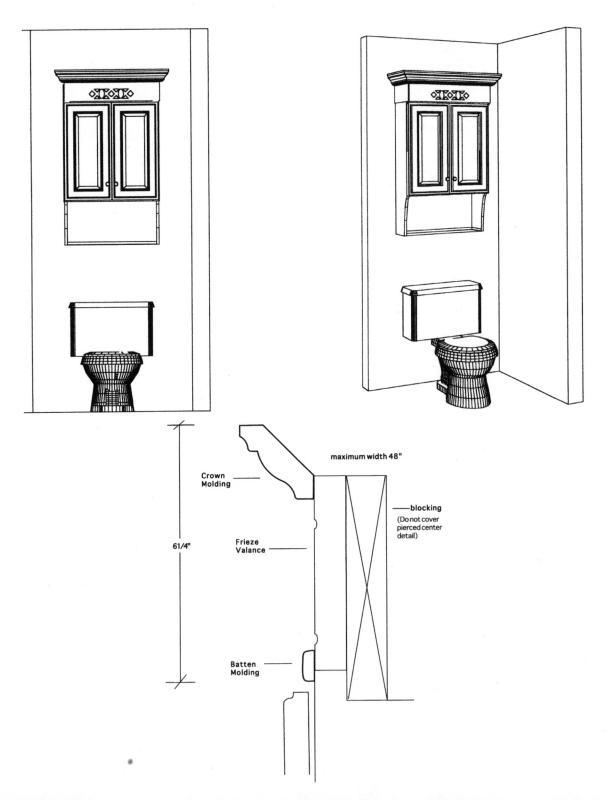

Crown
Molding

61/4"

Frieze
Valance

Batten
Molding

maximum width 48"

blocking
(Do not cover
pierced center
detail)

Vanity for Two

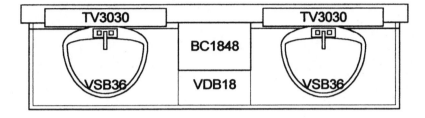

Cabinet List:

2 36″ vanity sink bases
1 18″ vanity drawer base
2 30″×30″ recessed medicine cabinets
1 18″×48″ bookcase
1 8′-0″ crown molding
1 8′-0″ base toe material
2 base toe kick cap covers
7 knobs or pulls
1 pint stain
1 putty stick

Additional Materials Needed:

• Miscellaneous fasteners and adhesives
• Countertop
• 2 lavs and faucets

Required:

• Recess medicine cabinets

Variations:

• Add skins and decorator matching doors to exposed sides
• Add crown molding to the top of the recessed medicine cabinets

A bookcase unit provides open shelving storage for baskets of cosmetics and toiletries. It also provides a measure of separation for each vanity area. Both users share a center drawer bank.

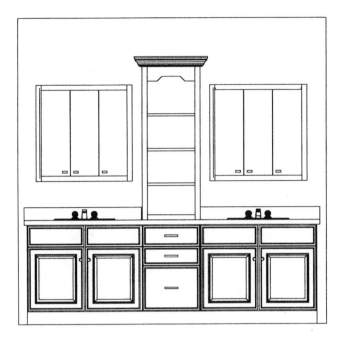

Vanity with Coastline Front

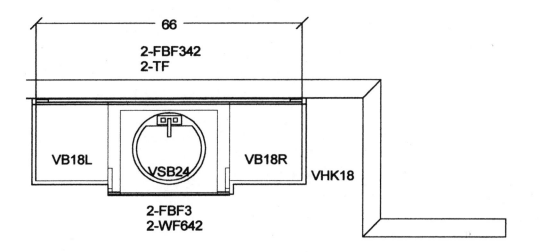

Cabinet List:

2 3″×42″ wall fluted fillers
2 tall fillers (trimmed)
2 18″ vanity base cabinets
1 18″ hamper insert
1 24″ vanity sink base
2 3″ fluted base fillers
2 6″×42″ wall fillers (trimmed)
1 36″ arched valance (trimmed)
1 8′-0″ base toe material
2 toe kick cap cover
1 8′-0″ crown molding
6 knobs or pulls
1 pint stain
1 putty stick

Additional Materials Needed:

- Miscellaneous fasteners and adhesives
- 1 lav and faucet
- 1 mirror
- Countertop with coastline front

Required:

- Pull VSB24 3″ from wall and adjacent cabinets
- Trim and attach fluted fillers to VSB24
- Install 3″×42″ wall fillers (trimmed in height) as fluted filler returns
- Trim valance and install as toe treatment
- Combine 42″ fluted wall fillers and trimmed tall fillers to frame the mirror

Variations:

- Add decorator matching doors to exposed sides of vanity

A few design details take this simple vanity from plain to custom in appearance. Begin by pulling the vanity sink base forward and away from each adjacent cabinet by 3″. Fluted and plain fillers, as well as an arched toe space, finish the look. The frame for the mirror is also made of fluted and plain fillers.

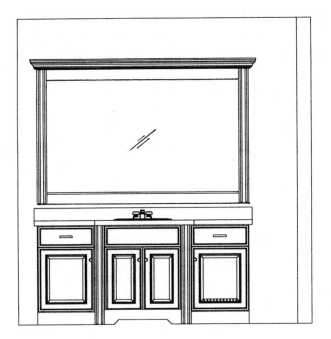

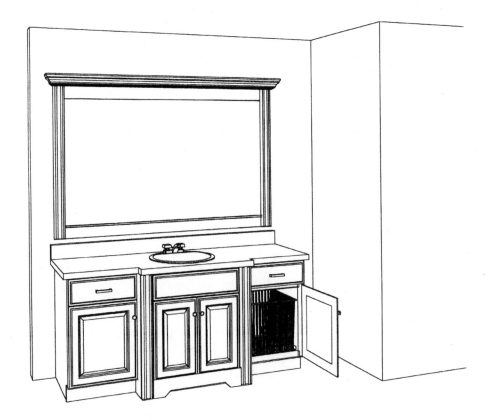

Vanity with Tambour Storage

Cabinet List:

2 18″ four-drawer bases
1 21″ sink base
1 6″ base filler (split)
1 tall filler (split)
1 24″×30″ wall cabinet
1 24″ straight tambour unit
2 18″×12″×84″ utility cabinets
12 utility shelves
2 8′-0″ base toe material
1 toe kick cap cover
1 8′-0″ crown molding
15 knobs or pulls
1 pint stain
1 putty stick

Additional Materials Needed:

- Miscellaneous fasteners and adhesives
- Dimensional lumber to block countertop extension
- 1 basin and faucet
- 1 mirror
- Countertop for 24″ deep cabinets with extension under tambour unit

Required:

- Minimum 1″ base filler at the wall
- Minimum 2″ base filler in the corner
- Minimum 1″ filler to left of the tambour stack
- Minimum 2″ tall filler notched for the countertop
- Block countertop extension in tambour area

Variations:

- Add decorator matching doors to exposed side on the utility cabinet
- Coastline sink base

This vanity arrangement is made from 24″ deep base kitchen cabinets to accommodate a standard 24″ wide tambour unit. The tambour unit is the perfect place to store the hair dryer and other items that are best kept out of sight. Careful placement of fillers is what makes this arrangement work.

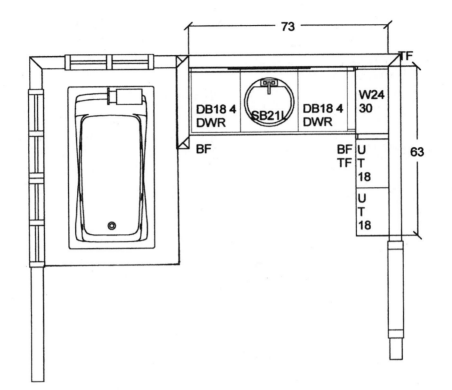

Vanity with Wall Cabinet Storage

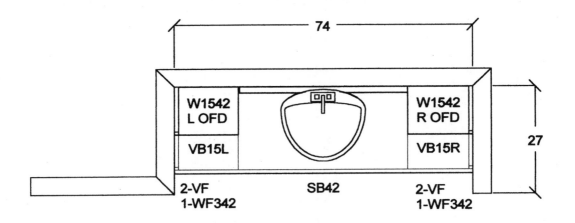

Cabinet List:

2 15″×42″ wall cabinets with open-frame doors and matching interiors
1 3″×42″ wall filler (split)
2 tempered glass inserts
2 15″ vanity bases
1 vanity filler (split)
1 42″ vanity sink base
2 8′-0″ crown molding
1 8′-0″ base toe material
8 knobs or pulls
1 pint stain
1 putty stick

Additional Materials Needed:

- Miscellaneous fasteners and adhesives
- Dimensional lumber
- 1 basin and faucet
- 1 mirror
- Countertop with additional backsplash material

Required:

- Minimum 1″ filler at each wall
- Build a platform to raise wall cabinets 4″
- Cover platform with backsplash material
- Cleat crown molding to wall between wall cabinets for a continuous line

Variations:

- Adjust to fit job-site dimensions
- Reduce depth of wall cabinets if additional counterspace is desired
- Select solid doors or semi-obscure glass for hidden storage

Traditional medicine cabinets often do not meet today's bathroom storage needs. This vanity design features 42″ high wall cabinets as storage for shampoos, lotions, medicines, and towels. By raising the cabinets level with the backsplash and wrapping the platform with additional backsplash material the cabinets are protected from occasional splashes.

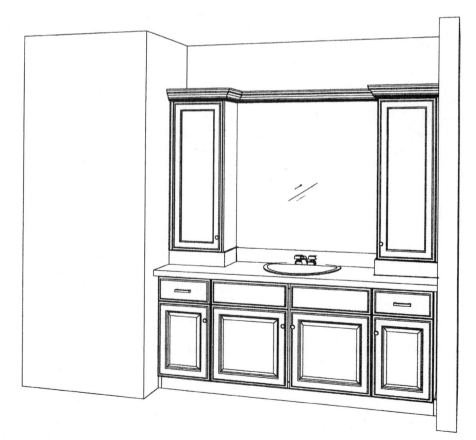

Wall to Wall Dresser

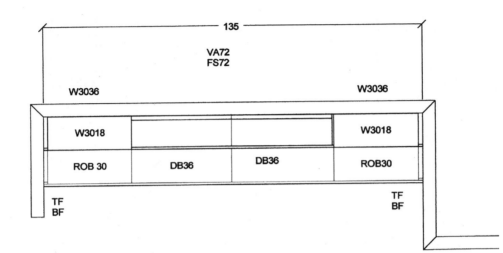

Cabinet List:

1 6″ tall filler (split)
2 30″×18″ wall cabinets
2 30″×36″ wall cabinets
1 tall skin (split)
1 72″ finished shelf
1 72″ arched valance
1 base filler (split)
2 30″ base cabinets with full-width rollout trays
2 36″ drawer bases
1 3″ tall filler
2 8′-0″ crown molding
2 8′-0″ base toe material
28 knobs or pulls
1 pint stain
1 putty stick

Additional Materials Needed:

- Miscellaneous fasteners and adhesives
- Mirror
- Matching wood countertop
- Lighting

Required:

- Trim finished shelf and install behind valance as a soffit board
- Split and trim tall skin to finish exposed sides of cabinet stack
- Trim 3″ tall filler as backsplash
- Install lighting behind valance

Variations:

- Adjust design to fit wall dimension
- Create a molding trim to the ceiling

Wall to wall storage replaces a freestanding dressers and ends the need to move heavy furniture during cleaning. Drawers can hold anything from underwear and sleeping attire to polo shirts. The cabinets with rollout trays are perfect for shoes and handbags. Select the lighting type carefully if the mirror is going to be used for applying makeup.

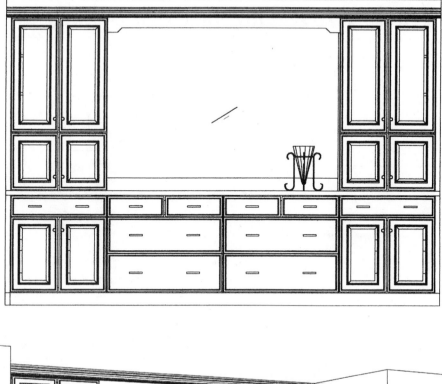

Window Seat with Recessed Bookcases

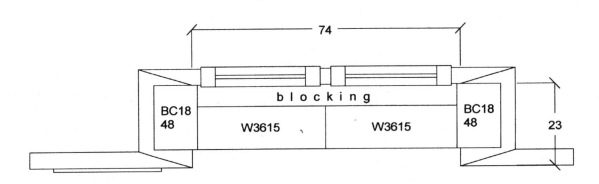

Cabinet List:

2 36″×18″ wall cabinets
2 18″×48″ bookcase units
2 8′-0″ scribe molding
1 8′-0″ crown molding
1 3″ wide tall filler
1 8′-0″ inside corner molding
4 knobs or pulls
1 pint stain
1 putty stick

Additional Materials Needed:

- Miscellaneous fasteners and adhesives
- Plywood
- Dimensional lumber
- Cushion

Required:

- Window recess with soffit above
- Pull and block wall cabinets to 18″ from wall

- Construct a 3″ high platform and cover with tall filler and inside corner molding
- Recess bookcases in side walls above the cushion height
- Trim top of bookcases with crown molding
- Make a top for the window seat with plywood. Finish edge with scribe molding

Variations:

- Omit recessed bookcases
- Add recessed lighting in the soffit

Many bedrooms in new homes have shallow box bay windows meant for a seating area. Usually conventional upholstered chairs are selected for an area like this. Another alternative is to build in a window seat and recess bookcases into the side walls, if space permits.

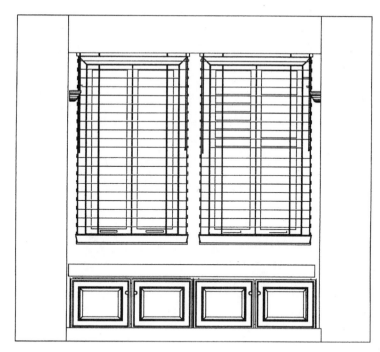

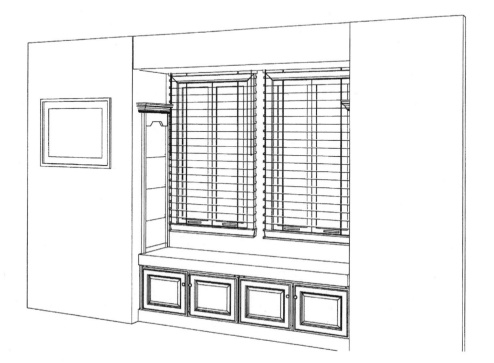

CHAPTER 3

Beverage Centers

Whether you call them satellite kitchens or beverage centers, mini kitchens are popping up all over the home. They add convenience to our lives, free up the main kitchen and make our leisure hours even more pleasurable. It is a whole new way of thinking about how we prepare meals and snacks.

The popularity of smaller scale appliances has made the design of these beverage centers more manageable. Undercounter refrigerators, wine coolers, drawer style dishwashers, and a wide variety of small sinks are just a few of the appliances available. Many undercounter appliances can be covered with wood panels that match the cabinetry. Blending the appliances into the cabinetry makes the beverage center seem more furniture-like and visually appealing.

When it comes to auxiliary kitchens, the most common place to find them is just off the kitchen or in the family room. Renewed interest in entertaining at home makes a small beverage area outside the kitchen the perfect addition to any house. It takes the pressure off the primary cook and provides a place to prepare snacks and beverages with ease.

The second most popular spot for a beverage center is in the master suite where they are often called morning kitchens or juice bars. In larger homes, a place within the master suite designed to grab a quick breakfast can be an efficient way to start the morning for busy executives. It doesn't take more than an undercounter refrigerator, some storage, counterspace and usually a small sink to make a great breakfast bar.

Because these beverage centers are often integrated into public living areas, aesthetics are extremely important. Fewer appliances also make it easier to focus on the overall beauty of the design. Furniture details such as elaborate top moldings or decorative light rail treatments are a given. Wall cabinets with mullion or open-frame doors and glass inserts are often treated with interior lighting and glass shelves. Even the toe space of the beverage center can be enriched with furniture toe treatments.

Beverage centers add to the comfort and convenience in our lives, and because they are often straight runs of cabinetry, they deserve careful thought and design attention.

Armoire Snack Bar

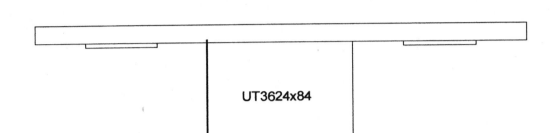

UT3624x84

Cabinet List:

1 36"×24"×84" utility cabinet
1 utility shelf
1 full width rollout shelf
1 36" frieze valance
1 8'-0" crown molding
1 6" tall filler
1 8'-0" inside corner molding
4 knobs or pulls
1 pint stain
1 putty stick

Additional Materials Needed:

- Miscellaneous fasteners and adhesives
- Dimensional lumber
- Countertop
- Bar sink and faucet
- Mini refrigerator

Required:

- Through-the-wall plumbing for the sink
- Turn the utility cabinet upside-down and remove toe
- Build a 4" high platform to support the inverted utility cabinet
- Cover platform with tall filler and inside corner molding
- Trim and install frieze valance at top of upper section

Variations:

- Replace hinges with those that open at 170° angles
- Add a two-piece wine rack to interior of the upper section
- The toe space can remain if a taller molding treatment is used
- Add tall skins and decorator matching doors to both ends of the cabinet
- Add additional cabinetry left and right of the armoire

Turn a standard utility cabinet into a hidden beverage center. By inverting it and adding a countertop and small sink. A small dorm-size refrigerator can be placed in the lower section. Just be sure to allow for sufficient ventilation per manufacturer's recommendations. A rollout shelf installed above the refrigerator can hold beverage accessories.

Bar with Bookcase

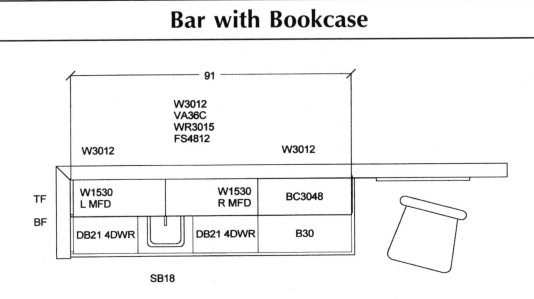

Cabinet List:

3 30″×12″ wall cabinets
2 15″×30″ wall cabinets with mullion doors and matching interiors
2 tempered glass inserts
1 30″×48″ bookcase
1 tall skin (split)
1 30″×15″ wine rack cabinet
1 36″ arched valance
1 piece beadboard paneling 30″×15″
1 piece finished shelving 30″×12″
2 21″ four-drawer base cabinets
1 18″ sink base cabinet
1 30″ base cabinet
1 base skin
1 8′-0″ base toe material
1 toe kick cap cover
21 knobs or pulls
1 pint stain
1 putty stick

Additional Materials Needed:

- Miscellaneous fasteners and adhesives
- Countertop
- Full-height tile backsplash
- Bar sink and faucet

Required:

- Install 12″ high wall cabinets on top of bookcase and wall cabinets
- Trim tall skin and apply to side of bookcase stack
- Trim finished shelf and install on top of the wine rack cabinet
- Minimum 1″ filler at the wall

Variations:

- Replace drawer base cabinets with standard 21″ base cabinets for cost savings
- Add decorator matching doors to exposed cabinet sides

Tucked in a corner this combination wet bar and bookcase unit would work well in a family or great room. Mullion door wall cabinets flank a wine rack cabinet with an open shelf area above it. The row of 12″ high cabinetry skims across the top of the unit adding extra storage.

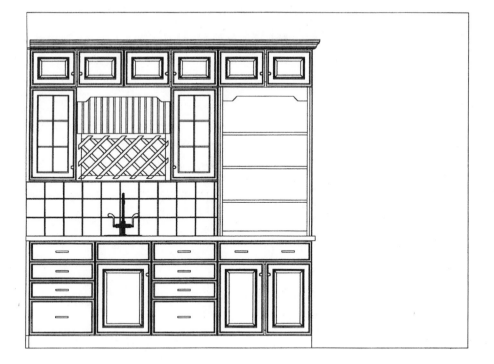

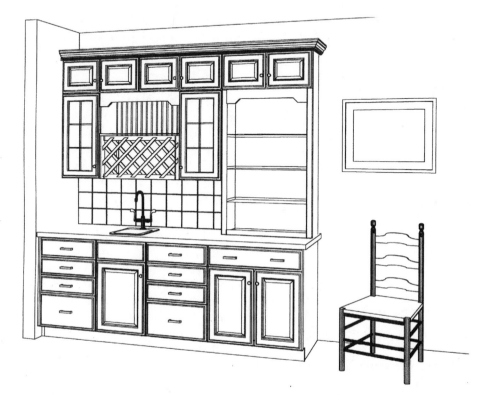

Basic Wet Bar

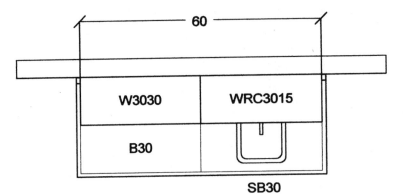

Cabinet List:

1 30″×30″ wall cabinet
1 30″×15″ wine rack cabinet
1 30″ stem glass holder
1 30″ base cabinet
1 30″ sink base cabinet
1 8′-0″ crown molding
1 8′-0″ base toe material
2 toe kick cap covers
8 knobs or pulls
1 pint stain
1 putty stick

Additional Materials Needed:

• Miscellaneous fasteners and adhesives
• Countertop
• Bar sink and faucet

Required:

• Attach stem glass holder below wine rack

Variations:

• Add mullion doors, tempered glass insets, glass shelves, and interior lighting to the 30″ wall cabinet
• Add a tray divider or other interior storage aids to the 30″ base cabinet
• Add skins and decorator matching doors to exposed cabinet sides

Just four cabinets are required to create this basic wet bar that fits on even a small wall space. Five feet of counterspace and a small bar sink make a convenient place to serve beverages of every kind. If additional drawers are needed, replace the 30″ base cabinet with a 15″ base cabinet and a 15″ bank of drawers.

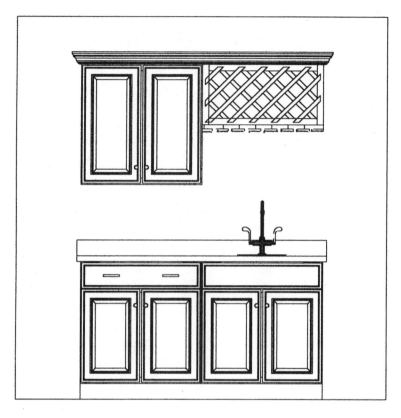

Beverage Center with Angled Ends

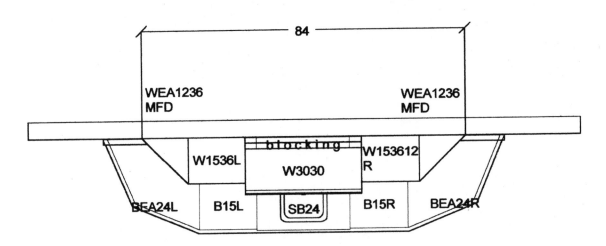

Cabinet List:

1 36″ high left end angle wall cabinet with mullion doors and matching interiors
2 15″×36″ wall cabinets
1 30″×30″ wall cabinet
1 30″ spice drawer with matching wood knobs
1 48″ decorative valance
1 48″ straight valance
1 36″ high right end angle wall cabinet with mullion doors and matching interiors
2 tempered glass inserts
1 24″ left end angle base cabinet
2 15″ base cabinets
1 24″ sink base
1 24″ right end angle base cabinet
2 8′-0″ crown molding
1 8′-0″ light rail molding
2 8′-0″ base toe material
16 knobs or pulls
1 pint stain
1 putty stick

Additional Materials Needed:

- Miscellaneous fasteners and adhesives
- Dimensional lumber
- Countertop
- Bar sink and faucet

Required:

- Stack 30″ wall cabinet, 30″ spice drawer, trimmed appliquéd valance and pull entire unit forward to 15″
- Cut straight valance as returns for decorative valance
- Install light rail on 36″ high wall cabinets only

Variations:

- Add rollout shelves to both 15″ base cabinets
- Add undercabinet lighting behind light rail

Dressy enough to fit in a dining room, this beverage center makes entertaining easy. The center section is stacked, staggered, and pulled forward. Mullion doors on the wall end angle cabinets are great for display.

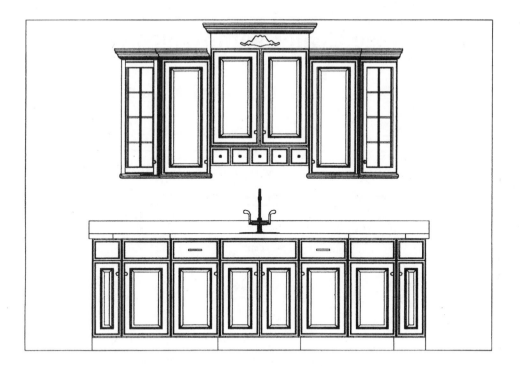

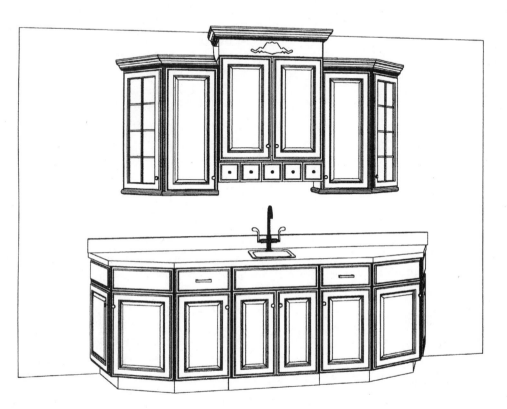

Beverage Center with Angled Front

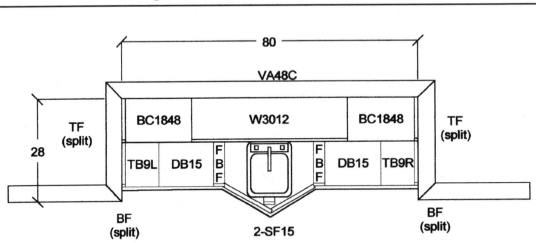

Cabinet List:

1 tall filler (split)
2 18"×48" bookcase units
3 48" finished shelves
1 48" arched valance
1 30"×12" wall cabinet
2 9" tray base cabinets
2 15" drawer bases
2 3" base fluted fillers
2 15" sink fronts
1 36"×36" sink front floor
1 8'-0" crown molding
2 6" tall fillers
12 knobs or pulls
1 pint stain
1 putty stick

Additional Materials Needed:

- Miscellaneous fasteners and adhesives
- Dimensional lumber
- Countertop
- Bar sink and faucet

Required:

- Minimum 1" filler at each wall
- Build a platform beneath the sink front floor
- Bevel edges of sink fronts at joints
- Use one finished shelf as a soffit board behind the valance
- Trim tall filler material as base toe material. Miter joint at point

Variations:

- Add interior tray dividers in tray base cabinets
- Add cutlery divider to top drawers
- Panel or tile entire wall between backsplash and valance

An interesting beverage center with an angled sink area is designed to be approached from either side rather than straight on. The cabinetry is symmetrically placed on either side of the sink area for a balanced look. Finished shelving captures the centered wall cabinet creating small open niches on either side.

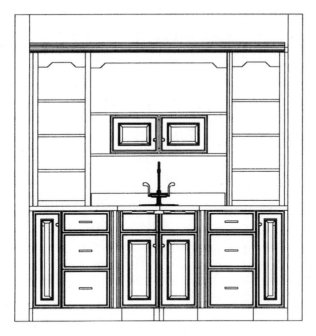

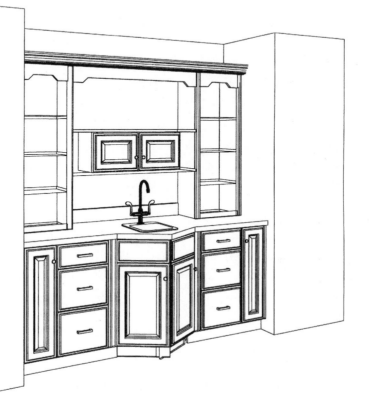

Billiard Room

Cabinet List:

1 wall filler
2 24″×30″ wall cabinets
2 15″×30 wall cabinets with mullion doors and matching interiors
2 tempered glass inserts
1 30″×15″ wine rack cabinet
1 decorative valance trimmed to 30″
1 72″ finished shelf (split)
4 36″ high fluted fillers
1 base filler
1 15″ base cabinet
1 dishwasher front kit
1 30″ sink base
1 15″ drawer base
1 9″ tray base cabinet
1 base skin
2 8′-0″ crown molding
2 8′-0″ base toe kick material
1 toe kick cap cover
15 knobs or pulls
1 pint stain
1 putty stick

Additional Materials Needed:

- Miscellaneous fasteners and adhesives
- Dimensional lumber for countertop cleat
- Countertop with snack bar overhang

- Dishwasher
- Undercounter refrigerator
- Sink and faucet

Required:

- Minimum 1″ filler at the wall
- Create support post for snack area from four fluted fillers
- Apply decorator matching door kit to dishwasher
- Cut 72″ finished shelf as soffit board behind valance and as top of wine rack

Variations:

- Add glass shelves and interior lighting for mullion door cabinets
- Add a tray divider and other interior storage aids to cabinets
- Panel wall above wine rack

A billiard table is often a guest magnet. Provide for every comfort for your guests by adding a snack area that includes a sink, dishwasher and undercounter refrigerator. A table leg made from fluted fillers, as well as cleating at the wall, supports the countertop overhang.

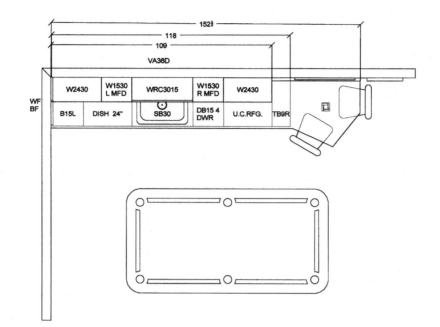

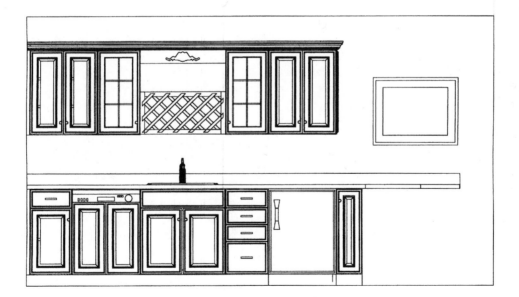

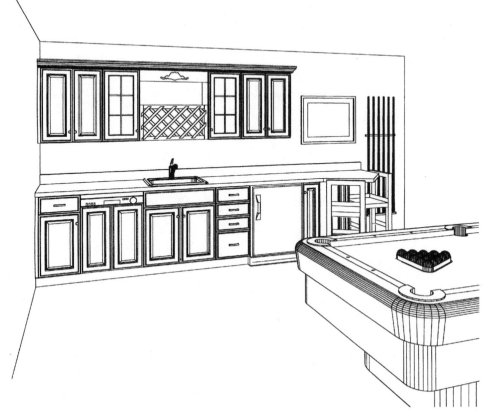

Breakfast Bar

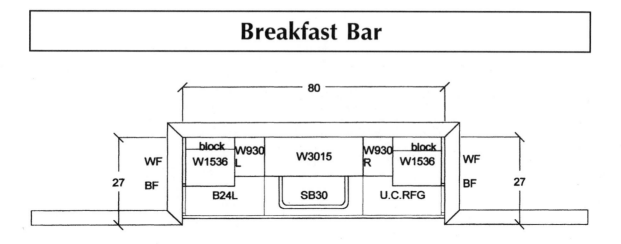

Cabinet List:

1 36″ wall filler (trimmed and split)
2 15″×36″ wall cabinets
1 tall skin (trimmed and split)
2 9″×30″ wall cabinets
1 30″×15″ wall cabinet
1 base filler (split)
1 24″ base cabinet
1 30″ sink base
2 8′-0″ crown molding
1 8′-0″ base toe material
12 knobs or pulls
1 pint stain
1 putty stick

Additional Materials Needed:

- Miscellaneous fasteners and adhesives
- Dimensional lumber
- Countertop
- Single-bowl sink and faucet
- Undercabinet microwave
- Undercounter refrigerator

Required:

- Minimum 1″ filler at each wall
- Pull 15″ wide wall cabinets forward and block
- Trim tall skin and finish exposed sides of 15″ wall cabinets

Variations:

- Change 15″ wide wall cabinets to mullion doors with matching interiors
- Adjust to fit job-site dimensions
- Add decorator wood doors on the under-counter refrigerator

This breakfast bar is designed to be located in the bedroom area for quick morning breakfasts. Staggered wall cabinets set off the design that includes an undercabinet microwave and refrigerator.

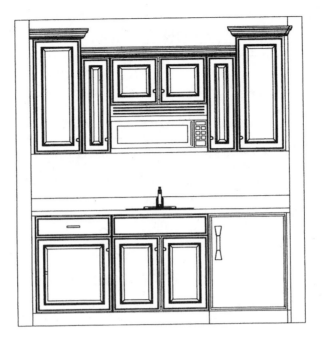

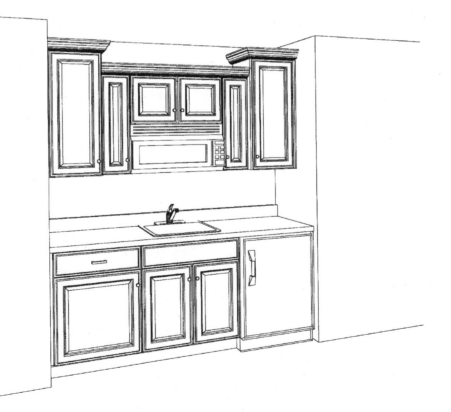

Coffee Bar

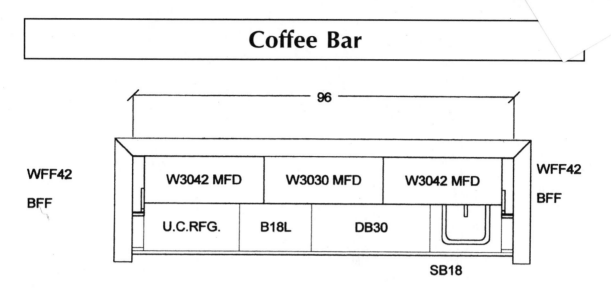

Cabinet List:

2 42″ fluted wall fillers
8 rosettes
2 6″×42″ wall fillers
2 30″×42″ wall cabinets with mullion doors
   and matching interiors
1 30″×30″ wall cabinets with mullion doors
   and matching interiors
1 30″×12″ finished shelf
6 tempered glass inserts
2 fluted base fillers
1 18″ base cabinet
1 30″ drawer base
1 18″ sink base cabinet
2 8′-0″ crown molding
1 8′-0″ base toe kick material
15 knobs or pulls
1 pint stain
1 putty stick

Additional Materials Needed:

- Miscellaneous fasteners and adhesives
- Dimensional lumber
- Under counter refrigerator
- Countertop with full-height backsplash
- Bar sink and faucet

Required:

- Block and install fluted wall fillers 15″ out
  from wall; use 6″×42″ plain fillers as returns
- Attach finished shelf to bottom of W3030
  MFD

Variations:

- Order some wall cabinets with solid doors
  for more concealed storage
- Add light rail and undercabinet lighting to
  wall cabinets

Coffee of every type is enjoying a tremendous popularity. This dedicated coffee bar can be tucked out of the way in a large kitchen, placed in the family or game room. It is outfitted with a bar sink and an undercounter refrigerator. A plumbed-in espresso maker would be the ultimate addition. The fluted wall fillers with rosette accents are pulled forward.

Deluxe Wet Bar

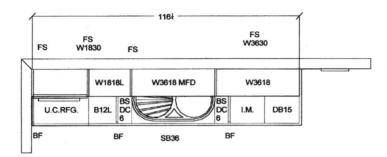

Cabinet List:

5 48″ finished shelves
2 stem glass holders
1 96″ tall skin (split)
1 18″×18″ wall cabinets
1 18″×30″ wall cabinets
1 36″×18″ wall cabinet with mullion doors and matching interiors
2 tempered glass inserts
2 36″ arched valances
1 36″×18″ wall cabinet
1 36″×30″ wall cabinet
1 base filler
1 12″ base cabinet
2 base spice drawers with matching wood knobs
2 base skins
1 appliance decorator matching door
1 36″ sink base
1 15″ drawer base
2 8′-0″ crown molding
2 8′-0″ base toe material
15 knobs or pulls
1 pint stain
1 putty stick

Additional Materials Needed:

- Miscellaneous fasteners and adhesives
- Countertop
- Tile for backsplash
- Sink/drainboard combination with faucet
- 24″ wide undercounter refrigerator that accepts wood panels
- 15″ icemaker
- Microwave to fit open area

Required:

- Measurement for wood panel on under-counter refrigerator
- Cut base skin to fit undercounter refrigerator trim kit, apply decorator door and install to front of appliance
- Minimum 1″ filler at wall
- Create open unit on left from finished shelves, stem glass holders and arched valance
- Apply tall skin to rear wall of open unit as paneling
- Use remaining part of tall skin to cover exposed joint on right wall cabinet stack
- Skin right side of 15″ drawer base

Variations:

- Adjust to fit job-site conditions and appliance specifications
- Add a light behind the center valance

This beverage center features an open shelf unit with ample space for storing glassware. Since this beverage center contains a microwave oven, undercounter refrigerator and icemaker as well as a sink with a drainboard, nearly a complete meal can be created in this environment. The backsplash area offers an opportunity to personalize the space with textural or hand painted tile.

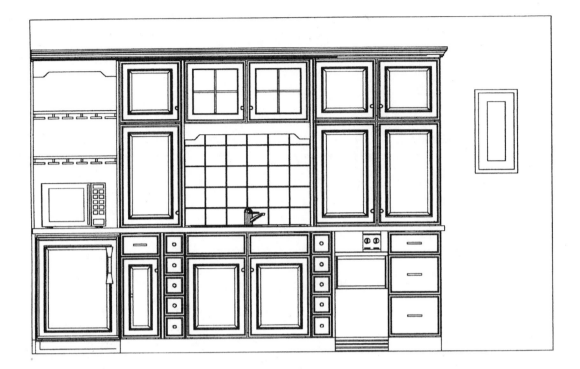

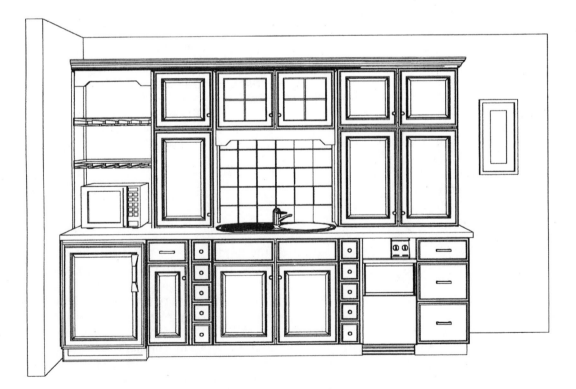

Dry Bar

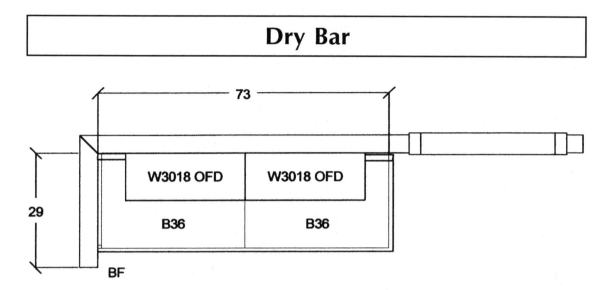

Cabinet List:

1 base filler
2 36″ base cabinets
2 30″×18″ wall cabinets with open-frame doors and matching interiors
4 tempered glass inserts
2 3″×96″ tall fillers
2 8′-0″ base toe material
1 base toe kick cap
12 knobs or pulls
1 pint stain
1 putty stick

Additional Materials Needed:

• Miscellaneous fasteners and adhesives
• Countertop

Required:

• Minimum 1″ base filler at wall
• Center the wall cabinets over the counter-top

• Trim tall filler as top molding and light rail, extending 1 1/2″ beyond the cabinet

Variations:

• Use ribbed or textured glass inserts instead of clear glass
• Reduce the base cabinet sizes to include an undercounter refrigerator
• Add skins and decorator matching doors to exposed ends of cabinets

Even when no plumbing exists, a handy and economical beverage bar can be created from four cabinets and a few miscellaneous parts. Tall filler material used as top and light rail molding gives a clean contemporary look.

Elegant Bar

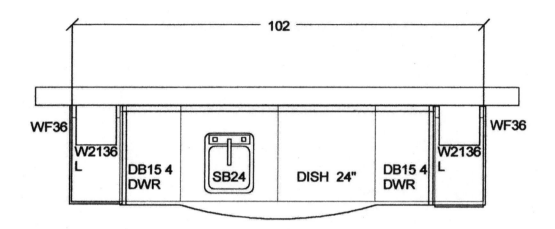

Cabinet List:

2 21″×36″ wall cabinets
2 36″ high wall fillers
2 15″ four-drawer bases
1 24″ sink base
1 set dishwasher panels
2 8′-0″ base toe material
12 knobs or pulls
1 pint stain
1 putty stick

Additional Materials Needed:

- Miscellaneous fasteners and adhesives
- Dimensional lumber
- Countertop with radius center, back and side splashes
- 2 caps for raised cabinets
- Bar sink and faucet
- 1 dishwasher
- 2 columns

Required:

- Soffit with recessed lights
- Install 21″×36″ wall cabinets perpendicular to wall with fillers
- Build platforms for end wall cabinets, allowing for toe recess

Variations:

- Change style of columns
- Change soffit to have an arched center

Thirty-six inch high wall cabinets are built up on a platform, topped with caps of matching wood or countertop material. These raised cabinets are the bases for decorative columns that adds to the formal look of the center. By providing sides splashes for the countertops, the backs of the raised wall cabinets are concealed.

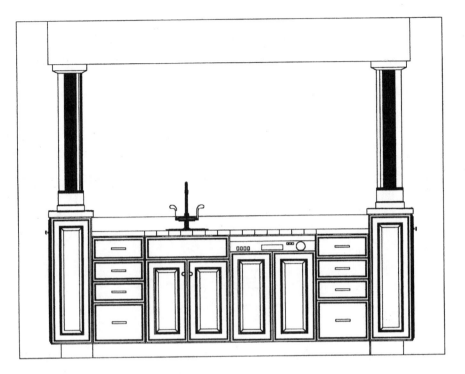

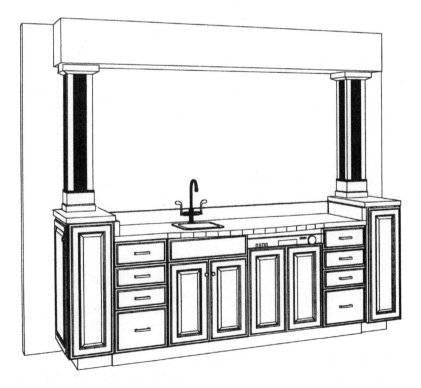

Game Room

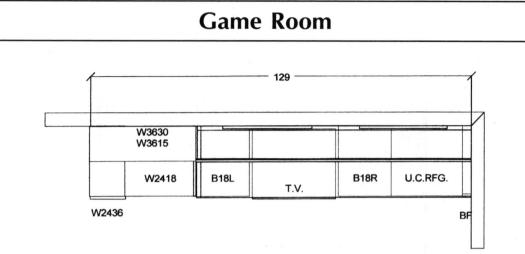

Cabinet List:

1 36″×15″ wall cabinet
1 36″×30″ wall cabinet
2 48″ wall skins
1 96″ tall skin
1 84″ tall skin
1 24″×36″ wall cabinet
1 36″ wall skin
1 36″ high wall decorator matching door
1 24″×18″ wall cabinet
2 18″ base cabinets
1 base filler
1 8′-0″ outside corner molding
2 8′-0″ crown molding
2 8′-0″ base toe material
12 knobs or pulls
1 pint stain
1 putty stick

Additional Materials Needed:

- Miscellaneous fasteners and adhesives
- Dimensional lumber
- Substrate material
- 3 countertops
- Microwave
- Undercounter refrigerator

Required:

- Build a platform for the raised microwave area

- Pull W2418 forward and block
- Right side of the microwave opening is made from substrate, tall skin material, and outside corner molding
- Finish the back of the W2436 and the wall behind the microwave with 84″ tall skin material and outside corner molding
- Create soffit board from substrate material, cover with tall skin, and cleat in place
- Skin both sides of the wall cabinet stack with 48″ high skins
- Minimum 1″ filler at wall
- Proper ventilation for television; consult manufacturer's specifications

Variations:

- Adjust design to fit appliances and job-site space
- Add lighting to soffit board

A family game room requires not only a place to store and prepare snacks but also a place for the television. This built-in incorporates both features and even provides a raised height microwave that makes it easy for the children to make a quick batch of popcorn. The open wall space above the counter is perfect for displaying artwork.

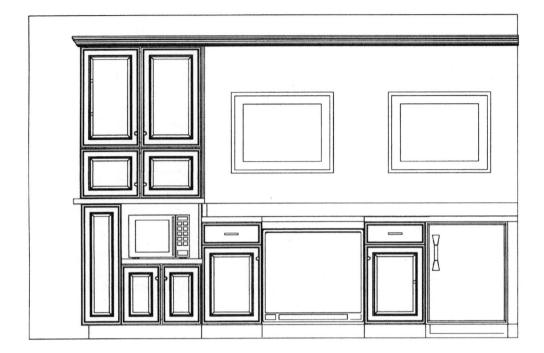

Granny Flat

Cabinet List:

2 84" high refrigerator panels
1 30"×18" wall cabinet
1 27"×30" wall cabinet
1 24"×30" corner wall cabinet
2 15"×30" wall cabinets
1 30"×15" wall cabinet
1 15" base cabinet
1 36" lazy susan cabinet
1 36" sink/range base
1 27" sink base
1 12" base cabinet
2 8'-0" base toe kick material
3 8'-0" crown molding
1 toe kick cap covers
18 knobs or pulls
1 pint stain
1 putty stick

Additional Materials Needed:

• Miscellaneous fasteners and adhesives
• Countertop
• Snack countertop and supports
• Dishwasher
• Refrigerator

• Cooktop
• Over-the-range microwave
• Single-bowl sink and faucet

Required:

• Pass-through with snack bar to living area

Variations:

• Add mullion doors to the 15" wall cabinets
• Add a cutlery divider and other interior storage aids to cabinets
• Add skins and decorator matching doors to exposed cabinet sides
• Add light rail molding and undercabinet lighting

Larger than most beverage centers this kitchen can easily be converted to a granny flat. Called that because when combined with a bedroom and a sitting area, it becomes a suite for an elderly parent. It is also ideal for a nanny or even bounce-back kids. The cabinetry and fittings here are not quite a whole kitchen, since the only oven is a microwave.

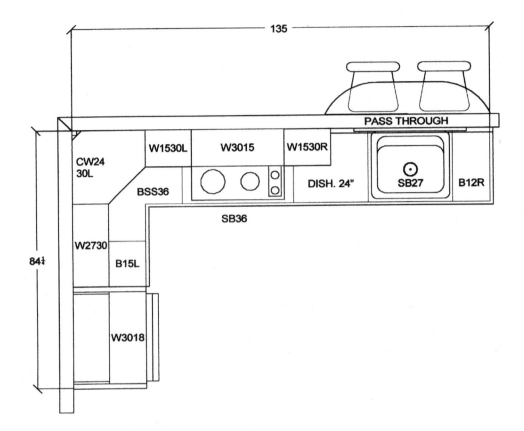

135

84¼

PASS THROUGH

CW24
30L

W1530L   W3015   W1530R

BSS36

DISH. 24"   SB27   B12R

SB36

W2730

B15L

W3018

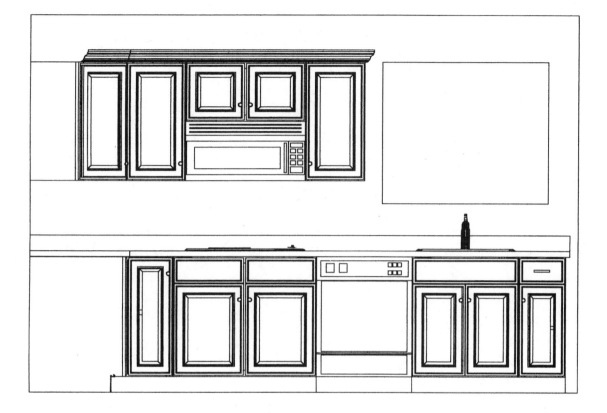

Kitchenette

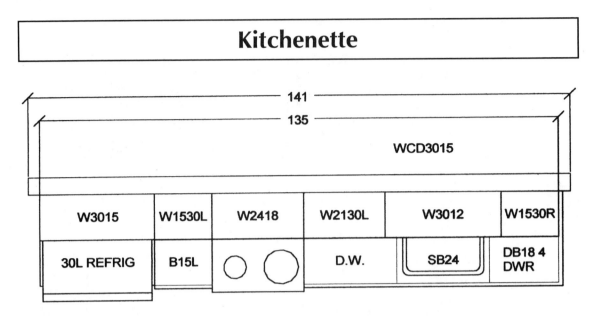

Cabinet List:

1 30″×15″ wall cabinet
2 15″×30″ wall cabinets
1 24″×18″ wall cabinet
1 21″×30″ wall cabinet
1 30″×12″ wall cabinet
1 30″×15″ plate rack cabinet
2 8′-0″ crown molding
2 8′-0″ base toe material
1 toe kick cap cover
17 knobs or pulls
1 pint stain
1 putty stick

Additional Materials Needed:

- Miscellaneous fasteners and adhesives
- Countertop
- 21″ single-bowl sink and faucet
- 30″ refrigerator
- 24″ range
- 24″ range hood

Required:

- Stack plate rack cabinet below 12″ high wall cabinet over the sink

Variations:

- Adjust dimensions to job-site conditions.
- Add a work island, if room permits, for additional storage and counterspace

Sometimes a beverage center can take the form of a full kitchenette. This works especially well in a basement recreation area where the area serves multiple usage. This kitchenette is not only a great place to mix up a fruit smoothie, but can also serve as a catering or canning kitchen. A full-size refrigerator stores extra beverages.

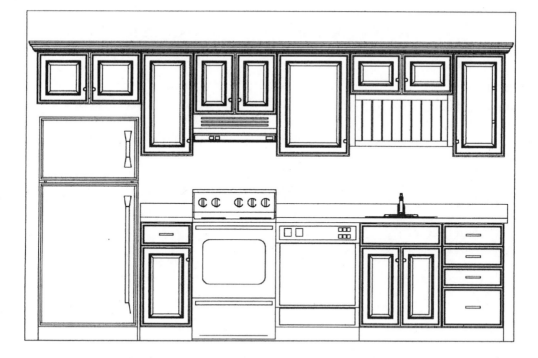

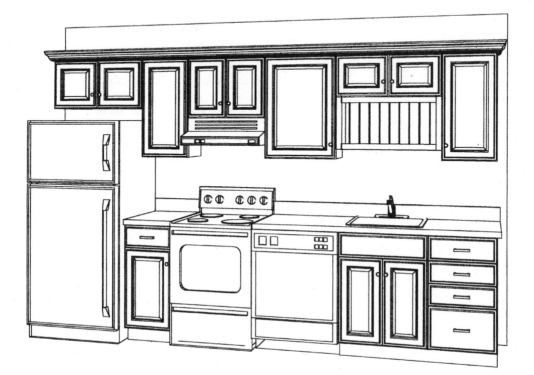

L-Shaped Beverage Center

Cabinet List:

2 18″×36″ wall cabinets reduced to 9″ deep
4 36″ wall skins
2 9″×36″ replacement doors as decorator matching doors
2 18″×36 wall cabinets
1 36″×30″ wall cabinet with mullion doors and matching interiors
2 tempered glass inserts
1 36″×15″ wall cabinet
1 tall skin (split)
1 30″ base cabinet
1 18″ four-drawer base
1 36″ lazy susan
1 27″ sink base
1 dishwasher return panel
2 base skins
2 base decorator matching doors
3 8′-0″ crown molding
2 8′-0″ base toe material
2 toe kick cap covers
2 counter top supports
19 knobs or pulls
1 pint stain
1 putty stick

Additional Materials Needed:

- Miscellaneous fasteners and adhesives
- Dimensional lumber

- 2 countertops
- Single-bowl sink and faucet
- Dishwasher
- Undercounter refrigerator

Required:

- 40 1/2″ high wall behind sink wall
- Stack, pull forward, and block center wall cabinets; finish sides with split and trimmed tall skin
- Skin exposed ends of B30 and dishwasher return, apply decorator matching doors

Variations:

- Add light rail below wall cabinets and add undercabinet lighting
- Add glass shelves and lighting to mullion door cabinet

For a family room or basement recreation area, this well-appointed beverage center has a raised countertop overhang that easily accommodates three people. A dishwasher return is required to conceal the unfinished end of the dishwasher. It is treated to a base skin and a decorator matching door.

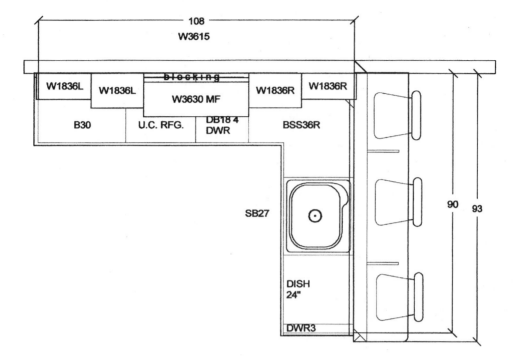

108

W3615

W1836L   W1836L   blocking   W1836R   W1836R

W3630 MF

B30   U.C. RFG.   DB18 4 DWR   BSS36R

90   93

SB27

DISH 24"

DWR3

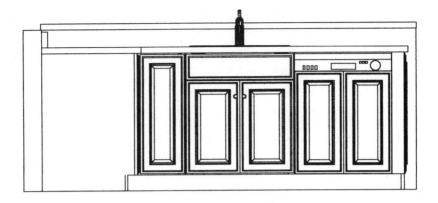

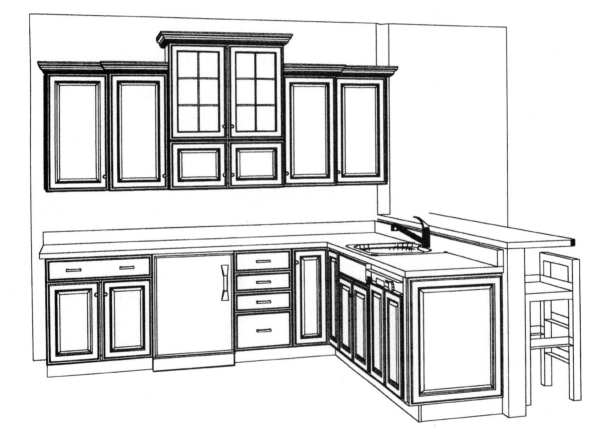

Mini Juice Bar

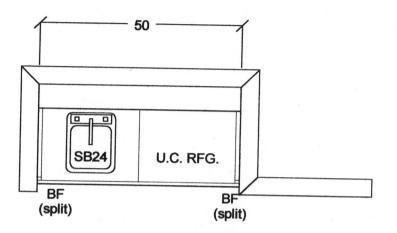

Cabinet List:

1 24″ sink base
1 base filler (split)
24″ of base toe material
2 knobs or pulls
1 pint stain
1 putty stick

Additional Materials Needed:

- Miscellaneous fasteners and adhesives
- Countertop
- 2 glass shelves and supports
- Bar sink and faucet
- Undercounter refrigerator

Required:

- Recess with soffit with recessed lights
- Minimum 1″ filler at each wall

Variation:

- Replace glass shelves with wall cabinets for additional storage

A tiny niche in the master bedroom area easily houses this mini juice bar. While it contains only a small sink and an under-counter refrigerator, that is all that is needed to prepare juice, coffee, and a quick bagel in the morning without ever leaving the master suite.

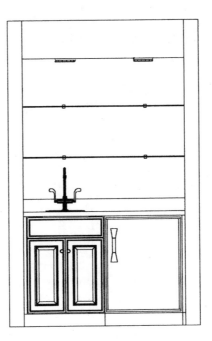

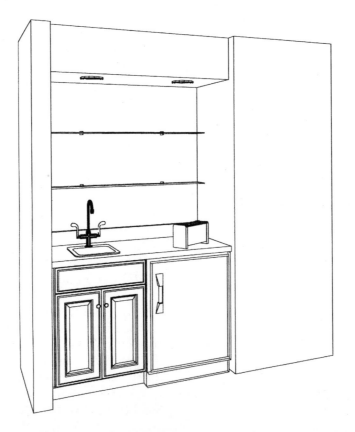

Morning Kitchen

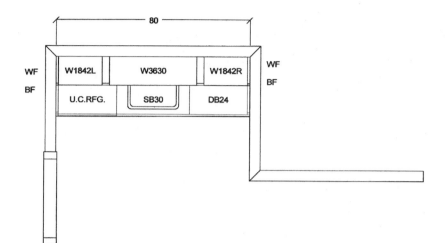

Cabinet List:

1 42″ wall filler (split)
2 18″×42″ wall cabinets
2 30″ fluted fillers
1 36″×30″ wall cabinet
1 36″ finished shelf
1 base filler (split)
1 dishwaser insert panel
1 appliance decorator matching door
1 30″ sink base
1 24″ drawer base
1 8′-0″ crown molding
1 8′-0″ light rail
1 8′-0″ base toe material
9 knobs or pulls
1 pint stain
1 putty stick

Additional Materials Needed:

- Miscellaneous fasteners and adhesives
- Countertop
- Single-bowl sink and faucet
- Undercounter refrigerator that accepts matching wood panels

Required:

- Measurements for wood panel on the undercounter refrigerator
- Cut dishwasher insert panel to fit undercounter refrigerator trim kit, apply decorator door, and apply to front of appliance
- Minimum 1″ filler at wall
- Install finished shelf flush with adjacent wall cabinets
- Install wall cabinets so that the molding goes to the ceiling

Variations:

- Change W1842s to mullion doors and matching interiors
- Adjust to fit site measurements

The morning kitchen is usually placed in the bedroom wing and provides guests and residents alike with the chance to begin the day with breakfast on the run. Adding a small microwave would expand the breakfast-making capabilities. The open shelf is a great place to store coffee mugs.

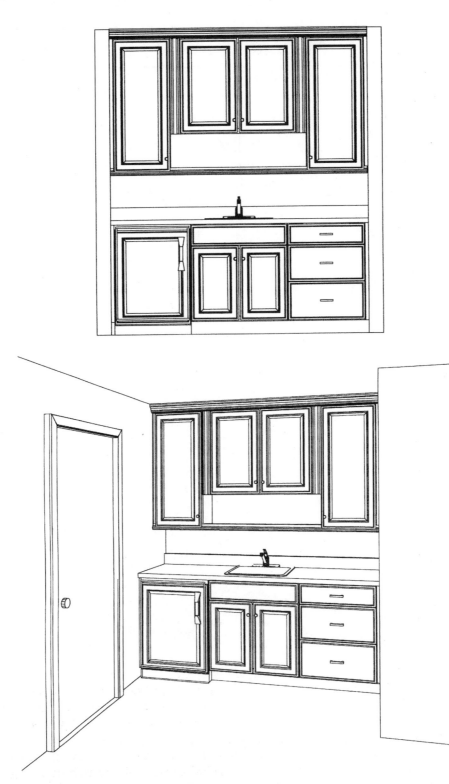

Patio Service Area

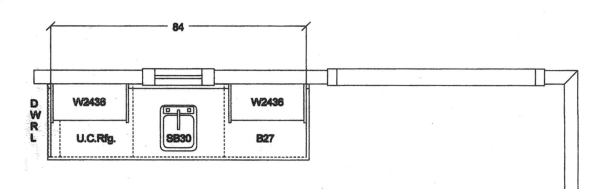

Cabinet List:

2 24″×36″ wall cabinets
5 48″ finished shelves
1 24″×12″ piece of paneling
4 42″ wall decorator matching doors
1 3″ base return panel
2 base skins
2 base decorator matching doors
1 30″ sink base
1 27″ base cabinet
1 8′-0″ base toe material
2 8′-0″ crown molding
2 toe kick cap covers
10 knobs or pulls
1 pint stain
1 putty stick

Additional Materials Needed:

• Miscellaneous fasteners and adhesives
• Countertop
• Bar sink and faucet
• Under counter refrigerator

Required:

• Cut four finished shelves to 42″ and install left and right, flush with bottoms of the W2436s

• Cut fifth shelf as top of niches
• Panel rear wall of niches
• Install 42″ decorator matching doors on finished sides
• Install base skins and base decorator matching doors on dishwasher return and B27

Variations:

• Order wall cabinets with mullion doors, matching interiors and tempered glass inserts
• Add rope or other decorator molding to the vertical edges of the finished shelves
• Delete decorator matching doors for cost savings
• Add light rail molding

If the patio is removed from the kitchen, a beverage center nearby will make entertaining much simpler. Here 36″ high wall cabinets are encased with finished shelving creating display niches above. Adding rope molding or other decorative molding to the vertical edges will add rich detailing.

Snack Center

Cabinet List:

2 24″×36″ wall cabinets
2 24″ appliance garages
2 tall skins (split)
1 wall skin
1 48″ arched valance
1 48″ finished shelf
1 3″ tall filler (trimmed)
1 24″ drawer base
1 base skin
1 45″ base cabinet
1 3″ base filler
2 36″×30″ wall cabinets
1 wall skin
2 8′-0″ crown molding
2 8′-0″ base toe material
1 toe kick cap cover
17 knobs or pulls
1 pint stain
1 putty stick

Additional Materials Needed:

- Miscellaneous fasteners and adhesives
- Dimensional lumber
- Table support
- 2 countertops
- Bar sink and faucet
- Undercounter refrigerator

Required:

- 34 1/2″ high wall behind wall cabinets in snack area
- Build a platform for wall cabinets used as bases
- Soffit with recessed lights to match front bar and snack area
- Trim finished shelf as a soffit board and install behind the valance
- Remove the center drawer box and "dummy" the drawer head on the B45 to accommodate the bar sink
- Minimum 1″ filler at walls
- Skin all exposed cabinet ends

Variations:

- Add decorator matching doors on exposed cabinet ends
- Adjust size to fit job-site conditions

When space is at a premium, 12″ deep wall cabinets can be built up on a platform and used as base cabinets. The wall between the tambour stacks can be paneled to match the cabinets, tiled for use as a place to display artwork, or can be used for a mirror.

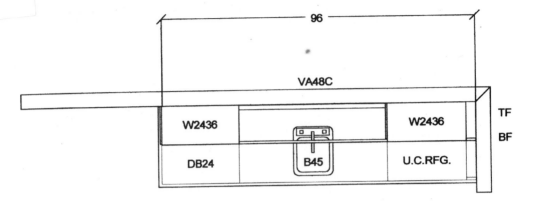

96

VA48C

| W2436 | | W2436 |

TF

BF

| DB24 | B45 | U.C.RFG. |

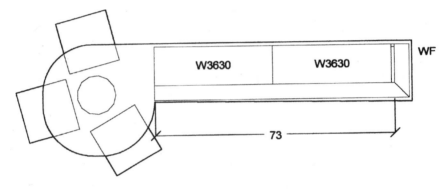

WF

| W3630 | W3630 |

73

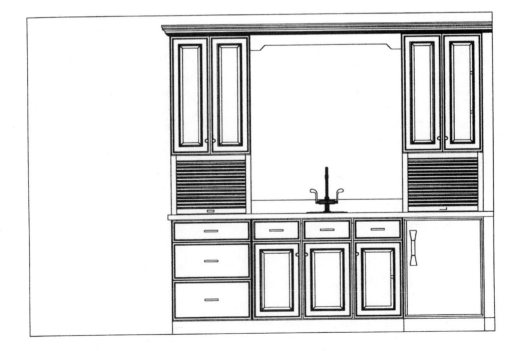

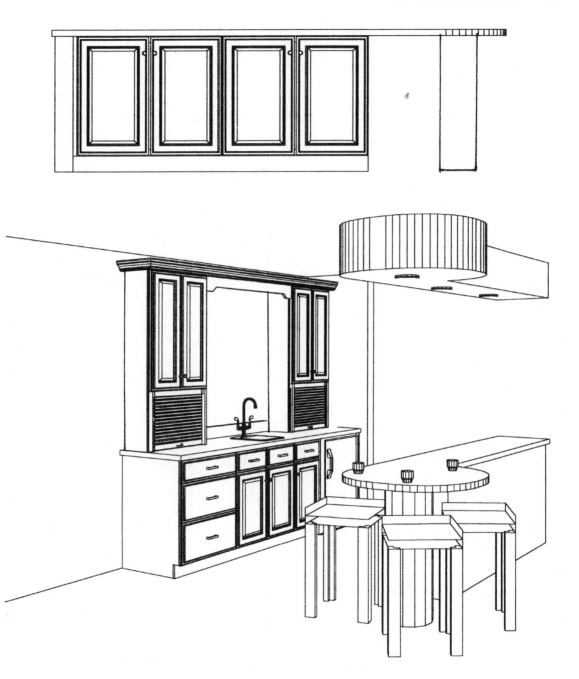

Tall Storage Beverage Center

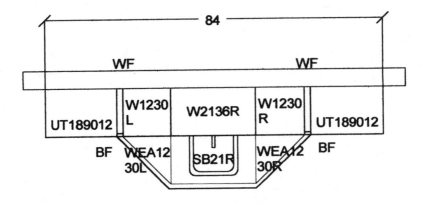

Cabinet List:

2 18″×90″×12″ utility cabinets
12 utility shelves
2 wall fillers
2 12″×30″ wall cabinets
1 21″×36″ wall cabinet
1 48″ finished shelf
2 base fillers
2 wall end angle cabinets
1 21″ sink base
2 8′-0″ crown molding
2 8′-0″ base toe material
2 toe kick cap covers
10 knobs or pulls
1 pint stain
1 putty stick

Additional Materials Needed:

• Miscellaneous fasteners and adhesives
• Dimensional lumber
• Countertop
• Bar sink and faucet

Required:

• Build platforms for angled wall cabinets allowing for toe recess
• Install wall end angle cabinets 12″ out from wall
• Wall and base fillers at utility cabinets

Variations:

• Add decorator matching doors to exposed ends of utility cabinets
• Choose the 12″ wide wall cabinets with mullion doors and matching interiors

This beverage center provides tall storage as well as a place to serve and clean up beverages. This unit would fit in a game room, bedroom wing, or family room. Varied height wall cabinets are tied together by finished shelving, creating open niches.

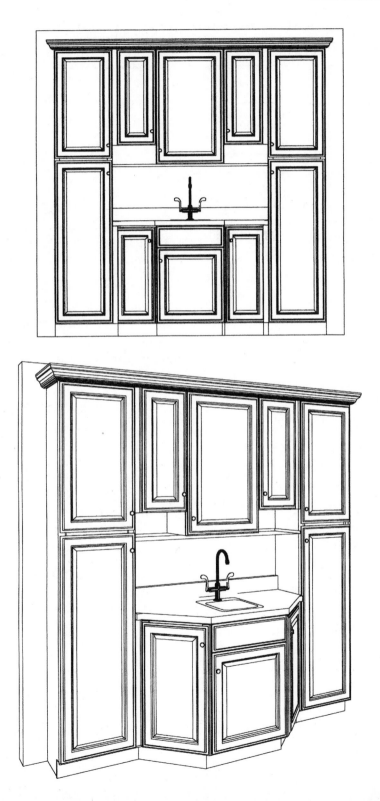

Two Section Beverage Bar

Cabinet List:

1 36″ wall filler
2 21″×36″ wall cabinets
1 36″ wall skin
1 30″ spice drawer unit with matching wood knobs
1 30′×18″ wall cabinet with mullion doors and matching interior
2 tempered glass inserts
1 30″×15″ wine rack cabinet
1 96″ tall skin (split)
2 36″ base cabinets
2 base skins
1 base filler (split)
1 18″ drawer bank
1 36″ sink base cabinet
1 18″ base cabinet
2 corbels
2 8′-0″ crown molding
2 8′-0″ base toe material
2 toe kick cap covers
19 knobs or pulls
1 pint stain
1 putty stick

Additional Materials Needed:

• Miscellaneous fasteners and adhesives
• Dimensional lumber

• 3 countertop sections
• Bar sink and faucet

Required:

• 73″ long by 40 1/2″ high wall behind front bar
• Minimum 1″ filler at each wall
• Stack spice drawers, mullion door cabinet, and wine rack together
• Pull forward and block center wall cabinet stack
• Split tall skin and cover both sides of wall cabinet stack
• Skin all remaining exposed cabinet ends

Variations:

• Add a tray divider or other interior storage aids to the base cabinets
• Add skins and decorator matching doors to exposed cabinet sides

A raised bar area obscures the view of bar clutter. The stacked and staggered height wall cabinets on the back wall provide a true design focal point. By pulling the center section forward 3″, adjacent top molding butts neatly into the side of the center stack.

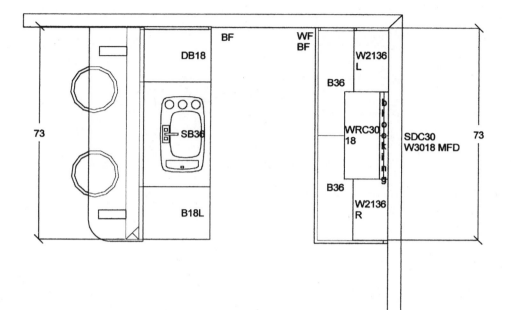

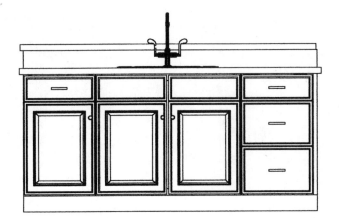

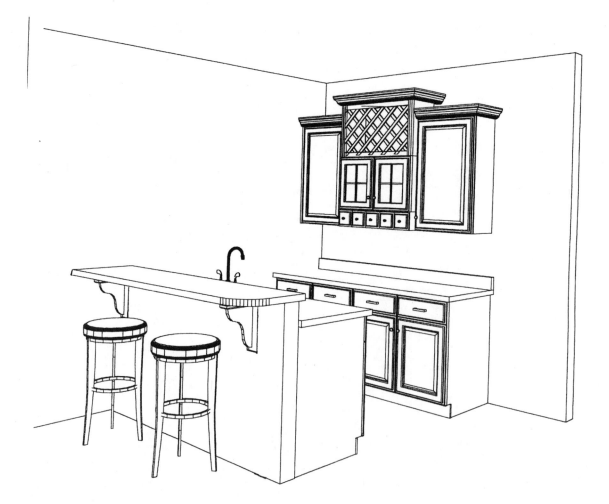

Wine Bar

Cabinet List:

1 36″ wall filler
2 30″×36″ wall cabinets
1 36″×30″ cathedral wall cabinet with mullion doors and matching interiors
1 36″ stem glass holder
2 tempered glass inserts
1 15″×36″ wall cabinet
1 30″×36″ wall cabinet
1 36″ wall skin
1 36″ decorator matching door
4 48″ finished shelves
1 36″ frieze valance
1 36″×15″ wall cabinet
1 36″×21″ piece of bead board paneling
2 base fillers
1 9″ tray base cabinet
2 base fluted fillers
1 24″ sink base
2 6″ base fillers
1 18″×30″ wall wine rack
1 18″ drawer base
1 24″ base end angle cabinet
1 36″ base cabinet
2 8′-0″ crown molding
2 8′-0″ base toe material
21 knobs or pulls
1 pint stain
1 putty stick

Additional Materials Needed:

- Miscellaneous fasteners and adhesives
- Dimensional lumber
- Countertop
- Bar sink and faucet
- Wine cooler

Required:

- Outside corner wall configuration
- Pull forward and install wall wine rack cabinet on a platform
- Attach fluted fillers to the sink base and install forward 3″
- Use 6″ base fillers as returns for fluted fillers
- Trim finished shelving as:
  - a soffit board behind the valance
  - two side panels
  - top shelf on W3615
- Apply beadboard paneling to open shelf area

Variation:

- Adjust dimensions to job-site conditions.

A sophisticated wine bar wraps around an outside corner wall. A base end angle cabinet and a wall cabinet that extends beyond the wall help make the transition with ease. The cabinet over the sink features cathedral mullion doors as an accent.

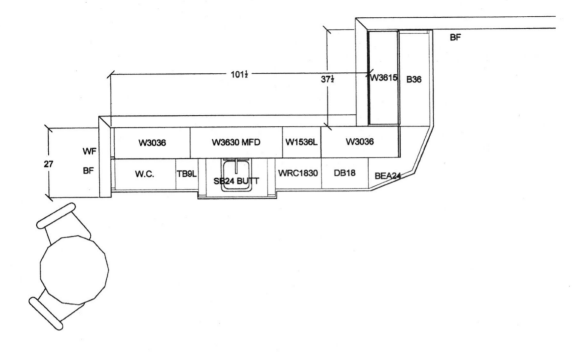

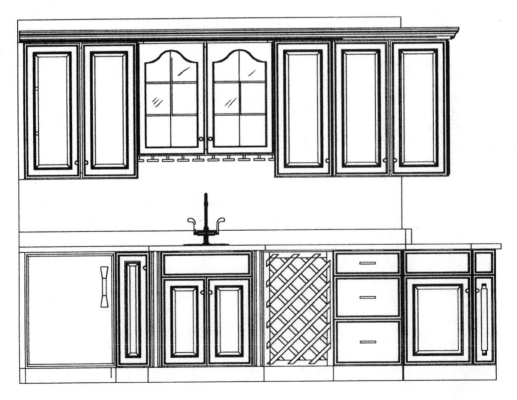

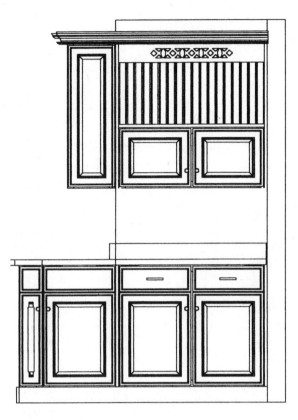

Wrap-Around Bar

Cabinet List:

2   18″×42″ wall cabinets with mullion doors and matching interiors
2   tempered glass inserts
4   42″ wall skins
1   36″ arched valance
1   36″×24″ piece paneling
1   36″×15″ plate rack cabinet
1   36″ under shelf unit
1   72″ finished shelf (split)
2   36″ base cabinets
1   30″ sink base
4   base fillers
1   blind base cabinet 45″/48″
2   blind swing-out shelves
1   15″ drawer base
1   3″×24″ dishwasher end panel
2   base skins
2   base decorator matching doors
2   96″×34 1/2″ paneling
4   countertop supports
2   8′-0″ crown molding
3   8′-0″ base toe material
3   base toe kick cap covers
1   8′-0″ outside corner molding
17 knobs or pulls
1   pint stain
1   putty stick

Additional Materials Needed:

- Miscellaneous fasteners and adhesives
- Dimensional lumber
- Substrate
- Countertop

- Bar sink and faucet
- Undercounter refrigerator

Required:

- Apply substrate to back of the wrap around bar and cover with paneling
- Cover raw edge of paneling at corner with outside corner molding
- Cut finished shelf, use half as a soffit board and install remainder on top of plate rack
- Apply finished paneling to back wall above plate rack
- Skin all exposed cabinet ends
- Apply decorator matching doors on base cabinets only

Variations:

- Add decorator matching doors to both ends of exposed wall cabinets
- Add a wainscoting treatment to the back of the bar
- Add glass shelves and interior cabinet lighting to mullion door cabinet

A wrap-around bar with a 36″ high snack bar is perfect for the family recreation area. The wall unit features a plate rack with an open shelf cabinet below. A dishwasher return panel encloses the side of the undercounter refrigerator. The cabinets with mullion doors show off glassware. The addition of substrate strengthens the back of the bar.

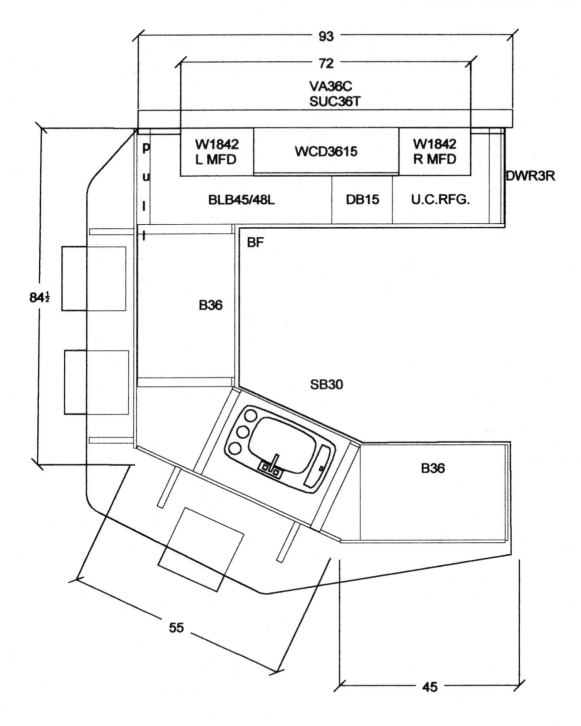

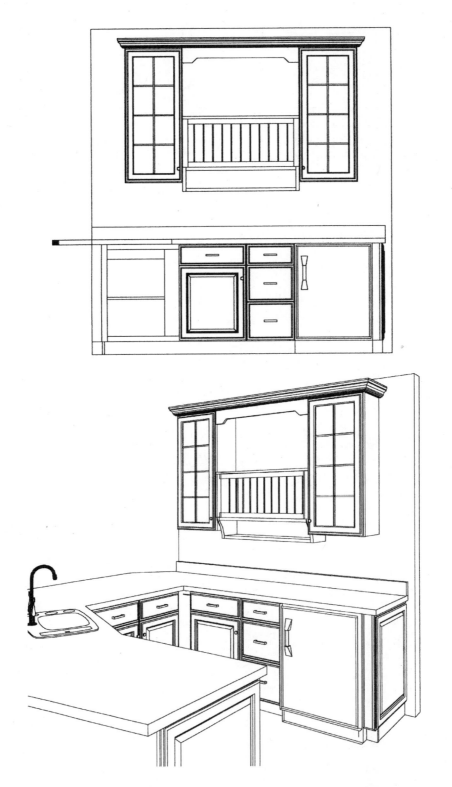

CHAPTER 4

Libraries, Offices, and Desks

Home offices are a fact as we begin the Twenty-first Century. Whether it is the heart of a home-based business, a place for the occasional telecommuter, or simply a space to surf the Internet, a well-thought-out office is on almost every homeowner's wish list today.

Design of an office or desk area depends on its planned usage. But it is always a good idea to over-design the space when it comes to wiring and work surfaces.

Technology and lifestyles change at a rapid rate. What seems to be more than enough power and spread-out space quickly becomes inadequate. Computers and other office equipment have very specific wiring and air circulation requirements. From a cabinet design standpoint, it is important to be completely familiar with the equipment specifications early in the design process so that spaces are well thought out and functional.

An office that is designed for a full-time home-based business is usually located in a dedicated room with its own private entrance. Professional offices also require space for scanners, copiers, and printers.

Then, there are the charging docks for PDAs (personal digital assistants) and cell phones. All in all, the design of the professional space must accommodate modern usage, and yet be an attractive part of the home.

Small desk areas are often found in medium to large kitchens. There are many negative points to having a true office in the kitchen such as spills, noise, and lack of space. Nevertheless, as many as 15 percent of all kitchen remodeling projects today *do* incorporate a space for a computer, for bill paying, for managing volunteer work, or for composing grocery lists.

Desk areas also can be part of a family room. Here, the focus is on a look that is totally compatible with the rest of the décor. Book storage is often incorporated here, too. Whether it is flanking the fireplace or incorporated in a desk area, an attractive place to store books and collectibles is highly desirable.

Of course, the ultimate is to have a separate library with walls lined with bookcases. But bookcase units as well as desks can be found anywhere in the home, and all of them can be created with attractive and economical stack cabinets.

Angled Wall Desk

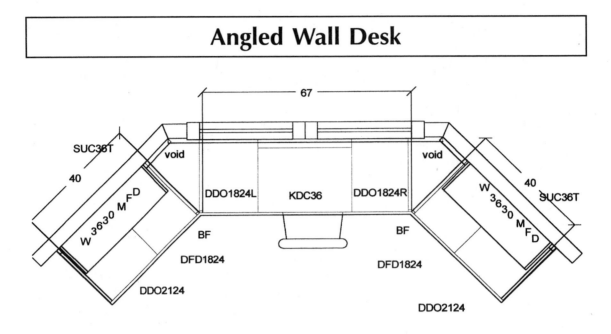

Cabinet List:

2 36"×30" wall cabinets with mullion doors and matching interiors
4 tempered glass inserts
4 30" wall skins
4 decorator matching doors
2 36" shelf undercabinet units
2 21" desk base cabinets
2 18" desk file cabinets
2 base fillers (split)
2 18" desk base cabinets
4 base skins
2 desk base decorator matching doors
1 36" trimmable kneehole drawer
2 8'-0" crown molding
2 base toe material
4 toe kick cap covers
17 knobs or pulls
1 pint stain
1 putty stick

Additional Materials Needed:

• Miscellaneous fasteners and adhesives
• Countertop

Required:

• Minimum of 1" filler at each angled base cabinet
• Skin and apply decorator matching doors on all exposed cabinet sides

Variations:

• Change mullion door wall cabinets to solid doors for more hidden storage

An angled desk, that could fit into a bay window area, features cabinets with mullion doors on either side of the window. One-inch fillers are required on both cabinets as they meet at the angle to allow doors and drawers to function freely.

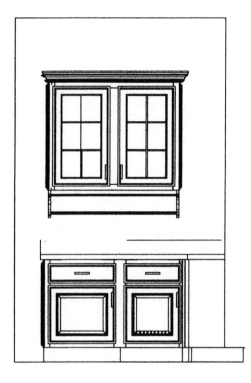

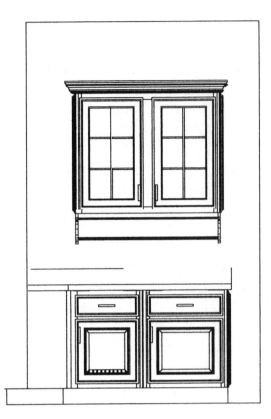

Barrister Bookcase

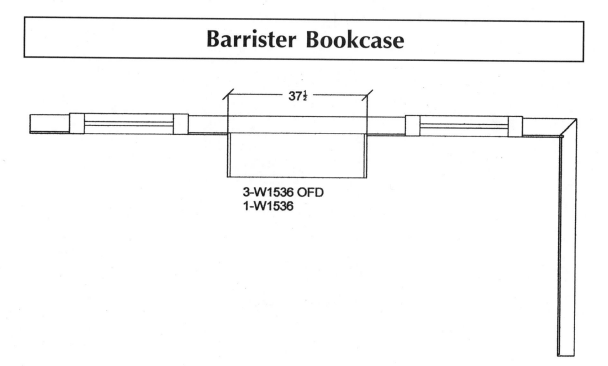

3-W1536 OFD
1-W1536

Cabinet List:

1 15"×36" wall cabinet
3 15"×36" wall cabinets with open-frame doors and matching interiors
3 tempered glass inserts
2 12"×60" finished shelves
1 8'-0" crown molding
1 8'-0" countertop edge molding
1 6"×36" wide wall fillers
1 8'-0" inside corner molding
4 knobs or pulls
1 pint stain
1 putty stick

Additional Materials Needed:

• Miscellaneous fasteners and adhesives
• Dimensional lumber for platforms
• 2 pair lid supports
• 2 pair positive locking supports

Required:

• Build 4" high platforms for bases
• Cover platforms with 6" filler material topped with inside corner molding
• Attach shelving vertically on both sides of the stack

Variations:

• Line insides of cabinet sides to cover shelf hole drillings
• Finish front edge of shelving, used as bookcase sides, with decorative molding

The barrister bookcase was originally designed to allow barristers, or British lawyers, to add a shelf at a time to their bookcases as their law book collection grew. Stacking wall cabinets horizontally creates this updated version that would be a great addition to any office or family room.

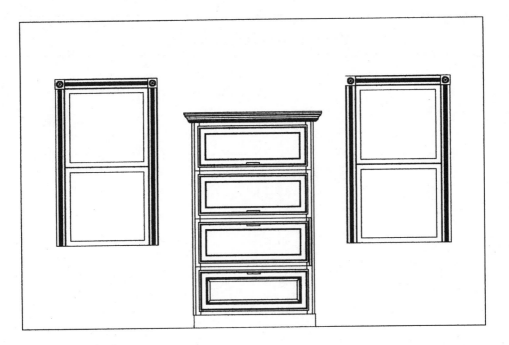

Bill-Paying Center

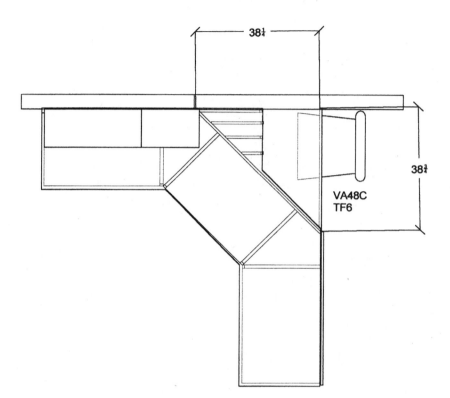

Cabinet List:

Peninsula designed in a 45° angle configuration
1 48" arched valance (trimmed)
1 tall 6" filler
1 pint stain
1 clear topcoat
1 putty stick

Additional Materials Needed:

- Miscellaneous fasteners and adhesives
- Desk countertop

Required:

- Extend the 36" high countertop over the lowered desk area to provide a space for the mail slots
- Stain and finish back of filler material

Variations:

- Raise area to 36" for a single-level work space

A tiny little space to pay bills is tucked into the back of an angled peninsula. A tall 6" filler is cut into mail slots so that bills can be organized quickly. An arched valance trims off the angled knee space.

Bookcase with Coastline Front

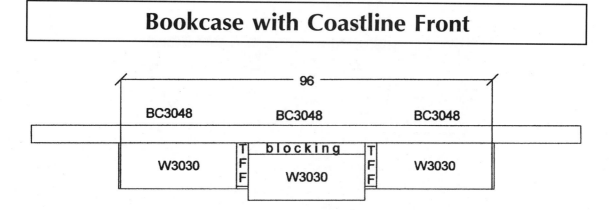

Cabinet List:

3 30″×48″ bookcase cabinets
3 30″×30″ wall cabinets
2 tall fluted fillers
2 84″ tall skins (split)
2 8′-0″ crown molding
2 6″ wide tall fillers
2 8′-0″ inside corner molding
6 knobs or pulls
1 pint stain
1 putty stick

Additional Materials Needed:

- Miscellaneous fasteners and adhesives
- Dimensional lumber

Required:

- Build 4″ high platforms for wall cabinets below bookcases
- Pull center unit forward 3″ and block
- Cover platforms with tall filler material topped with inside corner molding
- Split and trim tall skins to cover joints on all exposed sides

Variations:

- Vary top molding treatment
- Change shelves to tempered glass and add recessed lighting in the top

By pulling the center cabinets forward, creating a coastline affect, design interest is added to the top molding detail as well as the entire bookcase unit. The closed-door storage is great for concealing games or less attractive books, and the open shelves highlight books and decorative items.

Corner Office Desk

Cabinet List:

2 18"×24"×84" utility cabinets
12 utility shelves
2 18"×42" wall cabinets
2 shelf undercabinet units
2 21"×36" cabinets with mullion doors and matching interiors
2 tempered glass inserts
2 42" high wall fillers trimmed to fit
1 72" finished shelf (split)
1 48"×30" wall cabinet reduced to 9" deep
1 48" arched valance
2 18" wide desk drawer bases
2 18" wide file bases
1 keyboard tray
3 8'-0" crown molding
2 8'-0" base toe material
4 toekick cap covers
20 knobs or pulls
1 pint stain
1 clear topcoat
1 putty stick

Additional Materials Needed:

- Miscellaneous fasteners and adhesives
- Countertop
- Strip light

Required:

- Install strip light behind valance
- Trim finished shelves into two pieces and install vertically on both sides of the W4830

Variations:

- Exchange utility cabinet shelves for roll-out trays
- Add decorator matching doors on exposed ends of utility cabinets
- Change mullion door cabinets to solid doors for more hidden storage
- Order additional material to fill voids at angled wall fillers

Everyone loves a corner office, but if you don't have the view, then try this corner workspace arrangement. The center cabinet is reduced to 9" deep to give more room for the computer monitor. Twin utility cabinets can be fitted with a variety of shelves or roll-outs to suit storage needs.

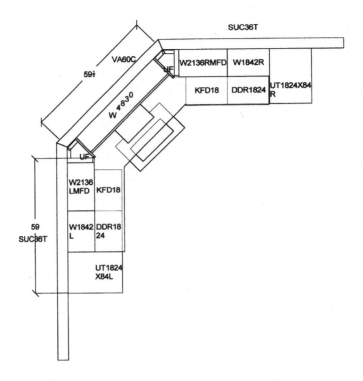

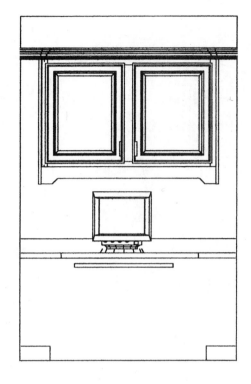

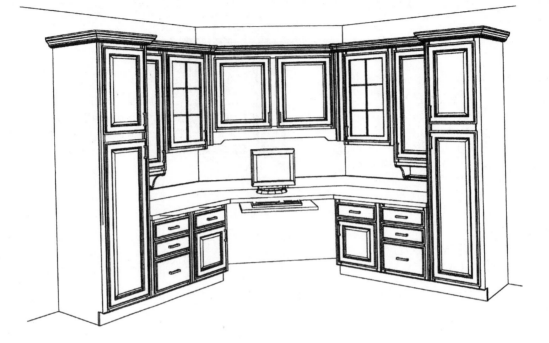

Desk Nook

Cabinet List:

1 36″×18″ wall cabinet
1 18″×18″ wall cabinet
2 decorator matching doors
1 42″ wall skin (split)
3 shelf undercabinet units
1 18″ desk file base
3 base skins
1 base decorator matching door
1 24″ desk drawer unit
1 18″ desk base cabinet
1 base filler
1 keyboard tray
1 8′-0″ crown molding
1 8′-0″ base toe material
3 toe kick cap covers
10 knobs or pulls
1 pint stain
1 putty stick

Additional Materials Needed:

• Miscellaneous fasteners and adhesives
• Dimensional lumber to cleat countertop in the corner
• Countertop with backsplash

Required:

• Minimum 1″ filler at wall
• Cut two skins from one 42″ wall skin
• Hanging height of wall cabinets is 78″ AFF
• Install cleat in corner to support counter-top

Variations:

• Change the wall cabinet doors to mullion style and add tempered glass inserts and matching interiors to the cabinets

An angled corner location is always good for computer monitors because of the extra depth in it provides. The design shown also lowers the chance of screen glare from the window since it is located behind the monitor. The mini wall hutch configuration gives convenient storage for office supplies. The open shelves below add charm and a place to store envelopes and other small office supplies.

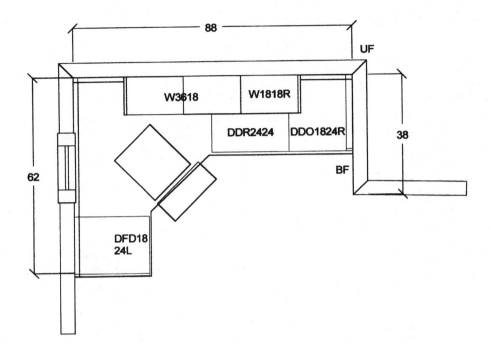

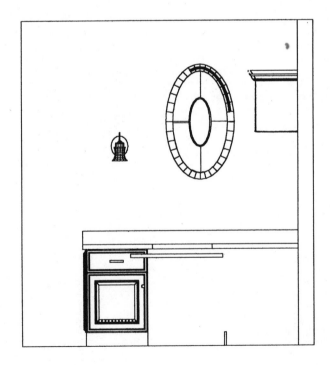

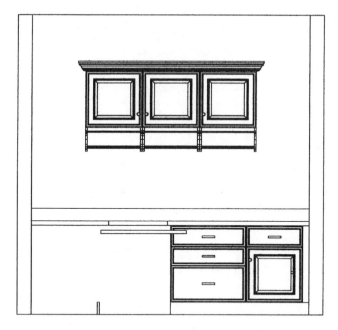

Desk with Angled Returns

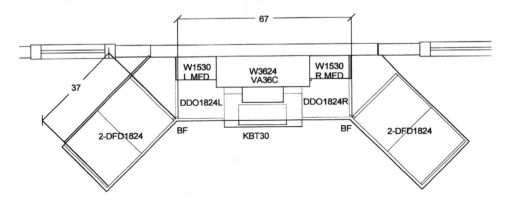

Cabinet List:

2 15"×30" wall cabinets reduced to 9" deep with mullion doors and matching interiors
2 tempered glass inserts
4 wall skins
2 9"×30" decorator matching doors
1 36"×24" wall cabinet
1 36" arched valance
2 18" desk base cabinets
2 base fillers (split)
4 18" desk file base cabinets
4 base skins
2 desk base decorator doors
1 30 keyboard tray
1 96"×48" piece of paneling
1 8'-0" outside corner molding
1 8'-0" crown molding
2 8'-0" base toe material
4 toe kick cap covers
16 knobs or pulls
1 pint stain
1 putty stick

Additional Materials Needed:

• Miscellaneous fasteners and adhesives

• Substrate material for rear of angled cabinets
• Countertop

Required:

• Panel rear of angled returns
• Minimum 1" fillers where angled cabinets meet
• Panel over substrate on rear of angled returns
• Apply outside corner molding to the corners
• Install valance flush with reduced-depth wall cabinets

Variations:

• Add decorator matching doors to rear of angled returns
• Add lighting behind valance

This angled cabinet arrangement adds a contemporary feeling to a home office. Work areas flare out left and right giving additional storage and workspace. The wall cabinets are staggered both up and down, as well as in depth, for visual appeal.

Desk with Back Storage

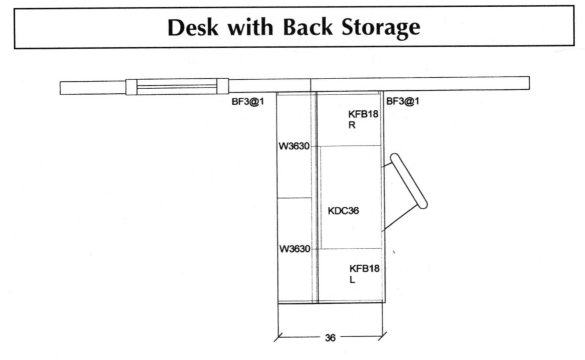

Cabinet List:

2 36"×30" wall cabinets
1 wall skin
1 30" decorator matching door
1 base filler (split)
2 file base cabinets
3 base skins
1 24"×24" decorator door
1 36" kneehole drawer
1 36"×28 1/2" piece of paneling
3 8'-0"×6" wide tall fillers
3 8'-0" inside corner molding
9 knobs or pulls
1 pint stain
1 putty stick

Additional Materials Needed:

- Miscellaneous fasteners and adhesives
- Substrate material for the kneehole space
- Dimensional lumber for a platform
- Upper and lower countertop with back-splash

Required:

- Build a 4" high platform for base
- Panel wall in knee space
- Cover platform with tall filler material topped with inside corner molding wrapping around the entire toe area

Variations:

- Change back storage to wall cabinets with mullion doors, tempered glass inserts, and matching interiors

This multipurpose desk is set at a right angle to a wall allowing the user to be included in activities in the adjacent rooms. Wall cabinets, installed on a platform, shield desktop clutter and add additional storage. The backsplash on the lower countertop easily covers the unfinished back of the wall cabinets.

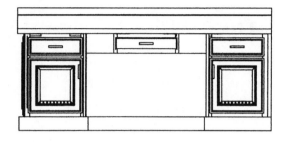

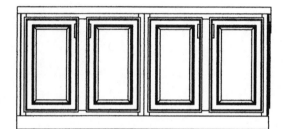

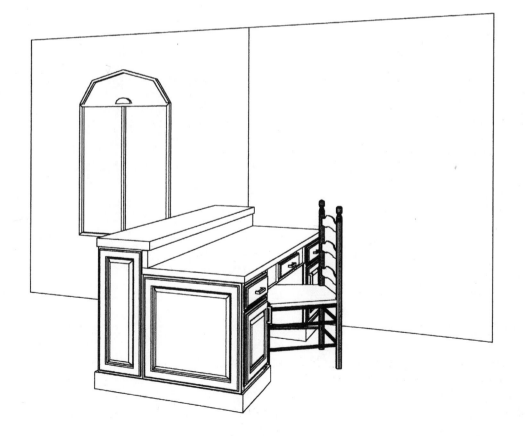

Desk with Mail Slots

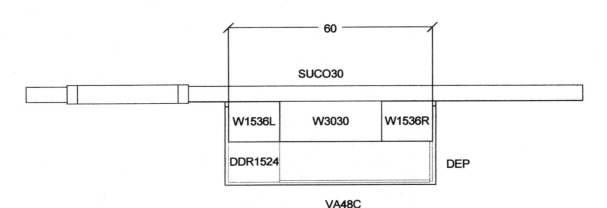

Cabinet List:

2 15″×36″ wall cabinets
1 30″×30″ wall cabinet
1 30″ shelf undercabinet organizer
1 15″ wide desk drawer base
1 48″ arched valance trimmed as knee space
   apron
1 desk end panel
1 8′-0″ crown molding
1 8′-0″ base toe material
2 toe kick cap covers
7 knobs or pulls
1 pint stain
1 putty stick

Additional Materials Needed:

• Miscellaneous fasteners and adhesives
• Countertop

Required:

• Trim arched valance to fit knee space

Variations:

• Change some or all of the wall cabinets to mullion door style with matching interiors
• Add skins and decorator matching doors on exposed ends

This 5′ wide hard-working desk is at home in the kitchen as much as in the family room. The shelf undercabinet organizer adds mail slots for organizing family correspondence. Lots of closed storage hides everything from cookbooks to games and address books.

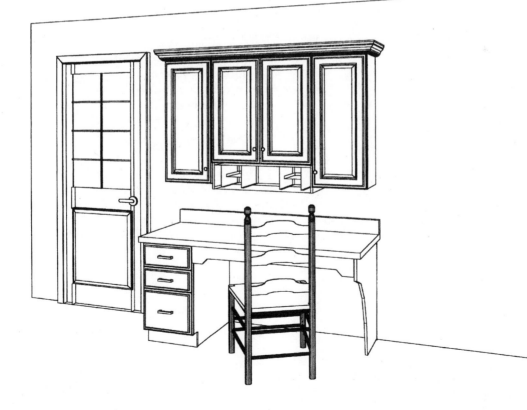

Fireplace Bookcases with Fluted Fillers

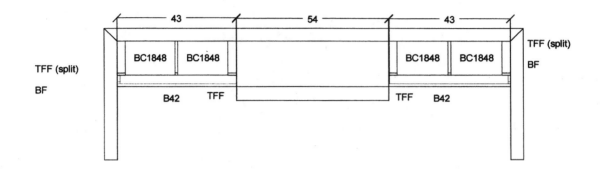

Cabinet List:

4 18″×48″ bookcases
1 tall filler
2 96″ tall fluted fillers (split)
8 rosette decorative blocks
2 42″ base cabinets reduced to 15″ deep
2 base fillers
1 8′-0″ crown molding
1 8′-0″ base toe kick material
8 knobs or pulls
1 pint stain
1 putty stick

Additional Materials Needed:

• Miscellaneous fasteners and adhesives
• 2 matching wood countertops

Required:

• Fireplace that is a minimum of 3″ deeper than the cabinets

• Cut each 96″ tall fluted filler in two 48″ lengths
• Minimum 1″ base filler at the wall
• Trim tall filler in two 1″ sections and install between bookcases to accommodate for the 1″ base filler at the wall

Variations:

• Cover filler, separating bookcases, with decorative molding such as rope molding
• Wall cabinets, pulled forward and used as base cabinets, can be a cost-effective alternative for the reduced-depth base cabinets.

Reduced-depth base cabinets work well when flanking a fireplace with bookcase units. By reducing the depth, space limitations are met, and there are still four working drawers to hold writing supplies or other necessities.

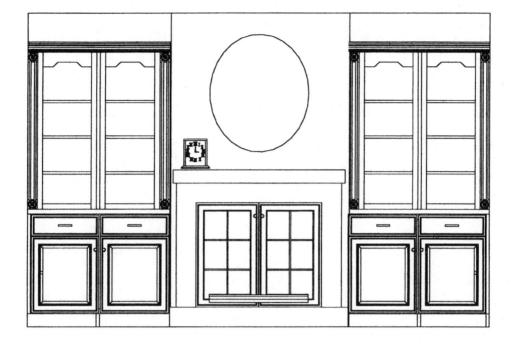

Fireplace Wall Units

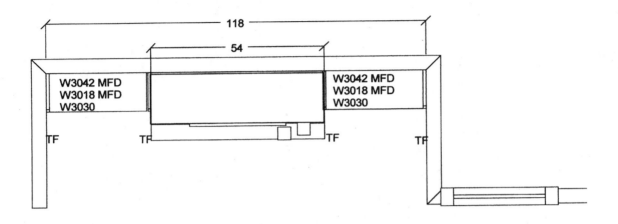

Cabinet List:

2 30"×30" wall cabinets
2 30"×18" wall cabinets with mullion doors and matching interiors
2 30"×42" wall cabinets with mullion doors and matching interiors
8 tempered glass inserts
6 tempered glass shelves
2 tall fillers (split)
1 8'-0" crown molding
1 8'-0" base toe material
12 knobs or pulls
1 pint stain
1 putty stick

Additional Materials Needed:

• Miscellaneous fasteners and adhesives
• Dimensional lumber for platforms
• Interior cabinet lighting

Required:

• Fireplace that is a minimum of 3" deeper than the cabinets

• Build 9" deep platforms and cover with base toe material
• Adjust platform height so that the molding goes all the way to the ceiling
• Minimum 1" filler at walls
• Install interior cabinet lighting

Variations:

• Delete glass inserts, shelves, and lighting and add shirred fabric behind each mullion door
• Order solid door cabinets instead of mullions for more hidden storage

An elegant pair of curio-style cabinets built in on either side of a fireplace is fitted with interior cabinet lighting and glass shelves. The base platform is recessed 3" to provide toe space. The wall cabinets are stacked and fitted to the ceiling with crown molding for a totally custom look.

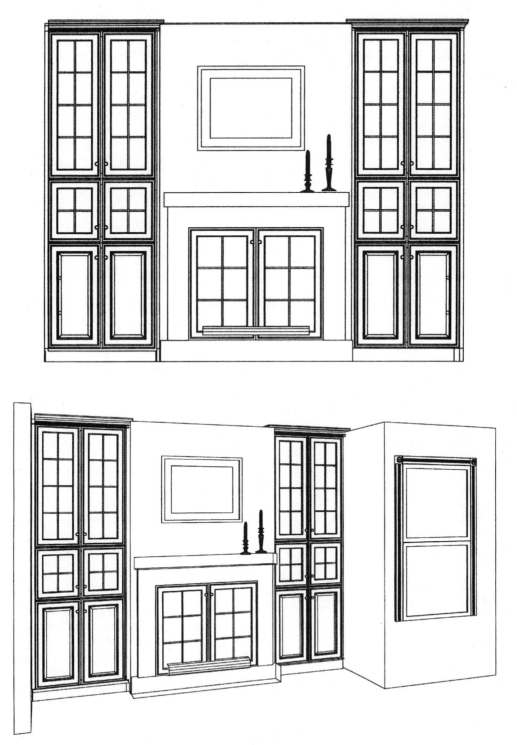

Flip-Down Desk

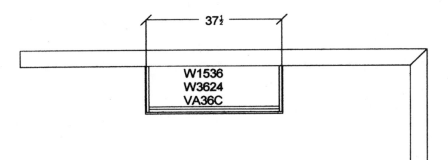

Cabinet List:

1 36″×24″ wall cabinet
1 15″×36″ wall cabinet (installed horizontally)
3 12″×72″ finished shelves
1 36″ arched valance
1 36″×48″ piece of paneling
1 8′-0″ crown molding
1 6″×36″ wall filler
1 8′-0″ inside corner molding
3 knobs or pulls
1 pint stain
1 putty stick

Additional Materials Needed:

• Miscellaneous fasteners and adhesives
• Dimensional lumber for platform
• 1 pair lid supports

Required:

• Flip-down door frame must be made of solid wood
• Build a 4″ high platform for base
• Cover front of platform with tall filler material topped with inside corner molding
• Attach one finished shelf vertically on both sides of the stack
• Cut remaining shelf into soffit board and center shelf
• Panel area behind open shelves
• Install lid supports to flip-down section

Variations:

• Line insides of cabinet installed horizontally to cover shelf hole drillings
• Add a light strip and an outlet inside of the cabinet

This flip-down desk makes a perfect spot to write grocery lists or pay bills. To make this unit, stack a wall cabinet, installed horizontally, on top of a standard 24″ wall cabinet. The combination makes the ideal work height. Finished shelving is used as a soffit board, a shelf, and to capture the sides of the stack.

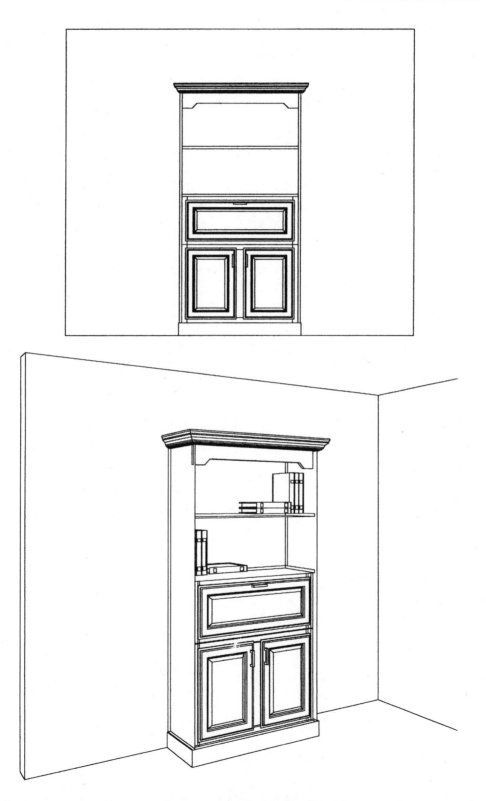

Glass Door Library Cabinets

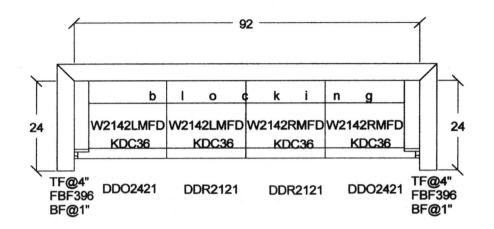

Cabinet List:

4 21″×42″ wall cabinets with mullion doors and matching interiors
4 clear tempered glass inserts
4 kneehole drawers trimmed to 21″ wide
2 tall 6″ fillers
1 8′-0″ tall fluted filler (split)
4 rosette blocks
2 24″ desk base cabinets
2 21″ desk drawer bases
20 knob or pulls
2 8′-0″ crown molding
1 8′-0″ base toe material
1 pint stain
1 putty stick

Additional Materials Needed:

• Miscellaneous fasteners and adhesives
• Dimensional lumber
• Plywood to cover void caused by pulling the wall cabinets forward
• Flat deck matching wood countertop

Required:

• Minimum 1″ filler at base cabinet line
• Block wall cabinets forward 6″

• Trim kneehole drawers to 21″ wide
• Install trimmed tall fillers with fluted fillers overlays
• Apply rosette blocks top and bottom

Variations:

• Change shelves to tempered glass and add interior cabinet lighting
• Unit can be made freestanding with the addition of finished end panels for exposed ends

A formal library wall made with 42″ high wall cabinets, pulled forward and stacked over kneehole drawers, is great for books or collectibles. Layering the fillers gives the look of fluted column and adds detail to the crown molding installation. Installing plywood flush with the top of the pulled forward wall cabinets closes the void and allows items to be displayed on top of the cabinets.

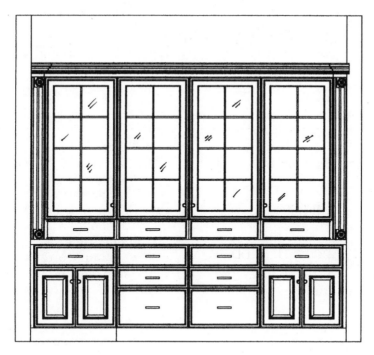

Guest Room Office

Cabinet List:

2 3/4″×24″ tall panels
1 3/4″×24″×36″ panel for television shelf
6 shelf pins
1 36″×1/4″ paneling for rear wall of TV/VCR area
2 18″ file base cabinets
1 36″×24″×24″ deep wall cabinet
1 30″×24″ wall cabinet
1 30″ mail organizer
1 15″×30″ wall cabinet
1 30″ wall filler
2 trimmable kneehole drawers
1 desk end panel
2 8′-0″ crown molding
1 8′-0″ base toe material
11 knobs or pulls
1 pint stain
1 putty stick

Additional Materials Needed:

- Miscellaneous fasteners and adhesives
- Dimensional lumber for blocking kneehole drawers
- 1 L-shaped countertop

- 1 matching wood countertop for television cabinet

Required:

- Adjust opening to fit actual television and VCR dimensions
- Block kneehole drawers in place
- Drill 3/4″ panels for shelf pins to support the VCR shelf
- Minimum 1″ filler at wall
- Follow manufacturer's specifications for ventilation and other electronic requirements

Variations:

- Add decorator matching doors to exposed side of television cabinet
- Expand to fit job-site conditions

If your home office has to occasionally serve as a guestroom, this corner desk/entertainment center combination will meet both needs. The addition of a sofa sleeper makes the space seem very business-like during the day and comfortable for your guests in the evening.

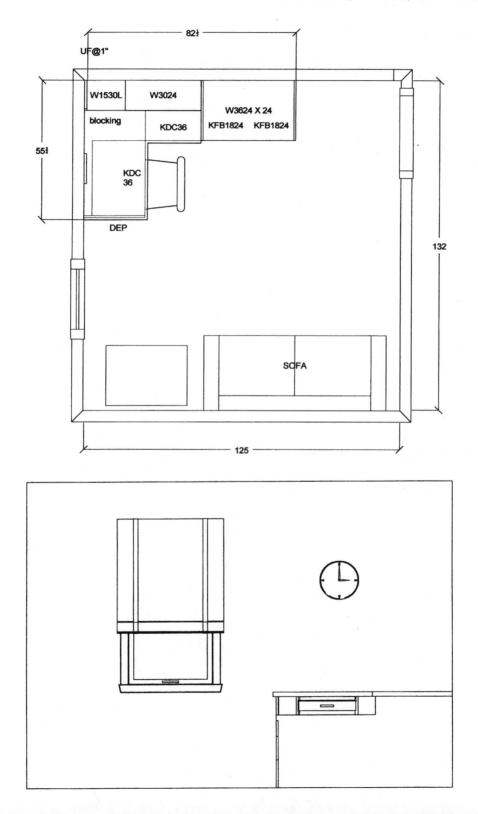

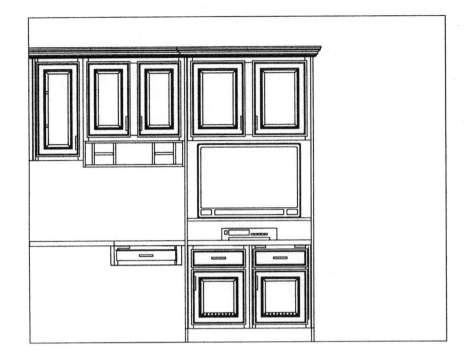

Home Office

Cabinet List:

1 18″ desk drawer base
1 trimmable 36″ knee drawer cabinet
1 18″ desk base cabinet
2 67″×28 1/2″ pieces of paneling
1 8′-0″ outside corner molding
1 30″×18″ piece of paneling
2 18″×18″ wall cabinets
2 24″ desk drawer bases
1 18″ desk base cabinet
2 48″ finished shelves used as vertical members
1 72″ finished shelf split for soffit board and shelf
1 8′-0″×6″ tall filler split as a light rail and credenza valance
1 8′-0″ crown molding
2 8′-0″ base toe material
4 toe kick cap cover
16 knobs or pulls
1 pint stain
1 putty stick

Additional Materials Needed:

• Miscellaneous fasteners and adhesives
• Plywood or other substrate for rear of desk
• 2 matching wood countertops

• Undercabinet lights

Required:

• Minimum 1″ filler at both walls
• Install undercabinet lights behind credenza light rail
• Apply substrate to rear of desk, cover with paneling
• Apply additional paneling to rear area of knee space
• Panel entire wall between and below wall cabinets

Variations:

• Add decorator matching doors to exposed cabinet ends
• Apply wainscoting treatment or decorator matching doors to rear of desk

When nothing but a professional office setup will do, this traditional desk with rear credenza may just be the answer. The credenza offers additional storage and a wide countertop for a copier, fax, or other office equipment. The arched desk countertop extends the work surface as well offering visitors knee space.

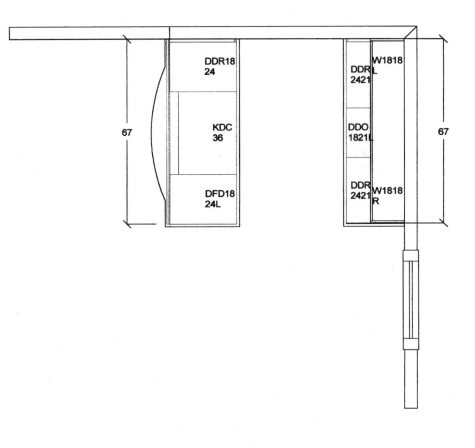

DDR18
24

KDC
36

DFD18
24L

67

W1818
DDRL
2421

DDO
1821L

DDR
2421

W1818
R

67

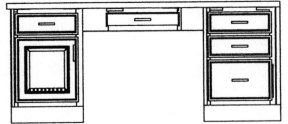

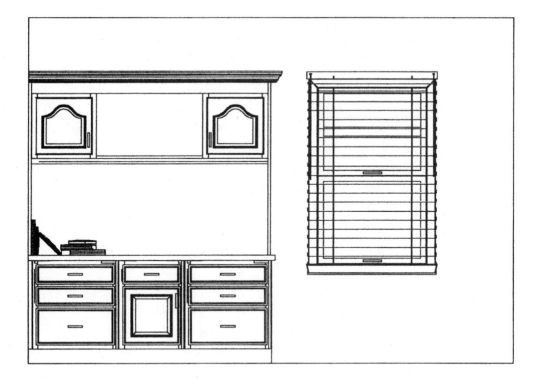

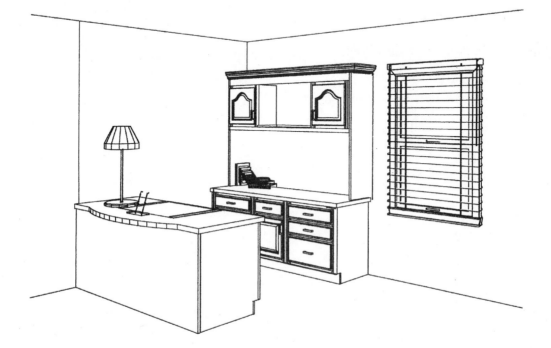

Home Office with Open Desk

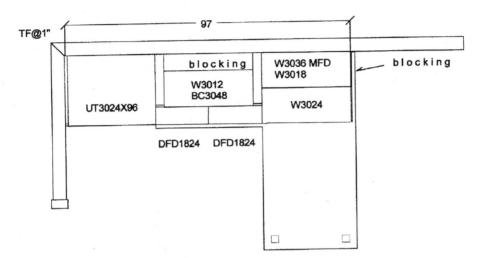

Cabinet List:

1 tall filler
1 30"×24"×96" utility cabinet
1 tall skin
7 utility shelves
1 30"×12" wall cabinet
1 30"×48" bookcase
2 tall fluted fillers trimmed to height
1 3/4" panel trimmed as return for fluted filler
1 30"×36 wall cabinet with mullion doors and matching interiors
2 tempered glass inserts
1 30"×18" wall cabinet
1 tall skin (split and trimmed)
2 18" desk base cabinets
1 30"×24" wall cabinet
2 8'-0" base toe material
2 8'-0" crown molding
16 knobs or pulls
1 pint stain
1 putty stick

Additional Materials Needed:

- Miscellaneous fasteners and adhesives
- Dimensional lumber to create a platform and blocking

- 2 turned legs
- Countertop

Required:

- Minimum 1" filler at the wall
- Pull forward 6" and block bookcase stack
- Pull forward 12" and block W3024 and install on a platform
- Cut one tall skin to finish the right side of the mullion door stack, as well as the right side of the pulled W30324 used as a base cabinet

Variations:

- Add pull-out shelf trays to the utility cabinet
- Change mullion door cabinet to open-frame door

Stacked and stair-stepped cabinets lend design interest to this home office with an open desk arrangement. Because some cabinets are stacked and others pulled, skin all exposed sides. Outsourced turned legs support the desk.

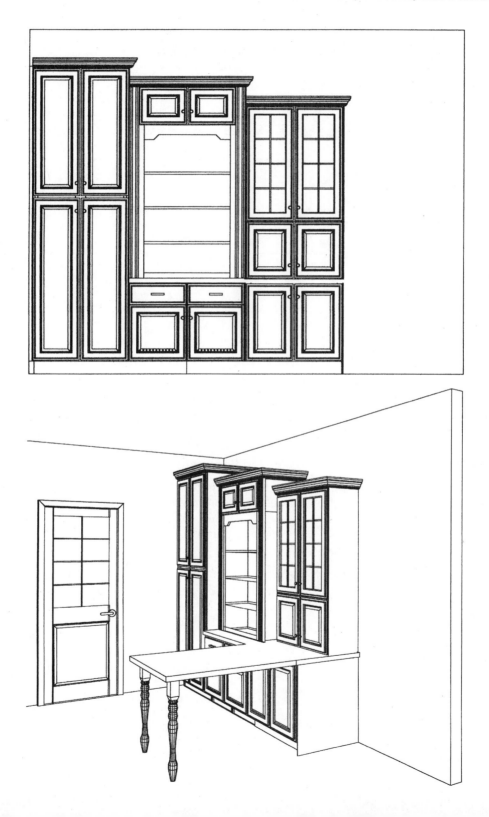

Homework Station

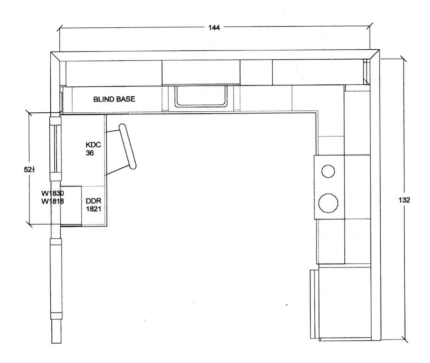

Cabinet List:

1 18″×18″ wall cabinet reduced to 10″ deep
1 18″×30″ wall cabinet reduced to 10″ deep
1 tall skin (split)
1 21″ deep desk drawer base
1 36″ trimmable kneehole drawer
1 8′-0″ crown molding
1 8′-0″ base toe material
2 toe kick cap covers
6 knobs or pulls
1 pint stain
1 putty stick

Additional Materials Needed:

• Miscellaneous fasteners and adhesives
• Countertop

Required:

• Panel the open portion of the blind base cabinet as it will be exposed
• Split and trim the tall skin to conceal the joint of the stacked cabinets

Variation:

• Adjust desk size to fit job-site condition

This 21″ deep desk butts into the side of a blind kitchen base cabinet to provide a place for a child to do homework in the kitchen. Because the desk area is shallow, the stacked wall storage cabinets are reduced to 10″ deep to keep the proportion and give more workspace.

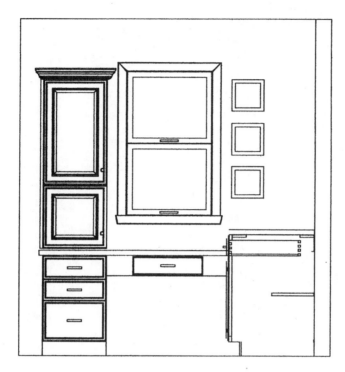

Island Desk

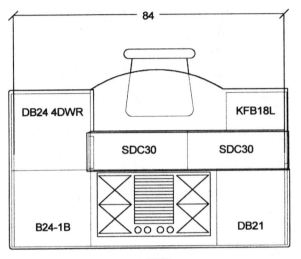

Cabinet List:

1 21″ drawer base
1 39″ sink base
1 24″ base cabinet
1 24″ four drawer base
1 48″×96″ piece of paneling trimmed as base skins
1 piece of paneling 48″×34 1/2″ to cover back of kneehole and pigeon hole areas
2 base skins
1 decorator matching door for file base
3 base decorator matching doors
2 30″ spice drawer cabinets with matching wood knobs
1 tall filler trimmed for letter slots
2 8′-0″ base toe material
6 toe kick cap covers
14 knobs or pulls
1 pint stain
1 clear top coat
1 putty stick

Additional Materials Needed:

• Miscellaneous fasteners and adhesives
• Substrate for kneehole area
• 3 countertops
• Backsplash material to wrap three sides of the spice drawers

Required:

• Panel the back of the SB39 and part of the DB21 to provide a finished knee space
• Skin exposed sides of base cabinets and apply decorator matching doors
• Cut tall filler into letter slots, stain and seal back

Variation:

• Delete decorator matching doors for a simpler look

This island features three different work heights. The traditional 30″ height for the desk section and 36″ high work area surrounds the cooktop. The 6″ high spice drawers create the third layer. They provide storage for small desk items and a protective and a visual barrier for the cooktop. Decorator matching doors make this island attractive from all angles.

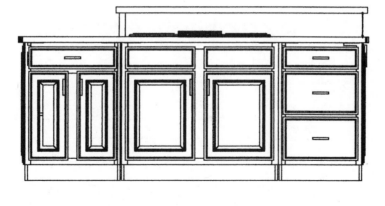

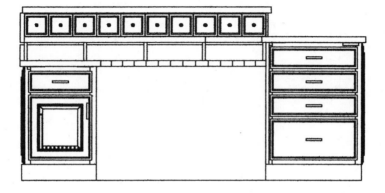

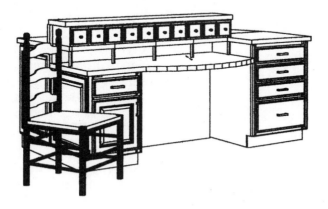

Kitchen Desk with Bookcase

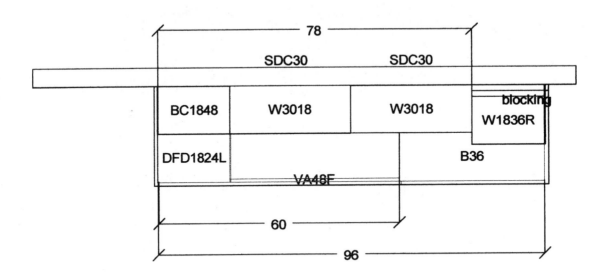

Cabinet List:

1 18″×48″ bookcase
2 48″ beaded skins
2 30″×18″ wall cabinets
2 30″ spice drawer units with matching wood knobs
1 18″×36″ wall cabinet
2 15″×36″ beaded skins
1 36″ base cabinet
4 beaded base skins
1 48″ frieze valance
2 8′-0″ crown molding
1 8′-0″ base toe material
4 toe kick cap covers
11 knobs or pulls
1 pint stain
1 putty stick

Additional Materials Needed:

- Miscellaneous fasteners and adhesives
- Dimensional lumber
- 2 countertops

Required:

- Pull 18″ wall cabinet forward 3″ and block
- Skin all exposed cabinet sides with beaded skins

Variations:

- Change solid doors to mullion door cabinets with matching interiors and glass inserts
- Change style of valance
- Add a light rail beneath the wall cabinets and install undercabinet lighting

This generous kitchen desk features a bookcase for decorative items as well as cookbooks. Two spice drawers set off the wall storage. The lower spice drawers are for office supplies and the upper are for family medications and vitamins. The 18″ wall cabinet is pulled forward 3″ for design interest and to allow the crown molding from the lower cabinets to butt into the deeper side.

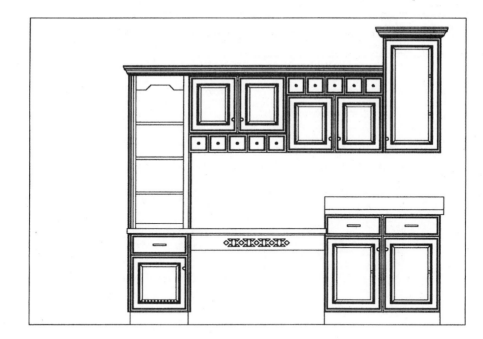

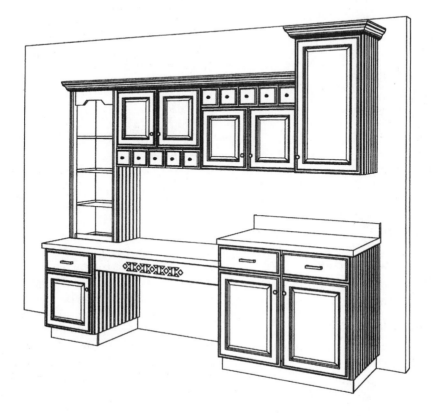

Kitchen Message Center

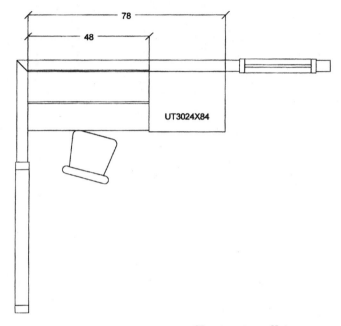

Cabinet List:

1 30"×24"×84" utility cabinet
6 utility shelves
1 48" decorative valance
3 48" shelves
4 corbels
2 8'-0" crown molding
1 8'-0" base toe material
2 toe kick cap covers
4 knobs or pulls
1 pint stain
1 putty stick

Additional Materials Needed:

- Miscellaneous fasteners and adhesives
- Dimensional lumber to fabricate cleat for countertop
- Countertop

Required:

- Trim one shelf and install as soffit board with valance in front
- Cleats at wall to support countertop

Variations:

- Change valance style
- Install small hanging lights in front of the shelves
- Install light rail molding to the bottom shelf and install undercabinet lighting
- Add decorator matching doors to right side of the utility cabinet

The open shelving in this message center tucked into a corner of a kitchen can hold cookbooks and family photos. Corkboard can be added to the area above the countertop to post notes and calendars. The countertop is installed at 36" high. That means the area can serve as additional kitchen workspace or a serving area when it is not being used as a message center.

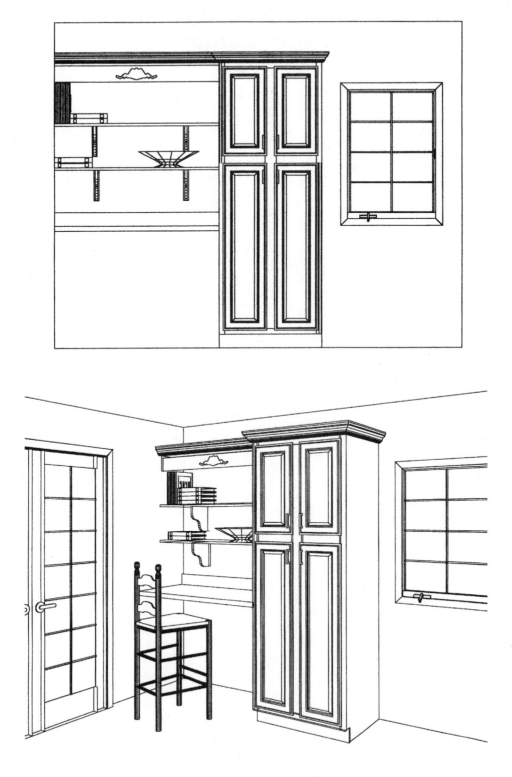

Library with Corner Desk

Cabinet List:

2 30″×48″ bookcase cabinets
2 30″×24″ wall cabinets
2 84″ tall skins (split)
2 36″ arched valances (trimmed to fit)
1 30″×30″ paneling
2 8′-0″ crown molding
2 8′-0″×6″ wide tall fillers
2 8′-0″ inside corner molding
4 knobs or pulls
1 pint stain
1 putty stick

Additional Materials Needed:

• Miscellaneous fasteners and adhesives
• Dimensional lumber for platforms
• Plywood for soffit board
• Countertop

Required:

• Build a 4″ high platform for wall cabinets below bookcases

• Cover platforms with tall filler material topped with inside corner molding
• Split and trim tall skins to cover joints on all exposed sides
• Cover plywood soffit board with paneling
• Trim one valance and install at top of workspace and one as skirt for knee space
• Minimum 1″ filler at wall

Variations:

• Add additional bookcase units (left and right) to fit job-site conditions
• Add lighting behind top valance

A corner bookcase arrangement can be expanded to fit most rooms. By stacking 48″ high bookcases over 24″ wall cabinets on a platform the work counter is the perfect height. This work area in the corner is a great landing space for books or to write letters.

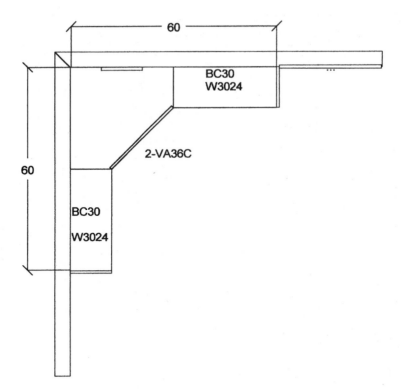

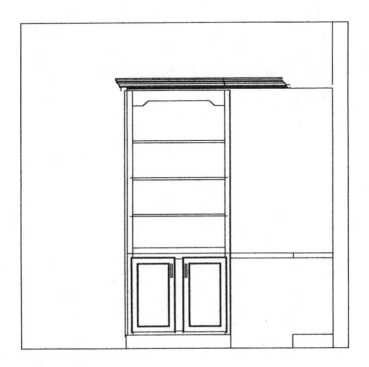

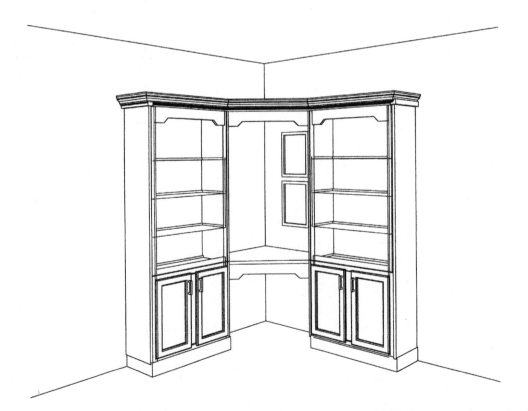

Library with Window Seat

Cabinet List:

6 30″×30″ wall cabinets
6 30″×48″ bookcases units
2 tall skins (split and trimmed)
3 3″ tall fillers
2 30″×15″ wall cabinets
1 6″×42″ wall filler (split and cut at 45° angle)
3 8′-0″ crown molding
1 8′-0″ countertop edge molding
3 8′-0″×6″ tall fillers
3 8′-0″ inside corner molding
16 knobs or pulls
1 pint stain
1 putty stick

Additional Materials Needed:

• Miscellaneous fasteners and adhesives
• Dimensional lumber for platform and blocking
• Plywood for deck of window seat
• Window seat cushion

Required:

• Build 4″ high platforms for base of all cabinets

• Cover platforms with tall filler material topped with inside corner molding as toe treatment
• Make deck for window seat with plywood and trim with countertop edge molding
• Pull 15″ high wall cabinets forward and cut 6″ wall fillers on 45° angles to create window seat
• Trim tall skins and cover all exposed sides

Variations:

• Adjust size to fit job-site conditions
• Increase or reduce the height of the cabinets below the bookcases to adjust overall height

Wall to wall bookcases and a built-in window seat are all made from stock wall cabinet sizes. The 15″ high wall cabinets are pulled forward 3″ and installed 3″ from each bookcase. Six-inch fillers are trimmed and installed at a 45° angle to soften the design.

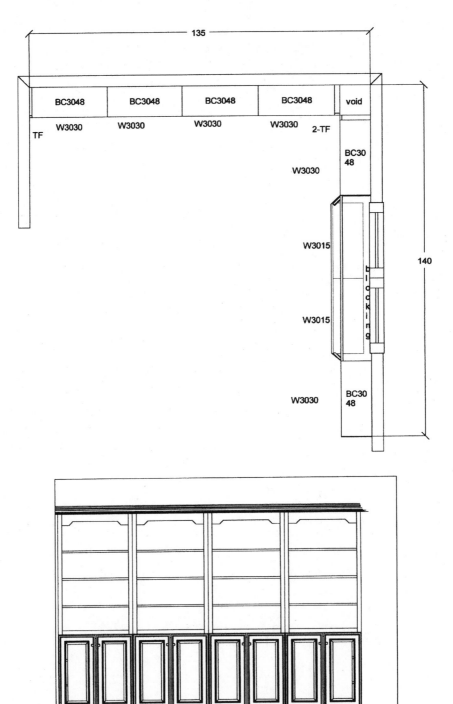

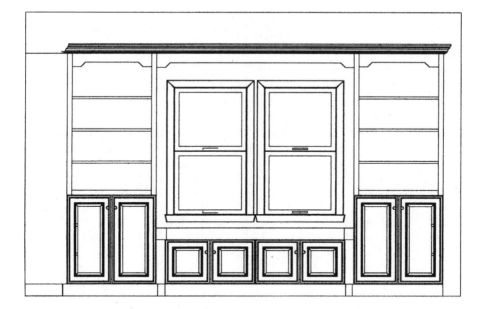

Mini Desk

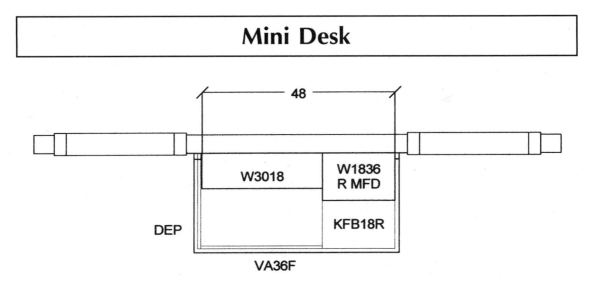

Cabinet List:

1 18″×36″ wall cabinet with mullion doors
   with matching interiors
1 tempered glass insert
1 30″×18″ wall cabinet reduced to 9″ deep
1 36″ frieze valance
1 desk end panel
1 18″ file base cabinet
1 8′-0″ crown molding
1 8′-0″ light rail molding
1 base toe material
2 toe kick cap cover
5 knobs or pulls
1 pint stain
1 putty stick

Additional Materials Needed:

• Miscellaneous fasteners and adhesives
• Countertop
• 1 undercabinet light

Required:

• Reduce depth on W3018 so that the top
  molding butts into the W1836

Variations:

• Add decorator matching doors to exposed
  ends
• Change valance style or add a kneehole
  drawer

This small well-proportioned desk will fit
into as little as 54″ of space including standard crown molding and countertop over-
hangs. This design works well in a kitchen
or family room. Light rail molding conceals
undercabinet lighting making it practical as
well as an attractive addition to any home.

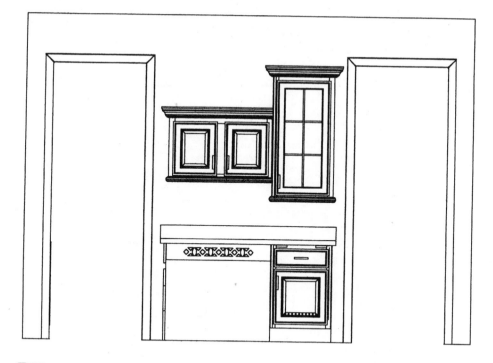

Office for Two

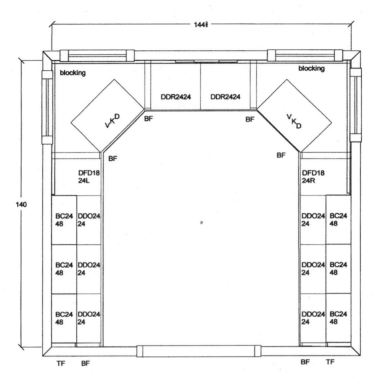

Cabinet List:

6 24″×48″ bookcases
2 tall fillers
6 24″ desk base cabinets
2 18″ desk file bases
2 kneehole drawer units
2 24″ desk drawer bases
4 base fillers
2 8′-0″ crown molding
3 8′-0″ base toe material
4 toe kick cap covers
30 knobs or pulls
1 pint stain
1 putty stick

Additional Materials Needed:

- Miscellaneous fasteners and adhesives
- Dimensional lumber for corner countertop blocking
- Countertop

Required:

- Trim one base filler as fillers on either side of the kneehole drawer
- Minimum of 1″ filler at each wall

Variation:

- Adjust size to fit job-site conditions

When two people enjoy working together but still need their own space, this office fills the bill. Each work area has its own set of bookcases and base storage. The area is approximately 12′ square and could be created in an unused bedroom or a special room in a new home set aside just for an office.

Office in a Closet

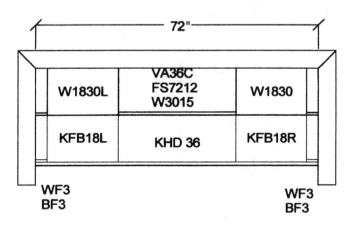

Cabinet List:

2 18"×30" wall cabinets
1 30"×15" wall cabinets
1 36" arched valance
1 72" finished shelf (split)
1 8'-0" light rail molding
2 wall fillers
2 18" file base cabinets
1 kneehole drawer
2 base fillers
1 8'-0" crown molding
1 8'-0" base toe material
2 toe kick cap covers
9 knobs or pulls
1 pint stain
1 putty stick

Additional Materials Needed:

• Miscellaneous fasteners and adhesives
• Countertop
• Undercabinet lighting

Required:

• Fillers must be wide enough to allow doors and drawers to clear the closet's return walls
• Select cabinets with narrow doors so that they can be opened and easily clear the closet header
• Closet depth should be a minimum of 27"
• Cut finished shelf into soffit board behind valance and as top to W3018

Variations:

• Finish wall in open shelf area with paneling
• If space is limited, use 21" desk base cabinets

An office in a closet? Why not? This compact desk can turn a spare bedroom into an efficient office. The open shelf area, above the 15" high wall cabinet, is ideal for books or family photos. The decorative light rail hides practical undercabinet lighting.

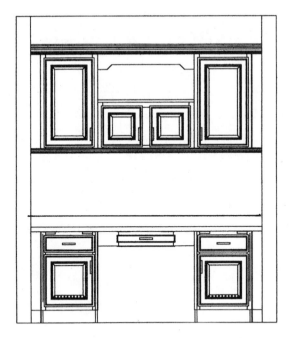

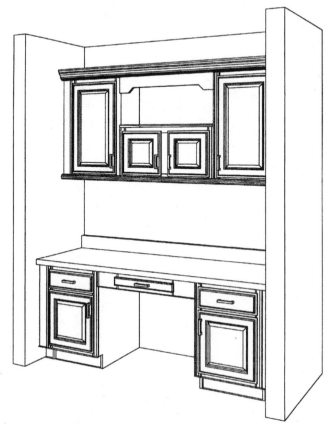

Partners' Desk

Cabinet List:

2 30″ drawer bases
3 base skins
8 base fluted fillers
2 18″×21″ file drawer base cabinets
1 36″×24″ wall cabinet
4 30″×12″ wall cabinets
2 30″×30″ wall cabinets with mullion doors
   and matching interiors
2 tall skins (split)
4 tempered glass inserts
2 33″×30″ wall cabinets reduced to 7″ deep
2 30″ wall fluted fillers
2 6″×30″ wall fillers as returns
3 8′-0″ crown molding
1 8′-0″ light rail molding
1 72″×18″ piece of 1/4″ paneling
3 3″ tall fillers
3 8′-0″ inside corner molding
2 8′-0″ base toe material
3 toe kick cap covers
34 knobs or pulls
1 pint stain
1 putty stick

Additional Materials Needed:

- Miscellaneous fasteners and adhesives
- Dimensional lumber
- 3 countertop sections

Required:

- Create returns for fluted fillers with 6″ wall fillers
- Create wainscot detail on rear wall from paneling, fillers, and inside corner molding
- Build a 4″ high platform for W3624 used as base
- Pull W3624 forward, block, and install on platform to support countertop
- Skin all exposed sides
- Fabricate two columns to support desktop from base fluted fillers
- Minimum 1″ filler at the wall

Variations:

- Add glass shelves and lighting to mullion door cabinets
- Add decorator matching doors to exposed side
- Delete wainscoted area or replace it with plain paneling

A deep desk area, that is ideal for playing games as well as spreading out paperwork, is accessible from both sides. Stacked cabinets offer furniture-like proportions. The centered cabinets are reduced in depth and flanked with fluted columns. A wainscoted back wall detail gives the look of a high-class men's club.

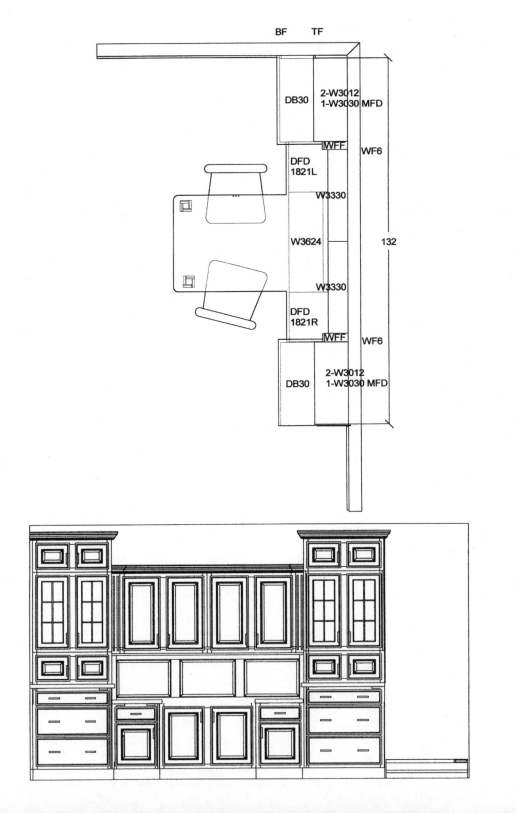

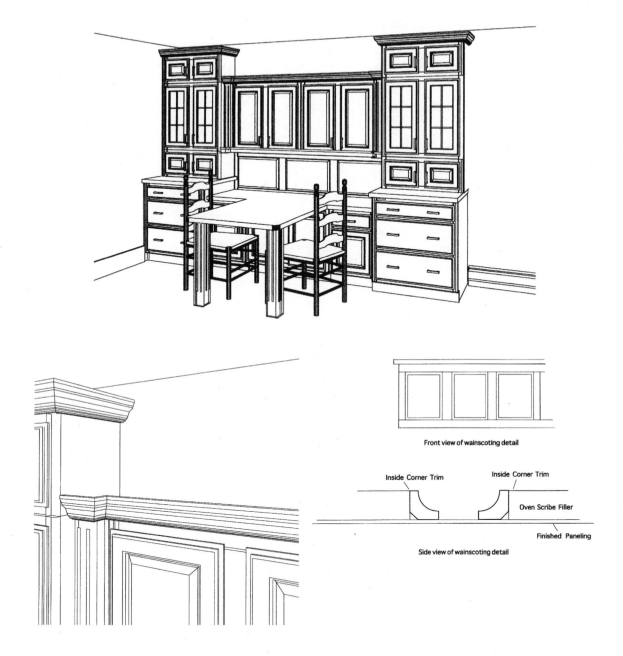

Front view of wainscoting detail

Inside Corner Trim

Inside Corner Trim

Oven Scribe Filler

Finished Paneling

Side view of wainscoting detail

Side Wall Credenza

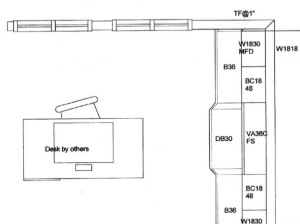

Cabinet List:

2 18″×30″ cathedral wall cabinets with mullion doors and matching interiors
2   tempered glass inserts
2 18″×18″ wall cabinets with square door style
1 tall filler
2 18″×48″ bookcase units
3 36″ finished shelves
3 48″ wall skins
1 36″ arched valance
1 36″×48″ piece of paneling
2 36″ base cabinets
1 30″ drawer base
2 6″ base fillers cut for 45° angle installation
1 base skin
2 8′-0″ crown molding
2 8′-0″ base toe material
1 toe kick cap cover
18 knobs or pulls
1 pint stain
1 putty stick

Additional Materials Needed:

• Miscellaneous fasteners and adhesives

• Matching wood countertop

Required:

• Trim tall filler to 1″, cut and install as base and wall fillers
• Pull drawer base 3″ from each wall and each adjacent cabinet
• Trim and install 6″ wall fillers at 45° angle on either side of drawers
• Trim one shelf to 11 1/4″ deep as a soffit board and install valance in front
• Panel wall in open shelf area

Variations:

• Add decorator matching doors to exposed end
• Add mullion doors and glass inserts on 18″ high wall cabinets

This 9′ long credenza is installed at right angles to the desk. The center section is open to the countertop to accommodate a fax machine or other office equipment. A matching wood top will give a true furniture look to this elegant built-in.

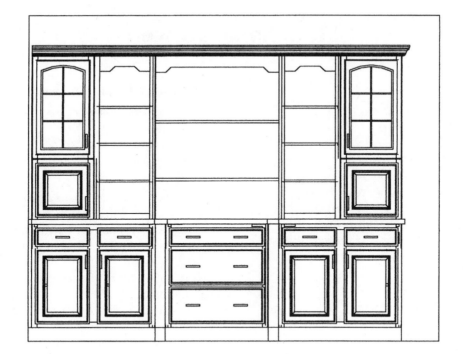

Traditional Office

Cabinet List:

1 tall filler trimmed
2 30″×18″ wall cabinets
2 30″×30″ wall cabinets with mullion doors and matching interiors
4 tempered glass inserts
1 30″×30″ wall cabinet reduced to 9″ deep
1 tall skin (split and trimmed)
1 18″ high wall decorator matching door
1 30″ high wall decorator matching door
2 tall fluted fillers
4 rosette blocks
1 3/4″ return panel (split and trimmed)
2 base fillers (trimmed)
2 18″×21″ desk base cabinets
2 18″×21″ desk drawer bases
1 24″×21″ desk base cabinet
2 18″×21″ desk file bases
2 96″×34 1/2″ pieces paneling
1 8′-0″ outside corner molding
3 24″×24″ decorator matching
1 base skin
2 base decorator matching doors
1 36″ trimmable kneehole drawer
2 8′-0″ crown molding
1 8′-0″ base toe material
4 toe kick cap covers
28 knobs or pulls
1 pint stain
1 putty stick

Additional Materials Needed:

• Miscellaneous fasteners and adhesives
• Substrate
• 2 Countertop sections

Required:

• Cover back of desk with substrate
• Cover rear of knee space and wall below reduced depth cabinet with paneling
• Panel rear of desk and apply decorator matching doors
• Trim 3/4″ return panels as returns for fluted fillers
• Minimum of 1″ filler at each wall
• Trim the tall skin to cover the exposed side of the right wall cabinet stack and as a base skin

Variations:

• Omit decorator matching doors
• Vary mullion and solid door arrangement

With every exposed end skinned and finished with decorator matching doors, this office has a rich elegant look. Construct it from dark cherry and it will take on a decidedly masculine air. The center cabinet is reduced to 9″ deep and is framed with fluted columns. The crown molding follows these depth changes, giving the back wall unit extra dimensions.

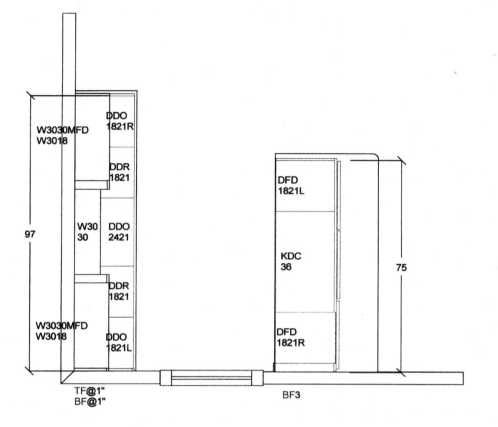

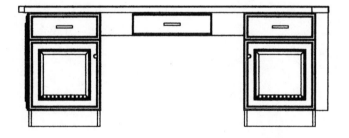

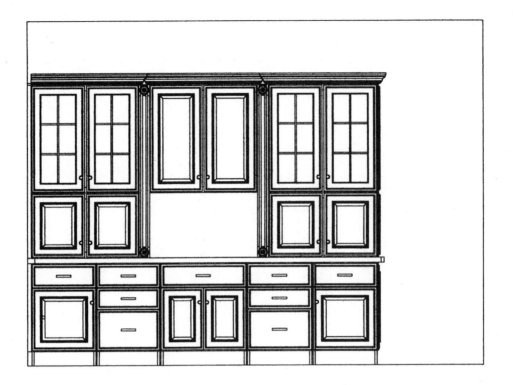

Two-Level Desk

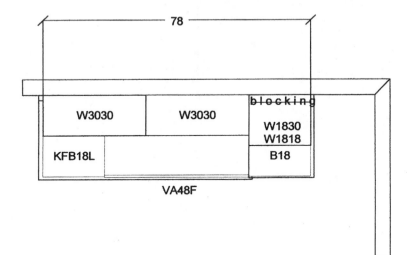

Cabinet List:

2 30″×30″ wall cabinets
1 wall skin
2 shelf undercabinet units
1 18″×30″ wall cabinet
1 18″×18″ wall cabinet
2 84″ tall skins (split)
1 18″ file base cabinet
1 18″ base cabinet
4 base skins
1 48″ frieze valance (trimmed to fit)
2 8′-0″ crown molding
1 8′-0″ base toe material
4 toe kick cap covers
10 knobs or pulls
1 pint stain
1 putty stick

Additional Materials Needed:

• Miscellaneous fasteners and adhesives
• Dimensional lumber for blocking
• 2 Countertop sections

Required:

• Pull forward 3″ and block stacked wall cabinets
• Skin all exposed sides
• Trim valance and install as skirt for knee space

Variations:

• Delete shelf undercabinet units, add light rail and undercabinet lighting
• Change cabinets to mullion door units with matching interiors and glass inserts
• Delete the decorative valance and add a keyboard tray

This versatile desk, with staggered height base and wall cabinets, can fit in a family room, study, or kitchen. The two stacked cabinets are pulled forward 3″ for design interest. This also allows the top molding from the lower cabinets to the left butt neatly into the side of the stack.

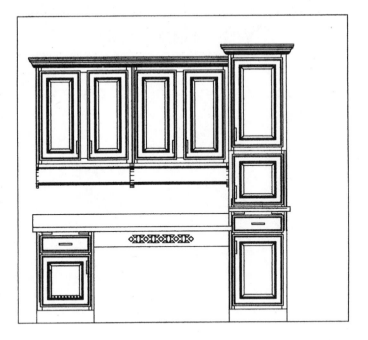

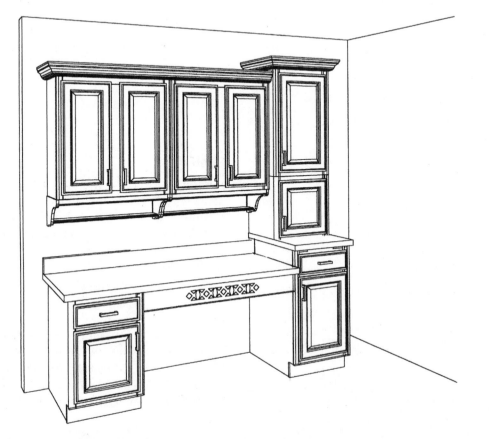

Work Island Desk

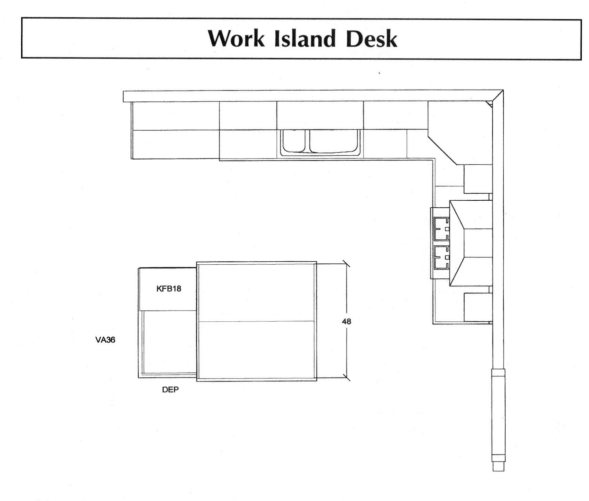

Cabinet List:

1 18″ file base cabinet
1 36″ arched valance (trimmed)
1 desk end panel
1 18″ piece of toe material
2 toe kick cap covers
2 knobs or pulls
1 pint stain
1 putty stick

Additional Materials Needed:

- Miscellaneous fasteners and adhesives
- Countertop

Required:

- Island with a minimum of 48″ finished end or side
- Hold desk in at least 1 1/2″ from island ends to allow for countertop overhang

Variation:

- Change arched valance to a kneehole desk drawer

The kitchen remains one of the most popular places to have a desk area. In this design the small desk area is placed on the end of a large island. A slim desk end panel is used to maximize the available knee space.

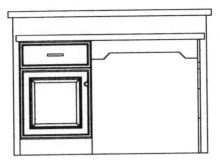

Wrap-Around Desk

Cabinet List:

1 18″×24″×84″ utility cabinet
6 utility shelves
2 30″×30″ wall cabinets with mullion doors and matching interiors
2 shelf undercabinet units
4 tempered glass inserts
1 27″×30″ corner wall cabinet
1 corner appliance garage (pulled to 27″)
1 30″×30″ wall cabinet
1 18″×36″ wall cabinet
1 18″×18″ wall cabinet
3 tall skins
1 base corner filler
3 18″ desk file bases
1 44″×28 1/2″ piece of base paneling
1 8′-0″ outside corner molding
6 base fluted fillers
2 8′-0″×6″ base fillers
1 21″ desk drawer base
3 15″ desk base cabinets
3 8′-0″ crown molding
1 8′-0″ base toe material
2 toe kick cap covers
26 knobs or pulls
1 pint stain
1 putty stick

Additional Materials Needed:

- Miscellaneous fasteners and adhesives
- Dimensional lumber to block wall cabinet stack and void
- Countertop

Required:

- Pull and block stacked wall cabinets and skin both sides
- Pull appliance garage forward and skin both sides
- Construct desk leg from fluted fillers
- Place 6″ fillers flat as returns for angled drawer base

Variations:

- Add decorator doors to back of desk area and exposed sides of cabinets
- Omit mullion door cabinets for more hidden storage

An office for the professional includes space for every piece of office equipment. Two separated niches are provided for a printer as well as a scanner, fax machine, and even a small copier. The stack of wall cabinets visually balances the tall utility cabinet that holds office supplies or reference books. The appliance garage is perfect for instantly hiding office clutter.

CHAPTER 5

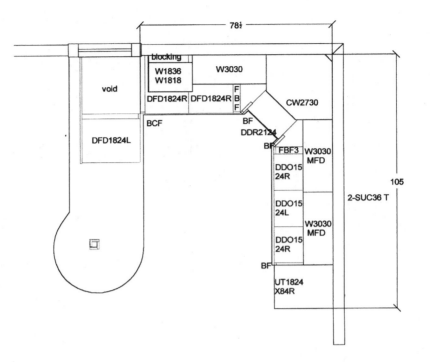

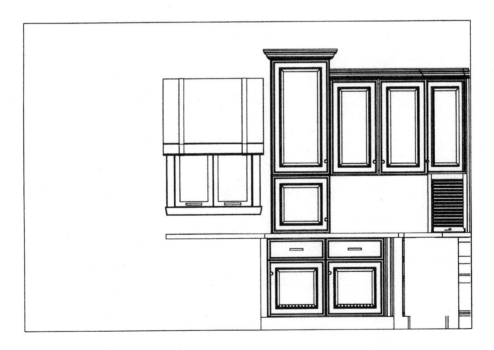

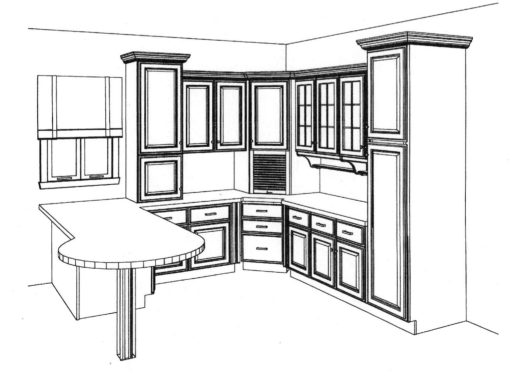

Craft Rooms, Potting Benches, and Workshops

Rooms dedicated to special uses are not new. Laundry rooms, game rooms, and home offices have become fairly standard. But more and more we are finding rooms dedicated to leisure time activities. Having a separate space for these activities makes it easy to leave hobby materials out and close the door when company comes. In this chapter we will look at rooms designed for some of the most popular hobbies: gardening, woodworking, and crafts of all kinds.

When craftrooms or workshops are set in a basement or garage, they are often unembellished. There is little need for top molding treatments or skinning exposed cabinet ends.

Door styles are usually simple. Countertops are selected for durability and appropriateness to the use. They will either be cost-effective laminate or sometimes something as simple as plywood. Flooring also needs to be durable and easy to clean. It may be anything from concrete in a garage workbench area to ceramic tile or synthetic material that will hold up under hobby spills.

The big thing here is function. A place to stash supplies is usually a top priority and storage solutions can come in many forms. Utility cabinets are a great choice, either with adjustable shelves or rollout shelf trays. Well thought-out wall and base cabinets also offer practical choices. Counter space that allows a project to be spread out, as well as a sit-down work area, complete the picture.

Once basic storage and counterspace are taken care of, then comes the opportunity to personalize the space to the given task. Woodworking areas may need the countertop extended to hold a vice or other clamp-on tools. Craft areas may require extra lighting, both natural and artificial. Most potting or flower arranging centers will benefit from a nearby sink for quick clean ups. Adding fluorescent lights to help start seedlings will make the space even more valuable for the true gardener. Adding locks to cabinets that store tools or any type of chemicals is a must.

One thing is certain, with today's busy lifestyles, people appreciate specially designed spaces that encourage their creativity and provide a respite from daily responsibilities.

Bonus Room Craft Area

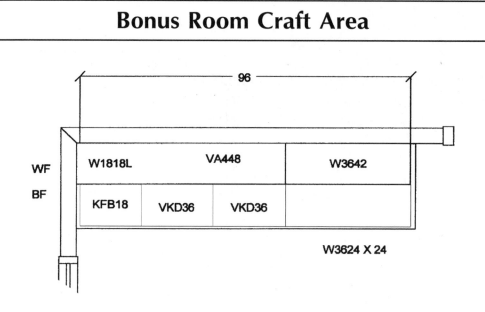

Cabinet List:

1 wall filler
1 18″×18″ wall cabinet
1 72″ finished shelf (trimmed)
1 48″ straight valance (trimmed)
1 36″×42″ wall cabinet
1 base filler
1 18″ file base cabinet
2 36″ trimmable kneehole drawers
1 36″×24″×24″ wall cabinet
4 18″ rollout shelf trays
2 6″×84″ wide tall fillers
9 knobs or pulls
1 pint stain
1 putty stick

Additional Materials Needed:

- Miscellaneous fasteners and adhesives
- Dimensional lumber
- Countertop
- Light strip

Required:

- Build a 21″ deep platform for W3624×24 used as a base cabinet
- Install four rollout shelf trays in W3624×24
- Install light strip behind valance
- Trim and install tall filler as toe material

Variations:

- Add corkboard to the rear wall
- Omit rollout shelves for cost savings

This design would fit well in an attic or bonus room over a garage because the overall height is approximately 72″ high without the top molding. The lower height works well with sloped ceilings. The 18″×18″ wall cabinet adds storage while leaving the counterspace free for a work area.

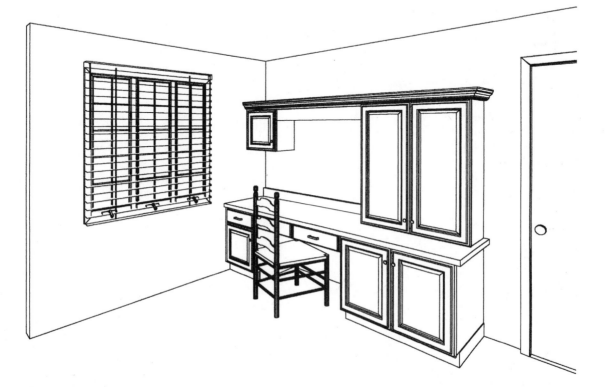

Craft Corner

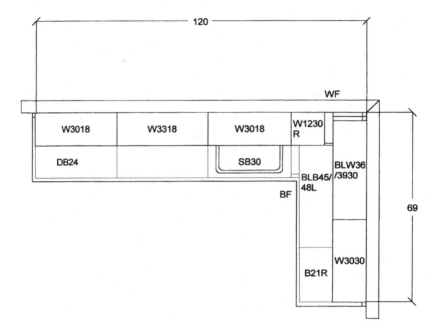

Cabinet List:

1 30"×30" wall cabinet
1 36"/39"×30" blind wall cabinet
1 wall filler
1 12"×30" wall cabinet
2 30"×18" wall cabinet
1 33"×18" wall cabinet
1 21" base cabinet
1 45"/48" blind base cabinet
1 base filler
1 30" sink base
1 24" drawer base
1 42" wall filler (trimmed)
2 8'-0" base toe material
4 toe kick cap covers
19 knobs or pulls
1 pint stain
1 putty stick

Additional Materials Needed:

• Miscellaneous fasteners and adhesives
• Countertop
• Sink and faucet

Required:

• Pull wall and base blind cabinets 3" from the wall
• Fillers at each blind cabinet
• Trim 42" wall filler as kneehole skirt

Variation:

• Adjust to fit site dimensions

Sometime working at a 36" countertop height is best and this craft corner meets that need. The shorter wall cabinets in the sink and main work area give extra headroom and provide a place to display finished projects above.

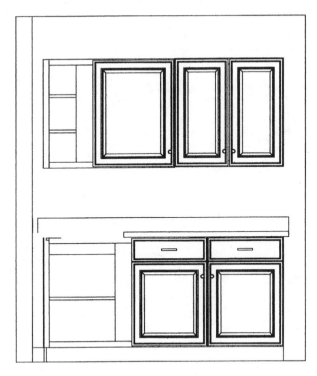

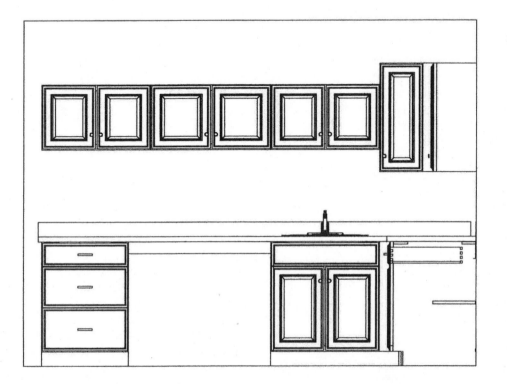

Craft Room

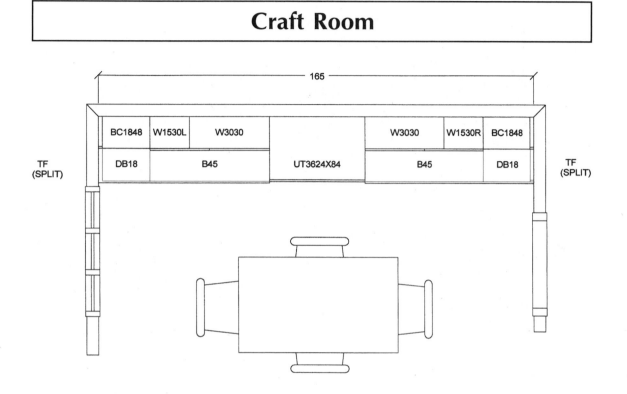

Cabinet List:

2 tall fillers (split)
2 18″×48″ bookcases units
2 15″×30 wall cabinets
2 30″×30″ wall cabinets
4 shelf undercabinet units (trimmed)
1 36″×84″ utility cabinet
6 utility shelves
2 18″ drawer base cabinets
2 45″ base cabinets
1 36″ frieze valance
1 72″ straight valance (trimmed)
2 8′-0″ crown molding
2 8′-0″ base toe material
28 knobs or pulls
1 pint stain
1 putty stick

Additional Materials Needed:

• Miscellaneous fasteners and adhesives
• Dimensional lumber
• 2 countertop sections

Required:

• Minimum 1″ filler at walls
• Trim tall fillers for use at bookcase and base cabinets
• Install frieze valance on top of utility cabinet, trim straight valances as returns

Variations:

• Adjust to fit job-site dimensions
• Replace four of the six utility shelves with four rollout shelf trays

A wall of storage in a spare room turns it into a craft room. The two sections of counterspace allow for multiple projects, and the tall utility cabinet can hold craft supplies or every kind.

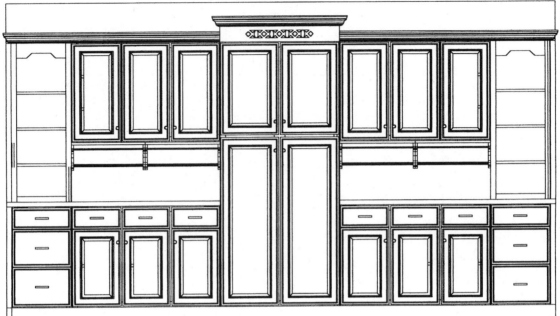

Craft Storage Wall

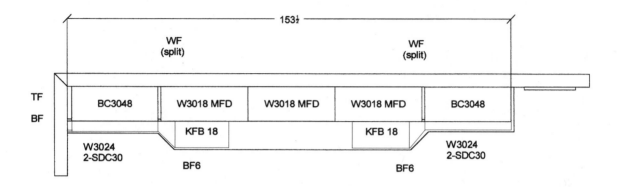

Cabinet List:

1 tall filler (trimmed)
2 30"×48" bookcases
4 30" spice drawer units with matching wood knobs
3 30"×18" wall cabinets with mullion doors and matching interiors
6 tempered glass inserts
1 8'-0" light rail molding
2 96" tall skins (split)
2 30"×24" wall cabinets
2 18" file base cabinets
2 base skins
2 6" base fillers
2 6" tall fillers (trimmed)
2 8'-0" crown molding
2 8'-0" inside corner molding
14 knobs or pulls
1 pint stain
1 putty stick

Additional Materials Needed:

- Miscellaneous fasteners and adhesives
- Dimensional lumber
- Countertop
- Light strip

Required:

- Trim tall filler, apply at wall at base and bookcase stacks
- Pull W3024's used as base cabinets forward 3"
- Build a toe kick height platform for W3024's
- Trim 6" base fillers as angled transitions to file base cabinets
- Install light strip behind light rail molding
- Create furniture toe treatment from trimmed 6" tall fillers and inside corner molding
- Skin all exposed cabinet sides

Variations:

- Add corkboard to the rear wall
- Order 18" high wall cabinets with solid doors for more closed storage

This storage wall also has a wide knee space for sit-down crafts and hobbies. The 48" high bookcases hold finished craft objects and reference material while the spice drawers can easily store paint brushes and other small craft supplies.

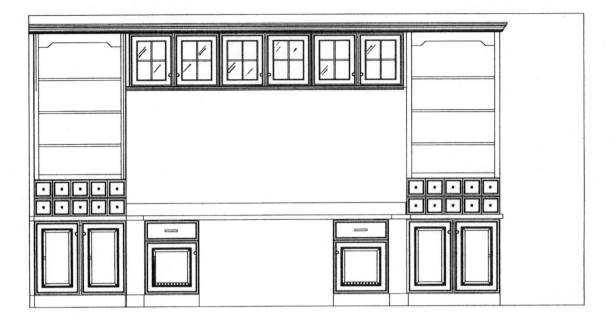

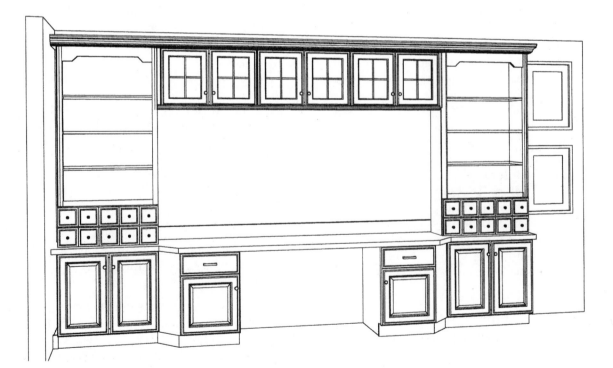

Craft Table

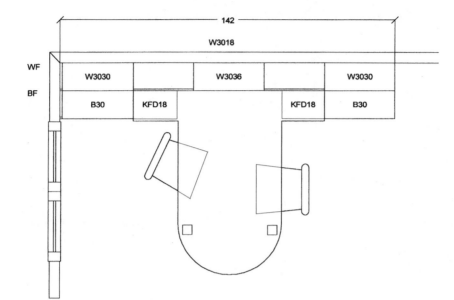

Cabinet List:

2 30″×30″ wall cabinets
1 30″×36″ wall cabinet
1 30″×18″ wall cabinet
1 tall skin (split)
2 36″ arched valances (trimmed)
3 48″ finished shelves (trimmed)
2 30″ base cabinets
2 18″ file base cabinets
1 8′-0″ base toe material
3 toe kick cap covers
2 8′-0″ crown molding
20 knobs or pulls
1 pint stain
1 putty stick

Additional Materials Needed:

- Miscellaneous fasteners and adhesives
- Dimensional lumber
- 2 table legs
- Countertop

Required:

- Minimum 1″ filler at wall
- Cleat countertop at rear wall for support
- Trim tall skin and cover sides of center cabinet stack
- Create open shelves left and right of center stack

Variations:

- Adjust width to fit job-site conditions
- Panel wall behind open shelving
- Skin remaining exposed cabinet ends
- Add rollout shelf trays to the 30″ base cabinets

A wall of storage with open shelving and a tall stack to hold craft supplies. The stacked cabinets in the center put supplies at an easy-reach. The broad worktable would be perfect for a quilter or two people working together.

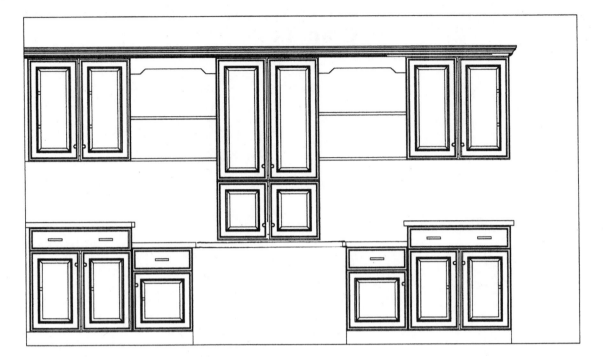

Flower Arranging Center

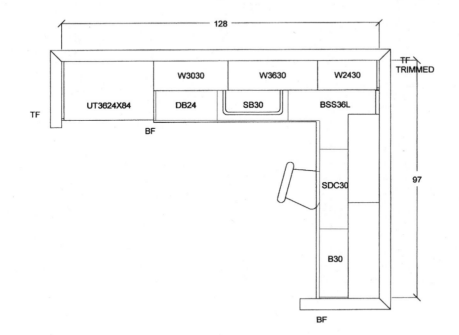

Cabinet List:

1 tall filler
1 36″×24″×84″ utility cabinet
2 utility shelves
4 rollout shelf trays
1 30″×30″ wall cabinet
1 36″×30″ wall cabinet
1 24″×30″ wall cabinet
1 24″ tambour unit
1 24″ drawer base
1 30″ sink base cabinet
1 36″ lazy susan
1 30″ spice drawer unit with matching wood
   knobs
1 30″ base cabinet
1 base filler
2 8′-0″ base toe material
2 toe kick cap covers
20 knobs or pulls
1 pint stain
1 putty stick

Additional Materials Needed:

- Miscellaneous fasteners and adhesives
- Countertop
- Sink and faucet
- 2 ventilated shelving units

Required:

- Pull spice drawer forward to 24″ off wall

Variations:

- Adjust to fit job-site conditions
- Substitute rollout shelf trays with adjust-able shelves for cost savings
- Add pull-out bins for collecting clippings for the compost pile

Spice drawers provides gardening gadget storage and a kneehole space for sit-down work area. The tall utility cabinet is outfitted with rollout shelf trays so that vases and other supplies are easy to access.

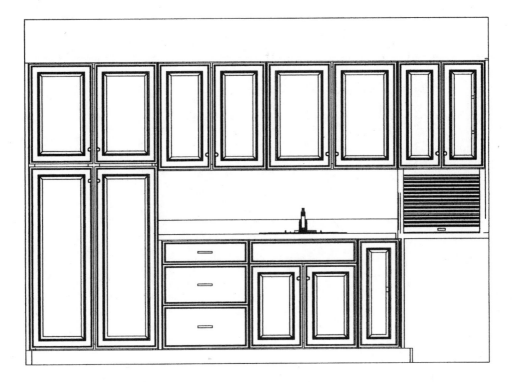

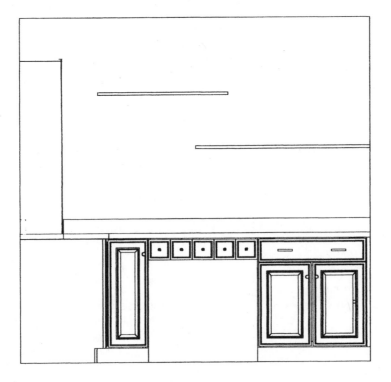

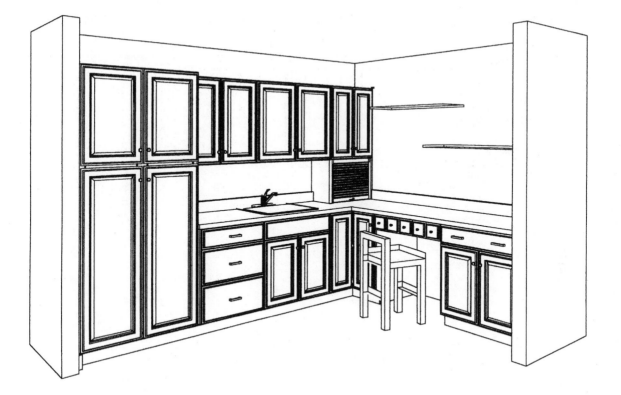

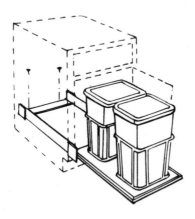

Full Service Workbench

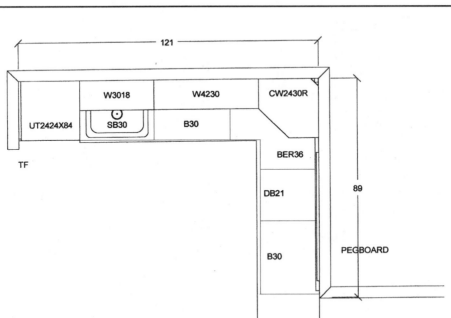

Cabinet List:

1 tall filler
1 24"×24'×84" utility cabinet
6 utility shelves
1 30"×18" wall cabinet
1 42"×30 wall cabinet
1 24"×24"×30" corner wall cabinet
1 30" sink base
2 30" base cabinets
1 36"×36" base corner easy-reach cabinet
1 21" drawer base
23 knobs or pulls
1 pint stain
1 putty stick

Additional Materials Needed:

• Miscellaneous fasteners and adhesives
• Countertop with extension
• Sink and faucet
• Pegboard

Required:

• Minimum 1" filler at wall

Variations:

• Adjust width to fit job-site conditions
• Replace utility shelves with rollout shelf trays
• Add additional wall cabinets in place of pegboard
• Add base toe material, if desired
• Add a lock to the tall cabinet for chemical storage

With tall storage, a sink, and extensive countertop, this workbench has just about everything a woodworker could want. The base easy-reach cabinet is shaped like a lazy susan but has an adjustable center shelf to easily store hand tools.

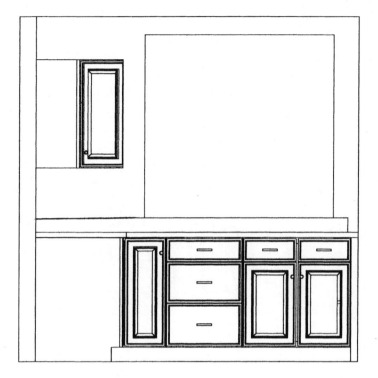

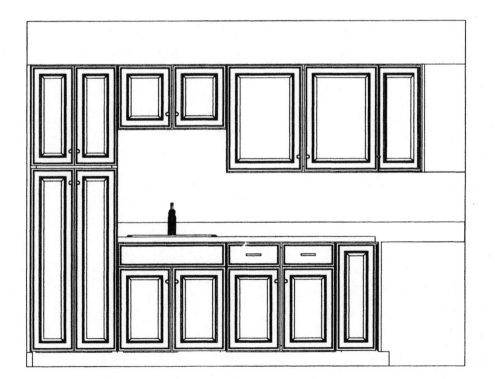

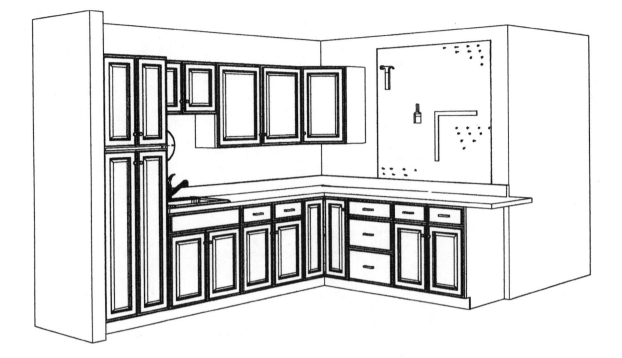

Garage Organizer

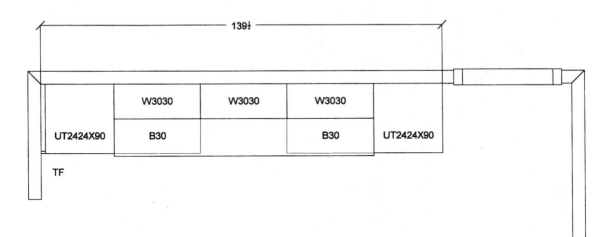

Cabinet List:

1 tall filler
2 24″×24″×90″ utility cabinets
12 utility shelves
3 30″×30″ wall cabinets
2 30″ base cabinets
22 knobs or pulls
1 pint stain
1 putty stick

Additional Materials Needed:

- Miscellaneous fasteners and adhesives
- Countertop
- Light strip

Required:

- Minimum 1″ tall filler at the wall
- Install light strip below wall cabinets

Variations:

- Add pegboard to rear wall
- Change one 30″ base to a sink base and add a sink
- Add base toe material and toe kick cap covers
- Add a knee space drawer

This combination workbench, potting area, and storage wall would make an untidy garage into a very organized space. Staggering cabinet heights gives extra storage in the utility cabinets while keeping everything in the wall cabinets in easy-reach.

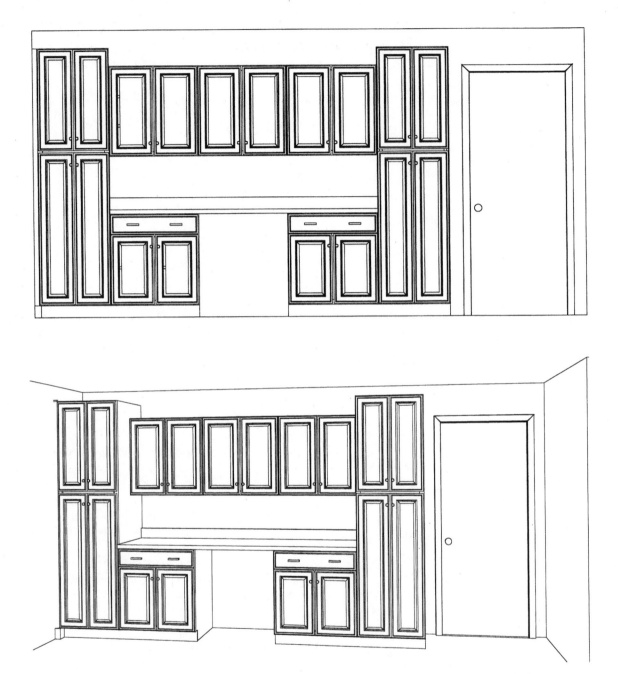

Garage Storage

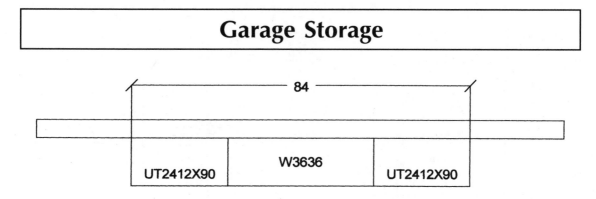

Cabinet List:

2 24″×12″×90″ utility cabinets
12 utility shelves
1 36″×36″ wall cabinet
1 36″×30 wall cabinet
1 8′-0″ base toe material
2 toe kick cap covers
12 knobs or pulls
1 pint stain
1 putty stick

Additional Materials Needed:

- Miscellaneous fasteners and adhesives
- Dimensional lumber
- Countertop

Required:

- Build a 9″ deep platform for W3630 used as a base cabinet

Variations:

- Adjust width to fit job-site conditions
- Add pegboard to the rear wall.

This 12″ deep storage wall contains over 50 cubic feet of storage space. There is just enough counter to use as a landing space for loading gardening or car-care supplies onto the shelves.

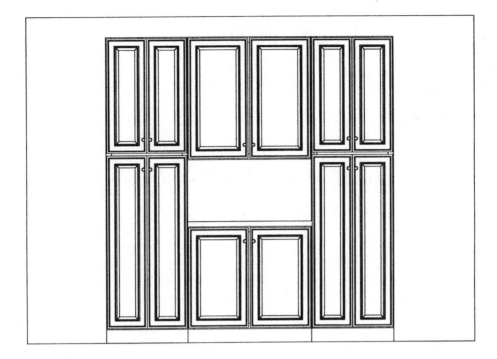

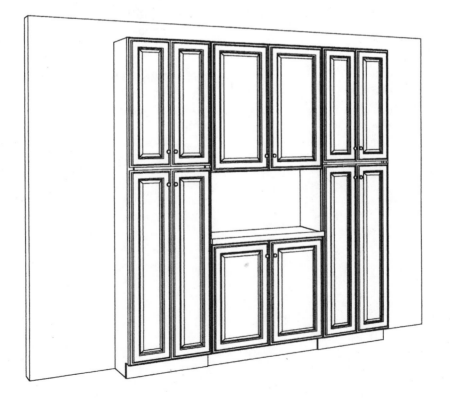

Gardening Station

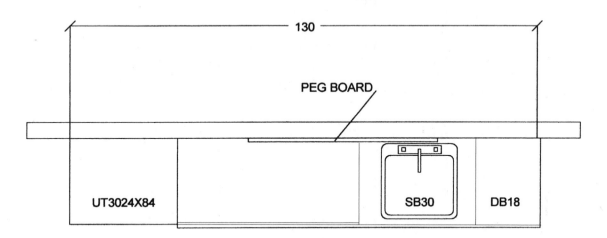

Cabinet List:

1 30″×24″×84″ utility cabinets
6 utility shelves
1 30″ sink base
1 18″ drawer base
7 tall fillers
1 8′-0″ base toe material
4 toe kick cap covers
9 knobs or pulls
1 pint stain
1 putty stick

Additional Materials Needed:

- Miscellaneous fasteners and adhesives
- Countertop
- Sink and faucet
- Pegboard

Required:

- Trim tall fillers, space 3/4″ apart, to create a slatted shelf
- Use extra filler material to cleat fillers to sides of the utility and sink base cabinets

Variations:

- Replace utility shelves with rollout trays
- Add a garbage disposal to the sink for from flower arrangement waste

A slatted shelf, that is created from filler material, allows air circulation for stored flowerpots. The tall cabinet easily holds gardening tools, containers, and flower arranging supplies.

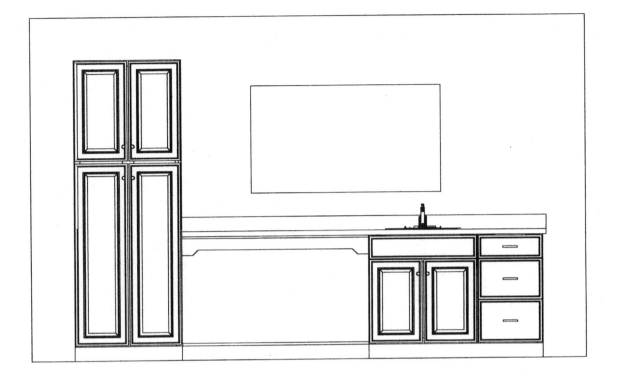

Garden Planning Center

Cabinet List:

1 wall filler
1 30″×18″ wall cabinet
2 18″×36″ wall cabinets
1 42″×18″ wall cabinet
1 24″×24″×36″ corner wall cabinet
1 base filler
1 30″ sink base cabinet
1 18″ base cabinets
2 trimmable 36″ kneehole drawers
1 6″ vertical spice drawer with matching wood knobs
1 21″ base cabinet
1 6″ base filler (split)
1 30″×30″ wall cabinet
1 24″×90″×12″ tall cabinet
6 utility shelves
2 8′-0″ base toe material
3 toe kick cap covers
21 knobs or pulls
1 pint stain
1 putty stick

Additional Materials Needed:

• Miscellaneous fasteners and adhesives
• Dimensional lumber
• Countertop
• Single-bowl sink and faucet
• 24″×30″ pegboard

• 1 fluorescent light strip
• 12 lineal feet of ventilated shelving

Required:

• Minimum 1″ filler at all walls
• Trim 6″ base filler and install 3″ in corner on sink wall and 1″ on utility cabinet wall
• Trim two kneehole drawers to fit 42″ opening
• Build a platform for W3030 to be used as a base cabinet
• Hang W4218 at 84″ and install fluorescent light strip below
• Install ventilated shelving below W4218 and between CW2436 and utility cabinet
• Clip countertop at utility cabinet

Variations:

• Adjust to fit job-site dimensions
• Increase cabinet height to ceiling

The counter height sit-down area provides a place to design garden layouts. The fluorescent light provides lighting for the sit-down area and encourages seedlings growing on the ventilated shelving. The vertical spice drawers are a great place to store packaged seeds.

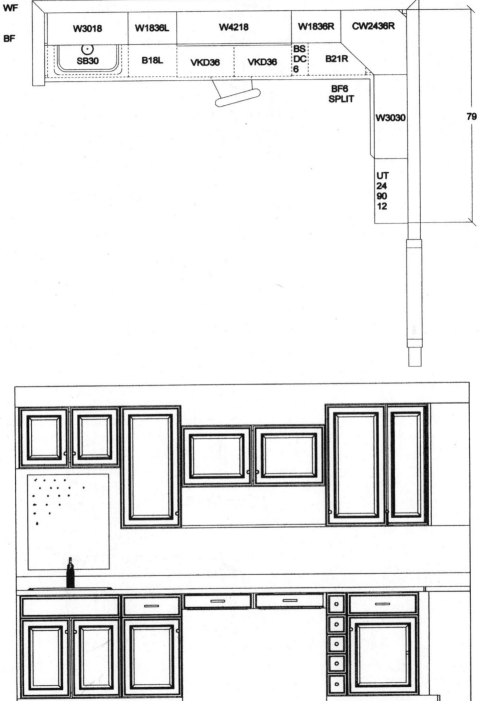

Handyman's Workbench

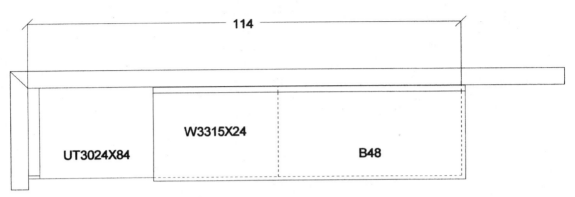

Cabinet List:

1 tall filler
1 30″×24″×84″ utility cabinet
2 utility shelves
4 rollout shelf trays
1 33″×15″×24″ wall cabinet
1 48″ base cabinet
2 8′-0″ base toe material
1 toe kick cap cover
10 knobs or pulls
1 pint stain
1 putty stick

Additional Materials Needed:

• Miscellaneous fasteners and adhesives
• Dimensional lumber
• Countertop
• 1 33″×24″ piece of 3/4″ plywood

Required:

• Minimum 1″ filler at wall
• Build a 21″ deep platform for W3315×24
  used as a base cabinet

• Install two utility shelves and four rollout
  shelf trays in utility cabinet
• Install plywood on top of W3315×24 for
  open storage

Variations:

• Add wall cabinets for additional storage
• Omit rollout shelves for cost savings
• Add locks on cabinets as required

With just enough storage and counter surface to make weekend home repairs almost fun, this workbench features a variety of storage types. The utility cabinet is outfitted with rollout shelves and the wall cabinet, used as a base, provides open storage. The 48″ base cabinet provides two drawers for hand tools.

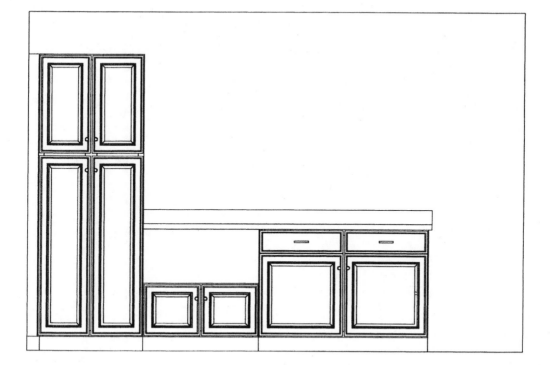

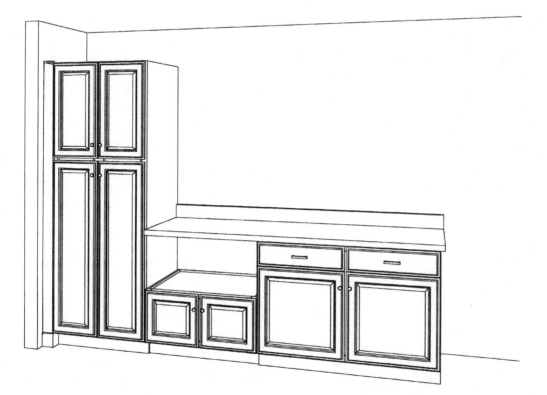

Hobby Room

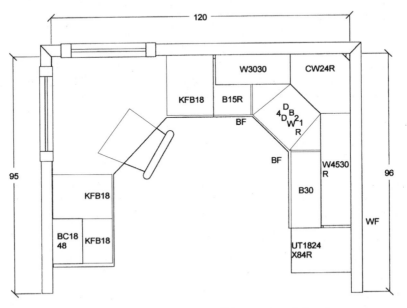

Cabinet List:

1 18″×24″×84″ utility cabinet
6 utility shelves
1 45″×30″ wall cabinet
1 wall filler
1 24″×24″×30″ corner wall cabinet
1 corner tambour unit
1 30″×30″ wall cabinet
3 shelf undercabinet units
1 18″×48″ bookcase unit
1 30″ base cabinet
1 21″ drawer base
1 base filler (split)
1 15″ base cabinet
3 file base cabinets
2 8′-0″ crown molding
2 8′-0″ base toe material
4 toe kick cap covers
24 knobs or pulls
1 pint stain
1 putty stick

Additional Materials Needed:

• Miscellaneous fasteners and adhesives
• Dimensional lumber
• 2 countertops

Required:

• Install 21″ drawer base in corner with 1″ fillers on each side to guarantee drawer clearance
• Install tambour unit below corner wall cabinet
• Cleat countertop in corners with dimensional lumber

Variations:

• Adjust to fit room dimensions
• Use rollout shelves in utility cabinet

Turn a small bedroom or the corner of a family room into a dedicated hobby room with built-ins. Cabinetry provides storage and a generous work surface for almost any hobby. The tambour unit is a great place to stash clutter.

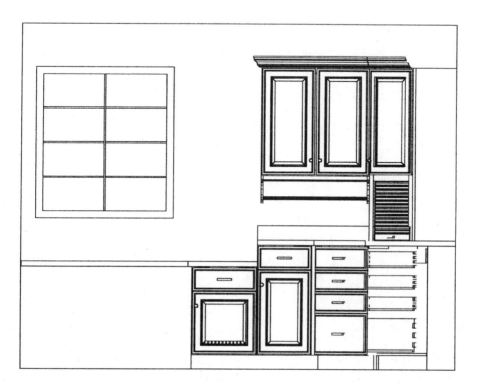

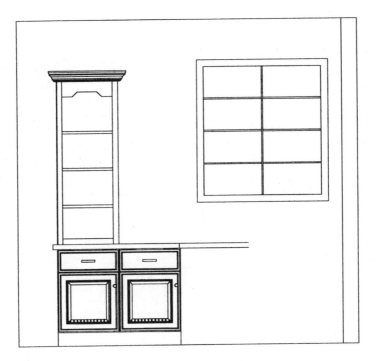

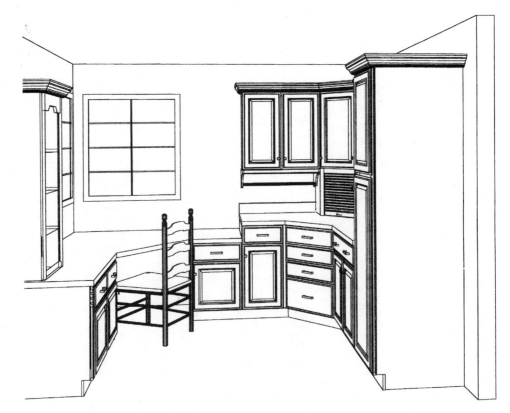

Potting Area

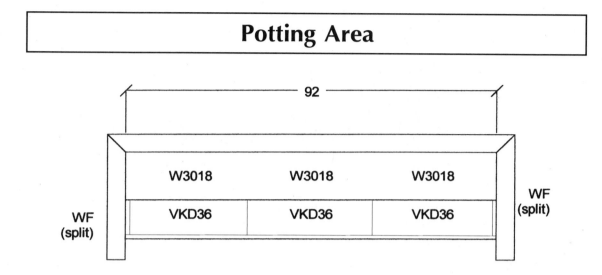

Cabinet List:

1 6″ filler split into four sections
3 30″×18″ wall cabinets
3 36″ trimmable kneehole drawers
9 knobs or pulls
1 pint stain
1 putty stick

Additional Materials Needed:

- Miscellaneous fasteners and adhesives
- Countertop
- 3/4″ laminate shelf
- 12″ deep ventilated shelving

Required:

- Minimum 1″ filler at each wall
- Hang wall cabinets at approximately 78″ off floor
- Install laminate shelf on top of wall cabinets
- Install ventilated shelving approximately 15″ off floor

Variations:

- Adjust width to fit job-site conditions
- Possible backsplash materials include corkboard, galvanized steel, and pegboard
- Install grow-lights beneath the wall cabinets

Short, easy to reach wall cabinets keep the area neat. A laminate shelf on top of the wall cabinets allows baskets, vases, and other gardening paraphernalia to be stored on top. The ventilated shelf below the counter is an ideal place for flowerpots.

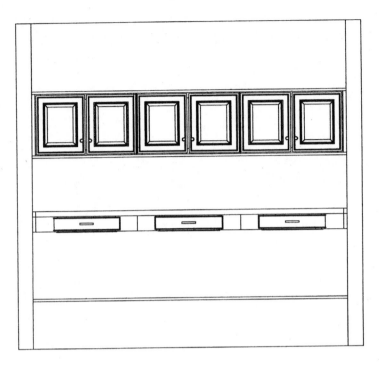

Potting Bench with Farm Sink

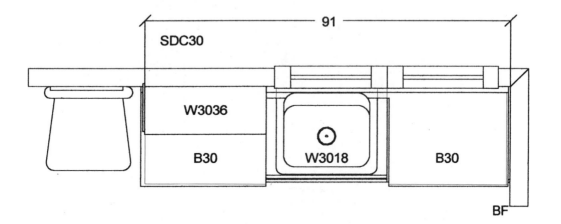

Cabinet List:

1 base filler
2 30″ base cabinets
1 30″×18″ front frame and doors only
1 sink front floor
1 6″ wall filer
1 30″×36″ wall cabinet
1 30″ spice drawer unit with matching wood
   knobs
1 8′-0″ crown molding
1 8′-0″ base toe material
1 toe kick cap covers
12 knobs or pulls
1 pint stain
1 putty stick

Additional Materials Needed:

- Miscellaneous fasteners and adhesives
- Dimensional lumber
- Countertop
- 30″ Farm sink and faucet

Required:

- Build 21″ deep platform for front frame
  and doors, cover with sink floor
- Trim and install 6″ filler on top of front
  frame and doors; scribe to fit sink
- Be sure to order the front frame and doors
  in a square style if the wall cabinet is in
  cathedral

Variations:

- Skin the sides of the wall cabinet to conceal the spice drawer joint
- Add a garbage disposal for plant clippings

This charming potting area looks like it be-
longs in a country cottage, but it would work
well in just about any home. The front
frame and doors act as a traditional sink
front but can be adapted to a farm sink with
the use of a filler.

Potting Nook

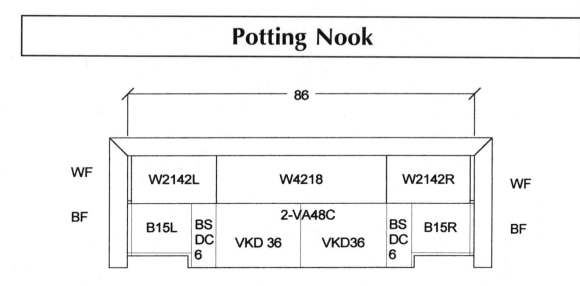

Cabinet List:

1 42″ wall filler (split)
2 21″×42″ wall cabinets
1 42″×18″ wall cabinet
1 base filler (split)
2 15″ base cabinets
2 6″ vertical spice drawer units with matching wood knobs
2 36″ trimmable kneehole drawers
2 48″ arched valances
1 48″×96″ paneling (trimmed)
1 8′-0″ crown molding
1 8′-0″ base toe material
1 8′-0″ scribe molding
8 knobs or pulls
1 pint stain
1 putty stick

Additional Materials Needed:

- Miscellaneous fasteners and adhesives
- Dimensional lumber
- Countertop

Required:

- Pull center cabinetry section forward to 27″
- Build a 24″ deep platform for opening below kneehole drawers
- Cover platform with paneling and scribe molding to cover raw edge
- Create false wall between vertical spice drawers and cover with paneling

Variations:

- Adjust to fit job-site dimensions
- Add rollout shelf trays to 15″ base cabinets
- Add lighting behind upper valance

Wall cabinets are hung so that the crown molding goes up to the ceiling in this eight-foot high nook. A pulled forward center section is open to house wicker baskets full of gardening paraphernalia.

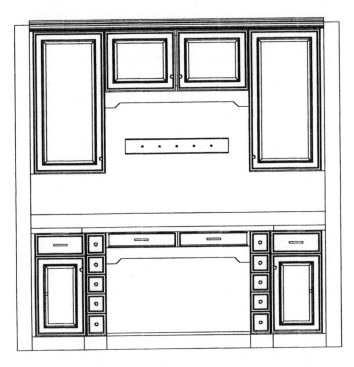

Scrapbooking Station

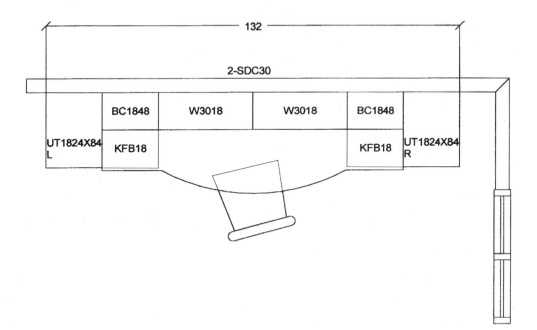

Cabinet List:

2 18″×24′×84″ utility cabinets
4 utility shelves
6 rollout shelf trays
2 file basket inserts
2 18″×48″ bookcase units
2 30″×18″ wall cabinets
1 60″ finished shelf (trimmed)
2 30″ spice drawer units with matching wood knobs
1 8′-0″ light rail
2 18″ file base cabinet
1 8′-0″ base toe material
4 toe kick cap covers
3 8′-0″ crown molding
12 knobs or pulls
1 pint stain
1 putty stick

Additional Materials Needed:

• Miscellaneous fasteners and adhesives
• Countertop
• Light strip

Required:

• Install shelves, roll out shelf trays and file basket inserts in utility cabinets
• Trim and install shelf below wall cabinets to conceal cabinet bottoms
• Install light rail molding below spice drawers
• Install light strip behind light rail molding

Variations:

• Enlarge utility cabinets if space permits for additional storage

The hobby of scrapbooking requires lots of storage. In this design, there are four file drawers to hold specialty papers. Bookcases store albums and reference books. Four file baskets hold paper supplies and spice drawers hold die-cuts, stickers, art pens, and other small supplies. The countertop is curved to create added workspace.

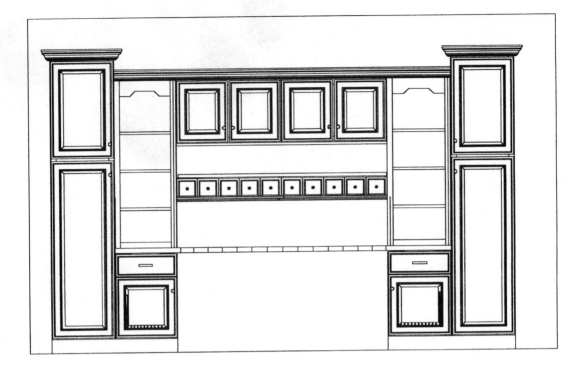

Wall Hung Workbench

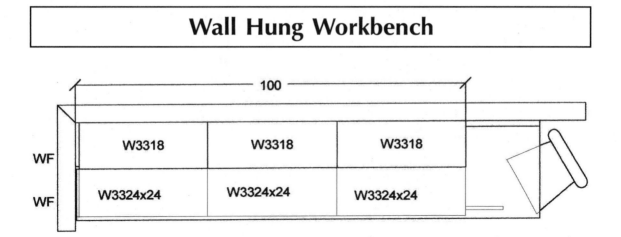

Cabinet List:

1 wall filler (split)
3 33″×18″ wall cabinets
3 33″×24″×24″ wall cabinets
1 counter support
12 knobs or pulls
1 pint stain
1 putty stick

Additional Materials Needed:

- Miscellaneous fasteners and adhesives
- Dimensional lumber
- Countertop
- Light strip

Required:

- Install 24″ high wall cabinets at 34 1/2″ off the floor
- Install light strip below wall cabinets
- Trim and install wall filler at wall on top and lower cabinets
- Create ledger strip from dimensional lumber to help support wall hung base cabinets

Variations:

- Add pegboard to the rear wall
- Add rollout shelves to 24″ deep wall cabinets

If keeping the workbench off the floor makes sense for a particular installation then consider using 24″ deep wall cabinets as the base. These cabinets are typically used over refrigerators but work well in this situation. The extended countertop provides a small sit-down area or a place to attach clamp-on tools.

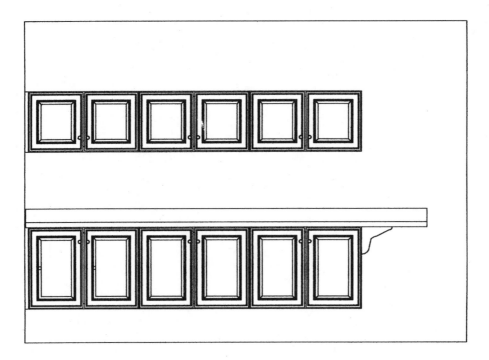

Weekend Workbench

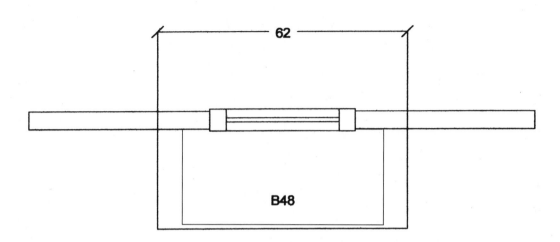

Cabinet List:

1 48″ base cabinet
4 24″ rollout shelf trays
4 knobs or pulls

Additional Materials Needed:

- Miscellaneous fasteners and adhesives
- Countertop with 6″ overhang left and right

Required:

- Install four rollout shelf trays in B48
- Enlarge cabinetry to fit existing space

Variations:

- Add base toe material and toe kick cap covers if desired
- Omit rollout shelves for cost savings

The most basic of workbenches is perfect for small weekend projects or repairs. The extensions on the countertop allow space for a vice or other clamp-on tool. Rollout shelf trays in the base give easy access to stored items.

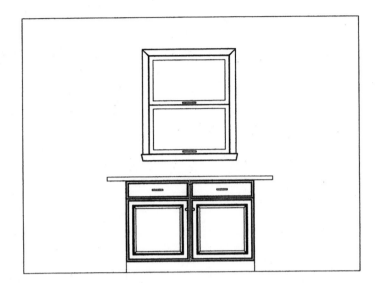

Work Bench

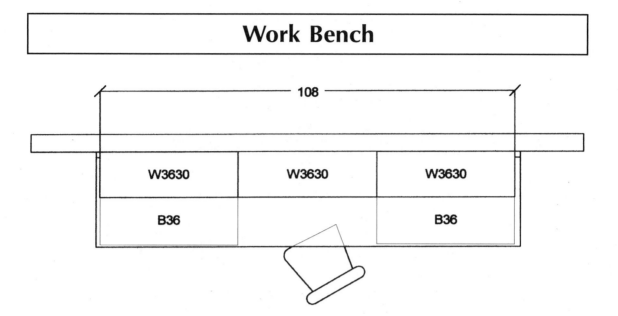

Cabinet List:

3 36"×30" wall cabinets
2 36" base cabinets
1 8'-0" base toe material
4 toe kick cap covers
14 knobs or pulls
1 pint stain
1 putty stick

Additional Materials Needed:

• Miscellaneous fasteners and adhesives
• Countertop

Required:

• Install wall cabinets at 84" off floor

Variations:

• Adjust width to fit job-site conditions
• Add a kneehole drawer

A basic workbench with a 9' counter span would be a welcome addition to any garage or basement. The countertop should be of a durable material such as hardwood or even plywood. Extend the countertop if a vise or other clamp-on tools are to be used.

Entertainment Centers

One of the most popular uses for built-ins created from stock cabinetry is the entertainment center. One reason for this popularity is that kitchens often open up to the family room. Having the cabinets in both rooms blend, if not match just makes sense. Another reason is the love affair that the world is having with audio-visual equipment of every kind.

Cabinet arrangements to fit today's electronic equipment can be designed in all sizes and levels of complexity. Not only are televisions getting larger, but it also seems that almost every year brings more components to intrigue the buyer. Add to that, the need for CD, video, and DVD storage and you have the basis for creating a very specialized built-in. Electronic systems have become essential elements of a modern home. They can vary from moderately sized units to ones that span the entire wall of a room.

The design process begins by gathering all audio-visual specifications. Not only are the individual dimensions important, but also speaker placement and required air circulation. It is always a good idea to make the openings for televisions slightly over-sized. This allows for the purchase of a larger unit in the future. Standard size cabinetry can then be combined in many configurations to accommodate the equipment. The finishing details of top and base molding, mullion, or other decorative doors create the final look.

Nothing is more important in setting up an entertainment center than the wiring. The best equipment and most beautiful cabinetry won't deliver the sound if it isn't hooked up properly. Consulting a professional audio-visual technician is the best thing you can do to ensure that your entertainment center sounds as good as it looks. It takes a team effort to create a really good system.

Entertainment centers are competing with fireplaces and winning the fight for wall space. Our electronic equipment deserves the perfect cabinetry to set it off.

Armoire Style Entertainment Center

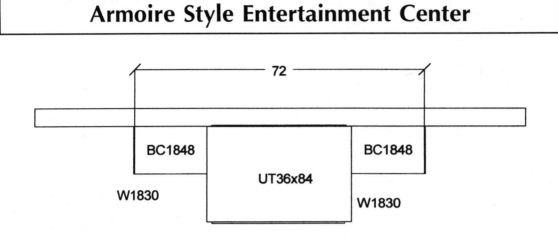

Cabinet List:

2 18″×30″ wall cabinets
2 18″×48″ bookcases
3 tall skins (split 1)
1 36″×84″ utility cabinet
1 utility shelf
2 36″ rollout shelves
2 8′-0″ crown molding
2 6″×96″ tall fillers
2 8′-0″ inside corner molding
6 170° angle opening hinges
6 knobs or pulls
1 pint stain
1 putty stick

Additional Materials Needed:

• Miscellaneous fasteners and adhesives
• Dimensional lumber
• Matching wood countertop
• Electrical and cable hookups
• Television

Required:

• Television specifications
• Build platforms for all cabinets

• Cover platforms with furniture toe treatment of 6″ tall fillers and inside corner molding
• Remove toe from utility cabinet and install on platform upside-down
• Block and install matching wood countertop and utility shelf in center section
• Install two rollouts in bottom of center section
• Skin all exposed sides

Variations:

• Line the upper section of the utility cabinet with plain or beadboard paneling
• Replace bookcase shelves with tempered glass shelves and add lighting

A combination of wall cabinets and an inverted utility cabinet is the basis for this entertainment center. Order 170° angle opening hinges, commonly used on lazy susans, and install on the upper doors to increase the standard opening.

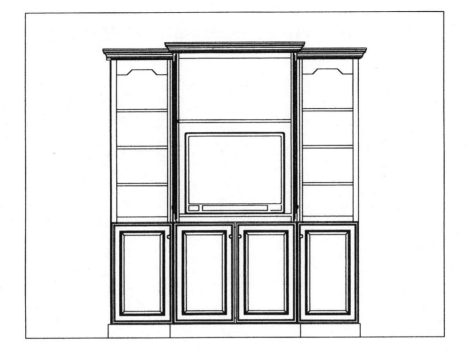

Big Screen Television Surround

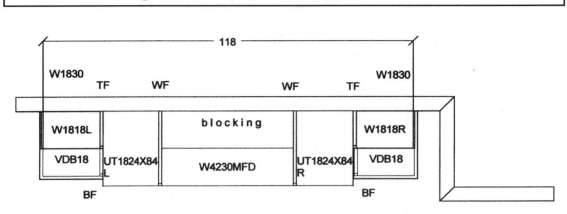

Cabinet List:

2 18"×30" wall cabinets
2 18"×18" wall cabinets
1 tall filler (split)
2 48" wall skins
2 18" vanity drawer bases
1 vanity filler (split)
2 base skins
2 18"×24"×84" tall cabinets
12 utility shelves
5 tall skins
1 42"×30" wall cabinets with matching interiors and mullion doors
2 tempered glass inserts
2 8'-0" crown molding
1 8'-0" base toe material
1 8'-0" scribe molding
6 toe kick cap covers
16 knobs or pulls
1 pint stain
1 putty stick

Additional Materials Needed:

- Miscellaneous fasteners and adhesives
- Dimensional lumber
- Plywood
- 2 countertops
- Electrical and cable hookups
- Big screen television

Required:

- Specifications for television
- Stack 18" wide wall cabinets and apply split tall skins on exposed ends
- Minimum of 1" filler at deeper cabinets
- Pull wall cabinet with mullion doors forward and block to 24"
- Skin all exposed sides
- Trim fifth tall skin as finish to bottom of W4230MFD. Finish raw edge with scribe molding

Variations:

- Adjust to fit television
- Change location of mullion doors
- Replace utility shelves with slid out shelf trays

Wall cabinets, vanity drawer bases and utility cabinets are combined to make a surround for a big screen television. The mullion door wall cabinet over the television must be pulled forward and blocked in place. Plywood is installed level with the top of the pulled forward cabinet so that decorative items can be placed on top.

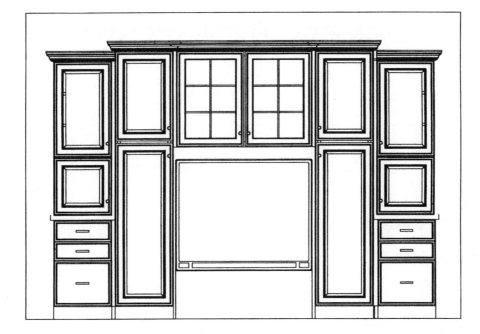

Bookcase Wall with Television

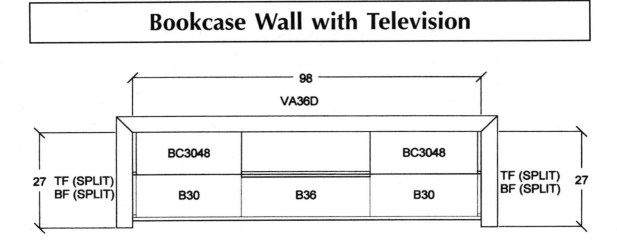

Cabinet List:

1 tall filler (split)
2 30"×48" bookcase units
1 72" finished shelf (split)
1 36" decorative valance
1 piece paneling 36"×48"
2 30" base cabinets
1 base filler (split)
1 36" base cabinet
2 8'-0" crown molding
2 8'-0" base toe material
12 knobs or pulls
1 8'-0" scribe molding
1 pint stain
1 putty stick

Additional Materials Needed:

- Miscellaneous fasteners and adhesives
- Matching wood countertop
- Electrical and cable hookups
- Television, VCR, and DVD player

Required:

- Specifications for all audio-visual equipment
- Split 72" finished shelf as soffit board and shelf. Use scribe molding as cleats
- Panel rear center wall providing a removable false back for the lower section to conceal wiring

Variation:

- Pull center base cabinet forward 3" for design interest

In just over 8' of wall space a bookcase and entertainment center combination fills many needs. The base cabinets can hold games, videos and DVDs. Open shelves house books and collectibles. The center section accommodates up to a 27" television as well as the VCR and DVD player.

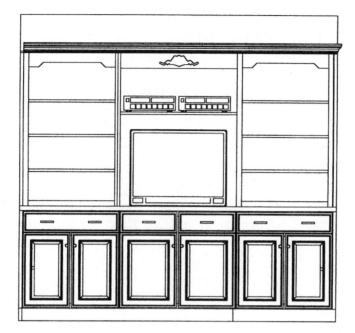

Contemporary Wall Unit

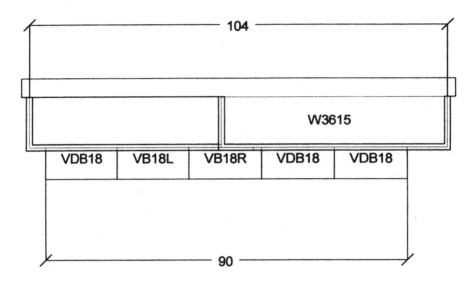

Cabinet List:

3 18″ vanity drawer bases
2 18″ vanity bases
1 36″×15″ wall cabinet
3 48″ finished shelves
3 60″ finished shelves
1 72″ finished shelf
1 48″×96″ paneling
2 8′-0″ light rail molding
1 8′-0″ base toe material
2 8′-0″ scribe molding
2 toe kick cap covers
15 knobs or pulls
1 pint stain
1 putty stick

Additional Materials Needed:

- Miscellaneous fasteners and adhesives
- Countertop
- Electrical and cable hookups
- Television, DVD, VCR, and receiver with portable speakers

Required:

- Specifications for all equipment
- Panel all areas behind open shelving to conceal wires
- Assemble open shelves using scribe molding as cleats
- Trim top two shelves with light rail molding for a contemporary look

Variation:

- Design can be reversed to have the taller unit on the left

This design has a contemporary, asymmetrical look and can house a number of audiovisual components as well as books or decorative accessories. The base of the unit is made from standard vanity cabinets and the upper section is fabricated from one wall cabinet and finished shelving.

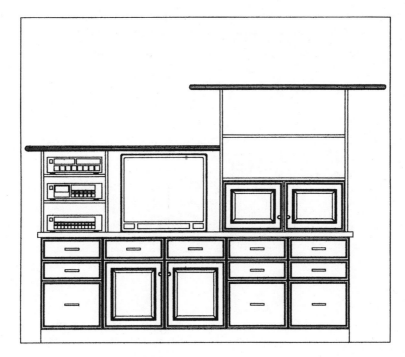

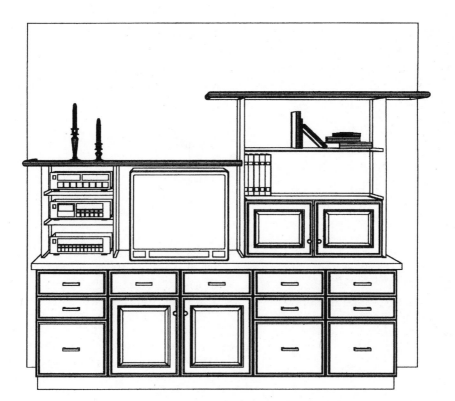

Desk and Entertainment Center Combination

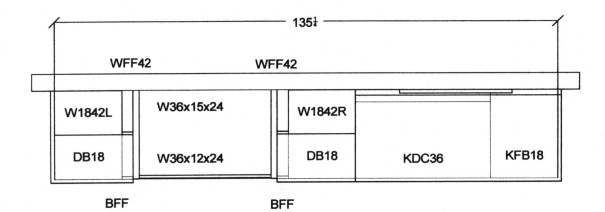

Cabinet List:

2 18"×42" wall cabinets
2 42" fluted wall fillers
1 36"×15"×24" wall cabinet
2 18" drawer bases
2 fluted base fillers
2 84" high refrigerator returns
1 36" arched valance
1 3/4"×96" tall end panel
2 tall skins
1 36"×12"×24" wall cabinets
1 36" kneehole drawer
1 18" file base
2 8'-0" crown molding
1 8'-0" base toe material
4 toe kick cap covers
15 knobs or pulls
1 pint stain
1 putty stick

Additional Materials Needed:

- Miscellaneous fasteners and adhesives
- Dimensional lumber

- 3 Countertop sections
- Electrical and cable hookups
- Television

Required:

- Build a platform for W3612×24
- Skin insides of refrigerator end panels
- Cut 3/4" tall end panel into soffit board and as tops of W3615×24 and W3612×24

Variations:

- Panel wall behind television with plain or beadboard paneling
- Add additional wall cabinetry above desk

A combination entertainment center and desk would be a great addition to any family room. Fluted fillers accent the wall and base storage cabinets. The television is raised off the floor approximately 17". The unit provides generous storage for videos and DVDs.

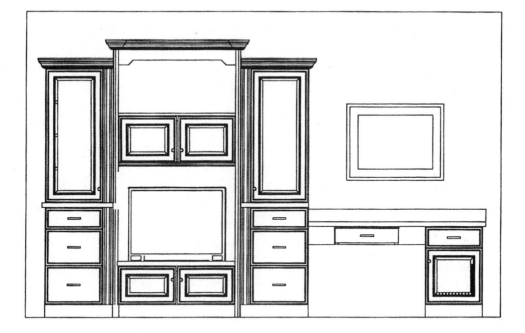

Entertainment Wall

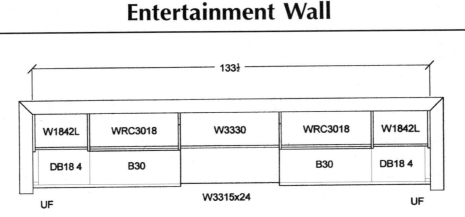

Cabinet List:

4 60″ finished shelves
2 72″ finished shelves (split)
2 18″×42″ wall cabinets
2 30″×18″ wine rack cabinets
1 33″×30″ wall cabinet
2 base fillers
2 18″ four-drawer bases
2 30″ base cabinets
1 33″×15″×24″ wall cabinet
1 3/4″ tall panel (split)
1 96″×34″ finished paneling
1 48″×34″ finished paneling
2 24″ frieze valances (trimmed)
1 72″ straight valance
1 48″ straight valance
2 8′-0″ crown molding
1 8′-0″ light rail molding
2 8′0″ base toe material
22 knobs or pulls
1 pint stain
1 putty stick

Additional Materials Needed:

- Miscellaneous fasteners and adhesives
- Dimensional lumber
- 2 countertop sections
- Electrical and cable hookups
- Television and DVD player

Required:

- Television specifications
- 2 1/4″ base fillers at each wall
- 60″ finished shelves are used for vertical panels
- 72″ finished shelves are split as soffit boards and tops of wine rack cabinets
- Panel all wall surfaces and exposed sides of the 30″ base cabinets
- Trim frieze and plain valances as shown
- Trim 3/4″ tall panel as television shelf and top to cabinet below

Variations:

- Add mullion doors, matching interiors, and glass inserts to wall cabinets
- Finish rear of wall behind television with wainscot detail
- Replace wine rack cabinets with 18″ wall high cabinets
- Add rollout shelves to 30″ base cabinets
- Use remaining base toe material to close the pierced openings of the frieze valances

At just over 11′ wide, this entertainment center will be the focal point of any family room. An attractive combination of open and closed storage areas provide space for wine, books, and games. The lowered television area makes it the perfect height for a seated viewer.

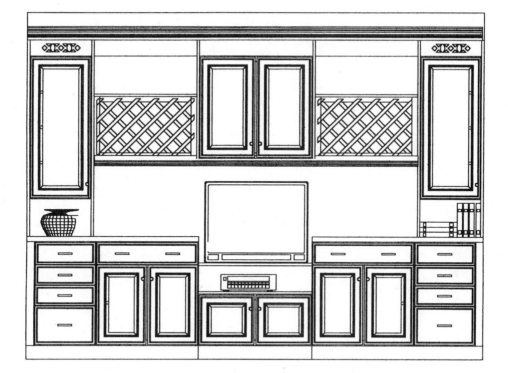

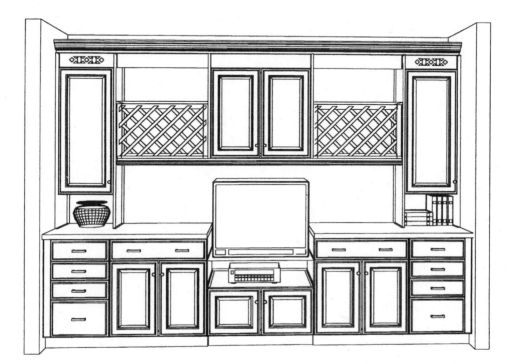

Family Room TV Cabinet

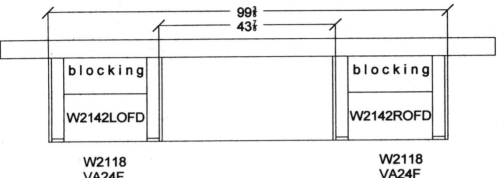

Cabinet List:

2 21″×18″ wall cabinet
2 21″×42″ wall cabinet with open-frame doors and matching interiors
2 tempered glass inserts
6 tempered glass shelves
2 24″ frieze valances (trimmed)
1 8′-0″ base toe material
5 3/4″×84″ tall end panels (trimmed)
4 tall fluted fillers (trimmed)
8 rosettes
2 8′-0″ crown molding
4 knobs or pulls
1 pint stain
1 putty stick

Additional Materials Needed:

• Miscellaneous fasteners and adhesives
• Dimensional lumber
• Electrical and cable hookups
• Television

Required:

• Television specifications
• Trim four 3/4″ tall panels to 24″ deep and to height
• Cut fifth tall panel as shelf and soffit board
• Build platform for wall cabinet stacks
• Pull and block wall cabinets to 24″ off wall
• Back pierced area of frieze valances with base toe material
• Cover platform with frieze valances

Variations:

• Adjust unit to fit television dimensions
• Apply decorator matching doors on the exposed sides of the tall end panels.

A minimalist approach to building-in a big screen television stills has plenty of style. Just big enough to hold the necessities and give a polished look, this unit features pairs of tall fluted fillers flanking the wall cabinet stack. The overall height is approximately 65″.

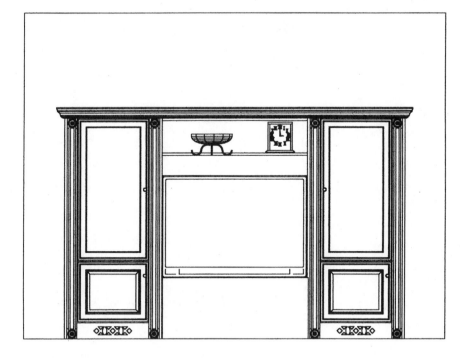

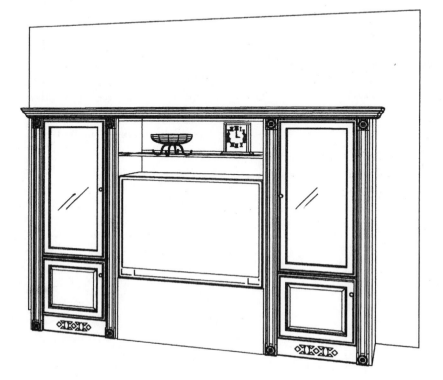

Fireplace with Big Screen Television

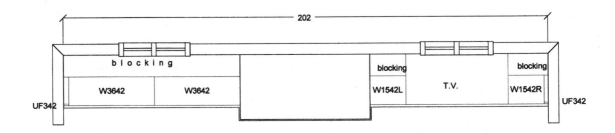

Cabinet List:

2   36″×42″ wall cabinets
2   15″×42″ wall cabinets
2   42″ wall fillers
2   8′-0″ base toe material
2   8′-0″ inside corner molding
6   knobs or pulls
1   pint stain
1   putty stick

Additional Materials Needed:

- Miscellaneous fasteners and adhesives
- Dimensional lumber
- Electrical and cable hookups
- Big screen television

Required:

- Specifications for television
- Build a platform for the wall cabinets, used as bases, and cover with base toe material

- Pull wall cabinets forward and block
- Minimum of 1″ filler at walls
- Install inside corner molding at the top of the cabinets, below the extended mantle
- Electrical and cable hookups

Variations:

- Adjust to fit television
- Add mullion doors and matching interiors on any, or all, wall cabinets

This built-in flanks a fireplace and requires an extension of the mantle to enclose the top of the cabinets. In this application, it is particularly important to understand the airflow requirements for the television.

Floating Entertainment Center

Cabinet List:

2 15″×36 wall cabinet with open-frame doors and matching interiors
2 tempered glass inserts
1 15″×42″ wall cabinet
3 3/4″×96″ tall end panels
1 6″×84″ filler (split)
3 knobs or pulls
1 pint stain
1 putty stick

Additional Materials Needed:

- Miscellaneous fasteners and adhesives
- 3 pairs of lid supports
- Electrical and cable hookups
- Plasma screen television

Required:

- Install cabinets on their sides with the hinges at the bottom
- Cut one 3/4″ panels to as support legs and cubbyhole shelf
- Split tall filler, as rear ledger strip, to help support cabinets
- Join 3/4″ tall panels with a scarf joint to create the top of the unit and bottoms to cubbyholes
- Attach lid supports to control the door opening

Variations:

- Adjust to fit job-site measurements
- Add a cushion to the cabinetry for extra seating
- Order additional paneling to line the open-frame door cabinets. This conceals shelf drillings. Matching interiors will not be needed. A shelf can also be added.

A low run of cabinetry provides a glass door cabinet under the plasma screen television for a DVD or other electronic equipment. A similar cabinet on the right gives a visual balance. The center cabinet gives hidden storage. Cubbyholes can hold baskets with remote controls.

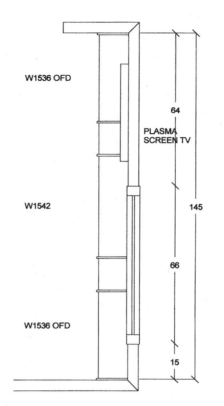

W1536 OFD

64

PLASMA
SCREEN TV

W1542

145

66

W1536 OFD

15

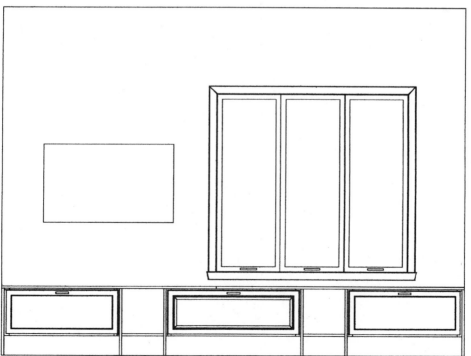

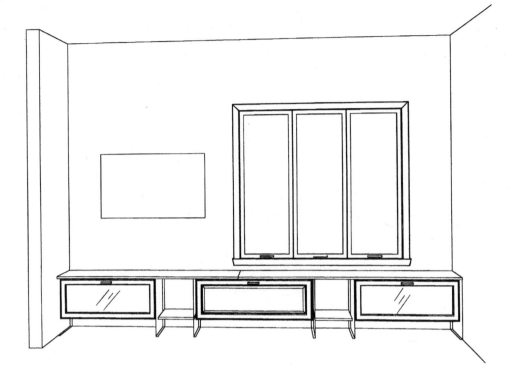

Inglenook

Cabinet List:

4 33″×15″ wall cabinets
1 wall filler (split)
2 18″×48″ bookcases
1 48″×96″ plain paneling (split)
1 8′-0″ outside corner molding
1 48″×96″ bead board paneling (split)
2 84″ tall 3″ fillers
2 8′-0″ base toe kick material
2 8′-0″ scribe molding
8 knobs or pulls
1 pint stain
1 putty stick

Additional Materials Needed:

- Miscellaneous fasteners and adhesives
- Dimensional lumber
- 2 matching wood caps for bookcases
- Plywood
- Cushion

Required:

- Panel bookcase backs and finish exposed corner with outside corner molding

- Pull wall cabinets forward 6″ and block with dimensional lumber
- Create seat from plywood and finish raw edge with scribe molding
- Construct 15″ deep platform for wall cabinets and finish with base toe material
- Minimum 1″ fillers at each wall
- Trim 3″ tall filler and install horizontally on wall level with bookcase unit
- Trim bead board paneling and panel between bench and 3″ filler

Variations:

- Adjust cabinet width to accommodate job-site conditions
- Use plain paneling on wall instead of bead board
- Add skins and decorator matching doors to exposed ends of bookcases

What could be more entertaining than sitting by the fireplace? This built-in inglenook created from wall cabinets and bookcases adds charm and storage. Pulling the wall cabinets forward 3″ gives a comfortable 15″ seat depth.

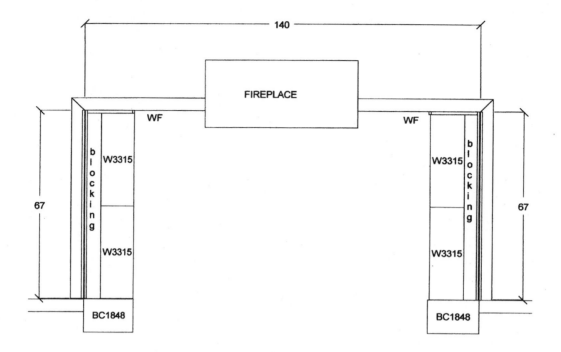

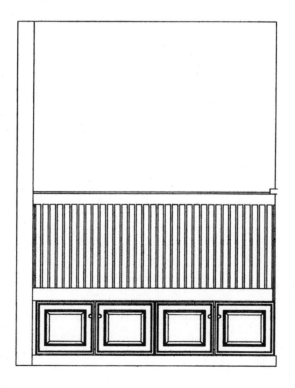

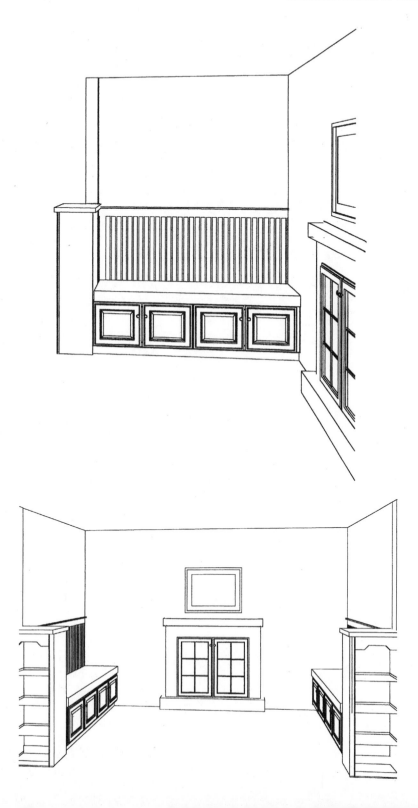

Kitchen Island with Television Niche

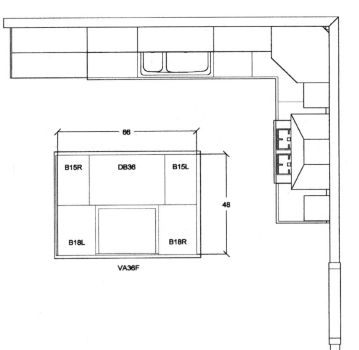

Cabinet List:

2 15″ base cabinets
1 36″ drawer base
2 18″ base cabinets
1 36″ frieze valance
3 48″×34 1/2″ paneling
2 8′-0″ base toe material
4 toe kick end caps
14 knobs or pulls
1 pint stain
1 putty stick

Additional Materials Needed:

- Miscellaneous fasteners and adhesives
- Dimensional lumber
- Substrate materila
- 2 countertop sections
- Electrical and cable hookups
- Television

Required:

- Specifications for the television
- Build a platform for television cover with countertop
- Trim paneling and apply to exposed sides of the island cabinets
- Apply substrate to cabinet in back of television opening, apply paneling

Variations:

- Adapt television to island size

When a small family area is adjacent to the kitchen, the back of the island may be the perfect place to put the television. A platform is built to the same height as the cabinet toe kick, and a countertop section is installed on top of the platform to support the television. A frieze valance finishes off the look and encourages airflow.

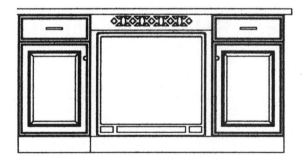

Low Television Cabinet

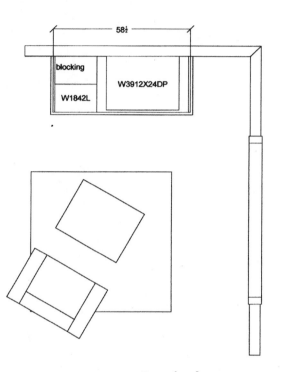

Cabinet List:

1 18″×42″ wall cabinet
1 39″×12″×24″ wall cabinet
1 3/4″×96″ tall end panel for cabinet sides
1 39″ piece of 3/4″ finished material for shelf below television
1 piece 48″×34 1/2″ paneling
2 4″ tall fillers (trimmed and mitered)
2 8′-0″ inside corner molding
3 knobs or pulls
1 pint stain
1 putty stick

Additional Materials Needed:

• Miscellaneous fasteners and adhesives
• Dimensional lumber to create platform and blocking
• 1 1/2″ thick wood top to match cabinetry

Required:

• 4″ high platform
• Split 3/4″ tall panel for sides of unit
• Panel open wall behind television
• Pull W1842 forward 12″ and block
• Furniture toe detail from fillers topped with inside corner molding
• Check television specifications

Variations:

• Add matching interiors and an open-frame door to the W1842

Compact but attractive, this low television cabinet works in even small dens or studys. With an overall opening of 39″×30″×24″ deep, it will fit most 31″ televisions. Adding a glass door cabinet and matching interiors makes the left cabinet a great place to display books or collectibles.

Media Center

Cabinet List:

3 3/4″×96″ tall end panels
2 3/4″×84″ tall end panels
2 42″ wall fillers
3 84″ tall fillers
2 12″×42″ wall cabinets with open-frame doors
2 30″×42″ wall cabinets with mullion doors and matching interiors
4 tempered glass inserts
2 48″ arched valances
1 60″ arched valance
1 48″×96″ paneling
2 45″×24″ wall cabinets
1 15″×24″ wall cabinet
1 33″×24″ wall cabinet
2 6″×96″ tall fillers
2 8′-0″ inside corner molding
15 knobs or pulls
1 pint stain
1 putty stick

Additional Materials Needed:

- Miscellaneous fasteners and adhesives
- Dimensional lumber
- Matching wood countertop
- Speaker cloth
- Electrical and cable hookups
- Television

Required:

- Television specifications
- Install 3/4″×96″ panels at the wall
- Build a platform for lower cabinets. Pull center section to 27″ and side sections to 24″. Block as required to support upper cabinets and television
- Trim and install 3/4″×84″ panels on either side of television area
- Frame television with filler material
- Pull open-frame and mullion door cabinets to 24″ and top with 3/4″ tall end panel material
- Use remaining tall end panels as soffit boards
- Install speaker cloth in open-frame door cabinets
- Panel walls in open niches

Variations:

- Adjust to fit site and television measurements

Wall to wall cabinets surround a big screen television. Standard wall cabinets are pulled forward to support the television and create a consistent line of cabinetry. A furniture toe treatment of tall fillers and inside corner molding give a finished looked to the base. The overall height of this unit is 96″.

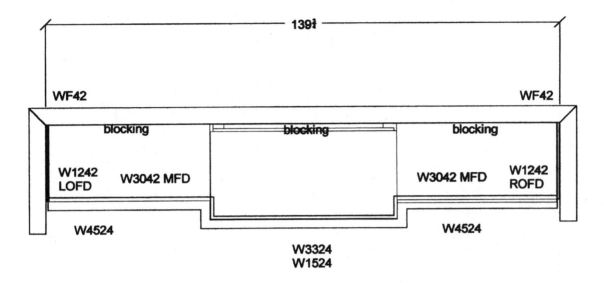

W1242
LOFD   W3042 MFD

W3042 MFD   W1242
ROFD

W4524

W4524

W3324
W1524

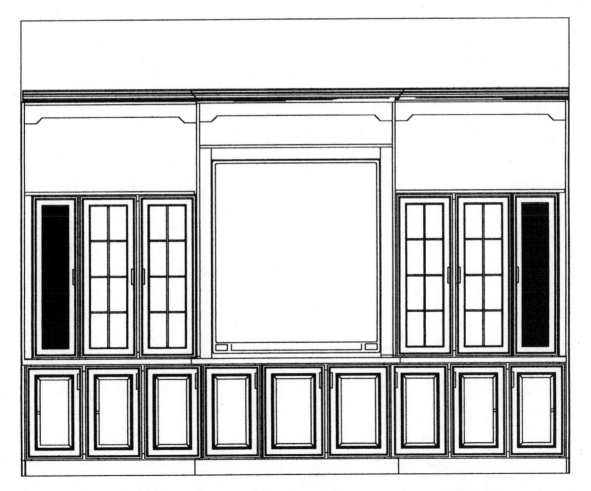

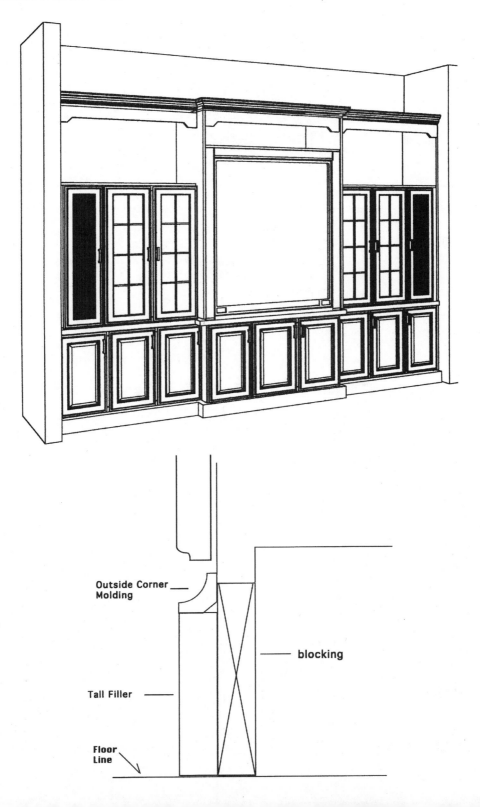

Outside Corner
Molding

blocking

Tall Filler

Floor
Line

Music Center

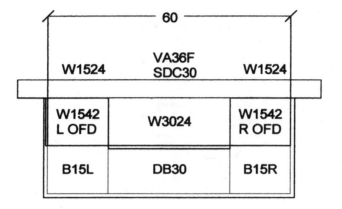

Cabinet List:

2 15″×42″ wall cabinets with open-frame doors
2 15″×24″ wall cabinets
1 30″×24″ wall cabinet
1 72″ finished shelf (split)
1 30″×36″ piece of paneling
1 30″ spice drawer unit with matching wood knobs
1 36″ frieze valance (trimmed)
2 tall skins (split)
2 15″ base cabinets
2 base skins
1 30″ drawer base
1 8′-0″ crown molding
1 8′-0″ scribe molding
1 8′-0″ base toe material
2 toe kick cap covers
16 knobs or pulls
1 pint stain
1 putty stick

Additional Materials Needed:

- Miscellaneous fasteners and adhesives
- Countertop
- Electrical hookups
- Speaker fabric
- CD, tape, and receiver

Required:

- Specifications for audio equipment
- Stack wall cabinets and skin exposed sides with split tall skins
- Insert speaker fabric in doors of W1542s with open-frame doors
- Apply paneling to the back wall, allowing for a false back to conceal wires
- Cut 72″ shelf into two sections. Use scribe molding as cleats
- Skin exposed base cabinet sides

Variations:

- Adjust dimensions to fit available space
- Add rollout shelves to base 15″ cabinets
- Add a furniture toe treatment to the base
- Delete the top row of wall cabinets for a room with a lower ceiling

Designed specifically for audio equipment, this tall entertainment center features wall cabinets outfitted with speaker fabric. Speakers are concealed behind the doors but are easy to access. This unit requires a room with a nine-foot ceiling.

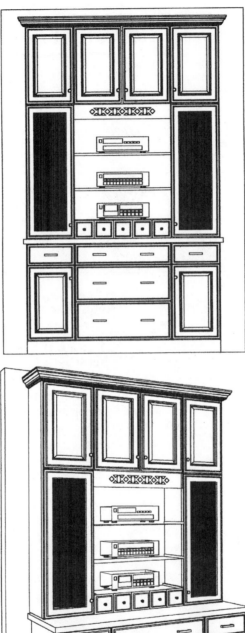

Southwestern-Style Entertainment Center

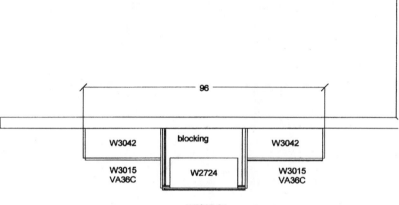

Cabinet List:

2 30″×42″ wall cabinets
2 30″×15″ wall cabinets
3 36″ arched valances
3 3/4″×84″ tall panels (split 1)
1 3/4″×96″ tall panel (split)
1 27″×24″ wall cabinet
2 42″ wall fillers (split)
1 33″×15″×24″ wall cabinet
1 piece paneling 36″×55″
2 8′-0″ crown molding
1 8′-0″ base toe material
12 knobs or pulls
1 pint stain
1 putty stick

Additional Materials Needed:

- Miscellaneous fasteners and adhesives
- Dimensional lumber
- Electrical and cable hookups
- Television
- DVD player
- VCR

Required:

- Specifications for all audio-visual equipment
- Build a 9″ deep platform for wall cabinets used as bases, cover with base toe material
- Pull 27″ wide wall cabinet forward, block in place
- Cut fillers to accent 27″ wide wall cabinet
- Cut 3/4″×96″ panel into tops for base wall cabinets
- Panel wall behind television and other openings

Variations:

- Adjust to fit audio-visual equipment
- Order 42″ wall cabinets with mullion doors, matching interiors, and glass inserts

Staggered filler trim gives a southwestern look to this entertainment center. Openings are provided for the television as well as two additional pieces of audio-visual equipment. Arched valances add a decorative treatment to the toe space.

Staggered Entertainment Center

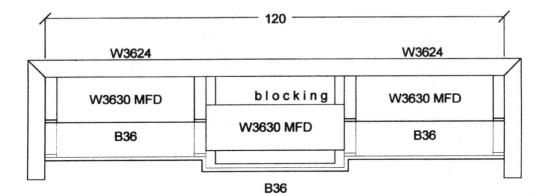

Cabinet List:

4 base fluted fillers
2 36″ base cabinets reduced to 21″ deep
1 36″ base cabinet
2 base skins
4 84″ tall fluted fillers (trimmed)
2 72″ finished shelves (trimmed)
8 rosettes
3 36″×30″ wall cabinets with mullion doors
   and matching interiors
6 tempered glass inserts
2 30″ wall skins
2 36″×24″ wall cabinets
2 8′-0″ crown molding
2 base toe material
2 toe kick cap covers
22 knobs or pulls
1 pint stain
1 putty stick

Additional Materials Needed:

- Miscellaneous fasteners and adhesives
- Dimensional lumber
- Countertop
- Electrical and cable hookups
- Television

Required:

- Television specifications
- Pull center W3036 with mullion doors forward to 20″ and block
- Skins sides of center base and pulled wall cabinet
- Trim finished shelves and install behind center two tall fluted fillers as returns
- Apply rosettes to upper fluted fillers only

Variations:

- Change locations of mullion door cabinets
- Change mullion doors to open-frame doors and install VCRs, etc., behind the doors
- If reduced cabinets are not available, consider pulling the center base cabinet forward
- Add glass shelves and interior cabinet lighting to mullion door cabinets

Fluted fillers set off each section of this staggered entertainment center. Rosettes are added to the upper fluted fillers as an accent. By reducing the end base cabinets and pulling the center wall cabinet forward, a custom look is achieved.

Stair-Stepped Entertainment Center

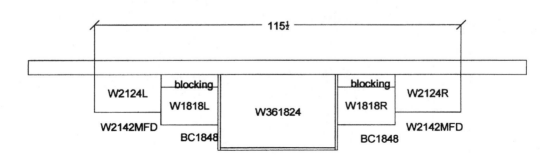

Cabinet List:

2 21″×42″ wall cabinet with mullion doors and matching interiors
2 tempered glass inserts
2 21″×24″ wall cabinets
2 tall skins (split)
2 18″×48″ bookcases
2 18″×18″ wall cabinets
3 3/4″×84″ tall end panels (split 1)
1 48″×96″ finished paneling
1 36″×18″×24″ wall cabinet
1 36″ arched valance
2 6″×96″ tall fillers
2 8′-0″ inside corner molding
3 8′-0″ crown molding
2 8′-0″ scribe molding
8 knobs or pulls
1 pint stain
1 putty stick

Additional Materials Needed:

• Miscellaneous fasteners and adhesives
• Dimensional lumber
• Plywood
• Matching wood countertop for beneath television
• Electrical and cable hookups

Required:

• Dimensions of television

• Build a 4″ high platform for entire unit allowing for bookcase stacks to be pulled forward 4″
• Cover platform with furniture toe made from tall filler and inside corner molding
• Panel back of area behind shelves and television with finished paneling
• Trim one 3/4″ panel as shelves above television
• Use scribe molding as cleats for shelves and to cover any gap in evening out the heights of the end units
• Create soffit board behind valance with plywood covered with remaining paneling
• Split tall end panels and cover exposed sides on all cabinet stacks

Variations:

• Omit end cabinet stacks for a smaller entertainment center
• Order 42″ high wall cabinets with solid doors for more closed storage

This entertainment center stair-steps up and down as well as in and out for a unique rhythm. Even the row of wall cabinets used as the base is at two different heights. Tall wood end panels capture the center section that houses open shelving and the television. A furniture toe treatment gives a solid look.

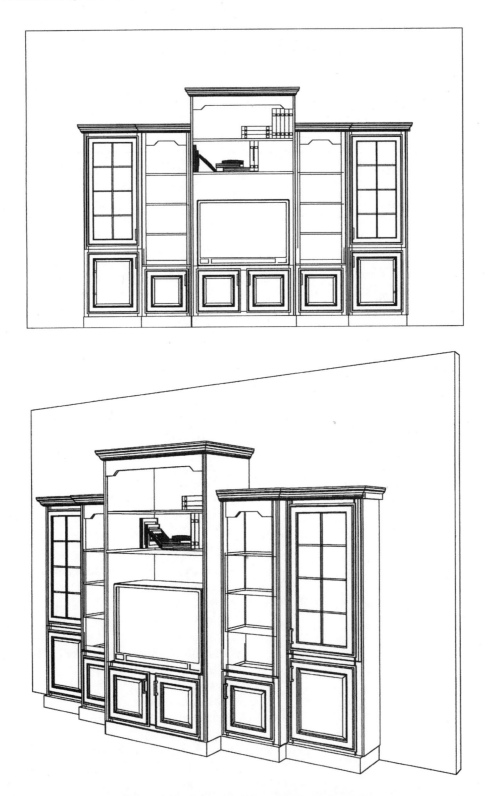

Storage Wall with Television

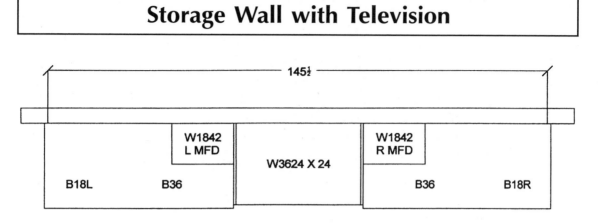

W3624x24

Cabinet List:

2 18″×42″ wall cabinets with mullion doors and matching interiors
2 tempered glass inserts
2 36″×24″×24″ wall cabinet
2 3/4″ tall end panels
1 36″×36″ piece of paneling
2 18″ base cabinets
2 36″ base cabinets
2 8′-0″ crown molding
2 8′-0″ base toe material
2 toe kick cap covers
18 knobs or pulls
1 pint stain
1 putty stick

Additional Materials Needed:

• Miscellaneous fasteners and adhesives
• Dimensional lumber
• 3 Matching wood countertop sections

• Electrical and cable hookups
• Television

Required:

• Television specifications
• Build a 21″ deep platform for lower W3624×24
• Panel wall behind television

Variations:

• Adjust to fit selected television and job-site dimensions
• Add skins and decorator matching doors to exposed cabinet ends
• Add glass shelves and in-cabinet lighting to the mullion door cabinets

Staggered height wall cabinets and open counterspace make this television and storage area welcome in nearly any home. Tall (84″ high) panels capture two deep wall cabinets and the television.

Tall Television Cabinet

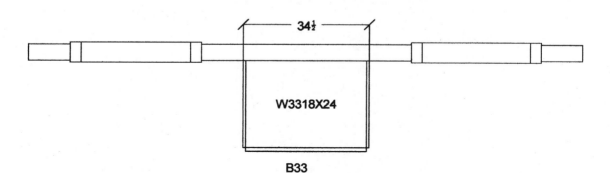

34½

W3318X24

B33

Cabinet List:

1   33″×18″×24″ wall cabinet
1   33″ base cabinet
2   3/4″×84″ tall end panels
2   sets of tall decorator matching doors
1   8′-0″ crown molding
1   6″×42″ wall filler (split)
6   knobs or pulls
1   pint stain
1   putty stick

Additional Materials Needed:

- Miscellaneous fasteners and adhesives
- Countertop
- Electrical and cable hookups
- Television

Required:

- Television specifications
- Attach decorator matching doors to exposed sides of tall end panels
- Cut 42″ wall filler as toe material and use remaining part as trim under wall cabinet

Variations:

- Panel bottom of wall cabinet
- Panel rear of television area
- Delete decorator matching doors for cost savings

When there is just a narrow wall space, this tall television cabinet provides extra storage and neatly houses a television. Tall decorator matching doors are applied to both exposed sides adding a furniture look.

Television Base

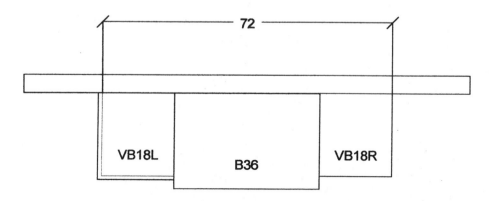

Cabinet List:

2 18″ vanity base cabinets
1 36″ base cabinet
1 8′-0″ base toe material
4 toe kick cap covers
1 8′-0″ crown molding
8 knobs or pulls
1 pint stain
1 putty stick

Additional Materials Needed:

- Miscellaneous fasteners and adhesives
- Dimensional lumber
- 3 countertop sections
- Electrical and cable hookups
- Television

Required:

- Television specifications
- Attach crown molding to the top of the B36. Add blocking to support countertop

Variations:

- Skin exposed sides of cabinets
- Add decorator matching doors

Just enough cabinetry to support a television in style, and provide a place for games, is wrapped up in this 72″ wide base unit. The crown molding applied to the top of the center base cabinet adds design flair and enlarges the countertop surface.

Traditional Style Entertainment Center

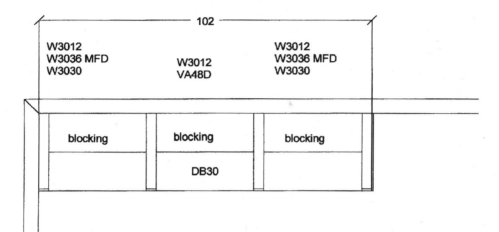

Cabinet List:

4 tall fluted fillers
3 30"×12" wall cabinets
2 30"×36" wall cabinets with mullion doors and matching interiors
4 tempered glass inserts
2 30"×30" wall cabinets
1 48" decorative valance (trimmed)
3 3/4"×84" tall end panels
1 36"×48" piece of paneling
1 36" drawer base cabinet
2 8'-0" crown molding
2 8'-0" base toe material
1 6"×30" wall filler
1 toe kick cap cover
20 knobs or pulls
1 pint stain
1 putty stick

Additional Materials Needed:

• Miscellaneous fasteners and adhesives
• Dimensional lumber
• Matching wood countertop
• Electrical and cable hookups
• Television

Required:

• Specifications for television
• Build a toe kick height platform for both wall cabinet stacks
• Stack wall cabinets, block, and pull forward to 24"
• Create returns for fluted fillers with blocking and 3/4" tall end panels
• Panel wall behind television
• Create returns to the toe kick at the bottom of the tall fillers with 6" filler material

Variation:

• Adjust to fit television

Stacked and pulled forward wall cabinets flank the center television column. These stacked cabinets combined with traditional fluted fillers create a more formal look. Fluted filler columns require returns made from the 3/4" tall end panels.

Wall Unit with Frieze Valance Accent

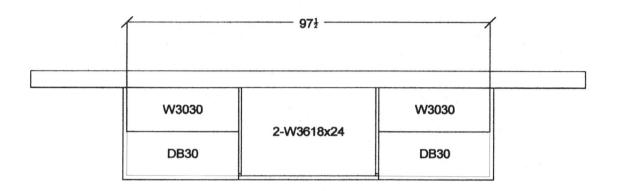

Cabinet List:

2 30″×30″ wall cabinets
2 36″ frieze valances (trimmed)
2 48″ wall skins
3 3/4″×84″ tall end panels (trimmed)
2 30″ drawer bases
2 base skins
2 8′-0″ crown molding
2 8′-0″ base toe material
2 toe kick cap covers
18 knobs or pulls
1 pint stain
1 putty stick

Additional Materials Needed:

- Miscellaneous fasteners and adhesives
- Dimensional lumber
- 2 countertops
- Electrical and cable hookups
- Television

Required:

- Specifications for television
- Build toe-kick height platform for lower W3618×24

- Trim two 3/4″ panels and attach to both sides of the center cabinets
- Trim third 3/4″ panel as top of lower W3618×24 and bottom of upper W3618×24
- Trim and back open area of frieze valances with toe kick material
- Build a platform for 30″ wall cabinets that is the height of the valances
- Stack 30″ wall cabinets on platform
- Skin all exposed cabinet sides

Variations:

- Adjust to fit television
- Panel rear wall behind television

This wall unit finishes out at just under six feet tall. Tall end panels capture the 24″ deep center section. Wall cabinets are stacked on a platform fitted with a frieze valances for a furniture look. Countertops can be made in matching wood for a dressier look.

Utility Areas

The nitty-gritty utility areas in the home really benefit from careful planning and additional storage. These areas are the family's daily point of entrance and are usually located between the garage and the main living spaces. It is here that the true workhorse rooms are located.

The family needs space to hang coats and prepare for the next day with book bags, brief cases, and sports equipment. Check out our Family Lockers on page 309 for a great solution to organizing the morning rush.

The laundry room often serves as a mud room when located near the garage, but many new homes today are calling for laundry rooms to be located in the bedroom wing or on the second-floor, or where the bulk of dirty laundry is generated. If the second story is the choice, be sure to provide a floor drain to handle washer leaks or overflows. Laundry rooms should provide ample counterspace for folding and a sink for soaking.

Sewing areas can be separate if one member of the family considers it a hobby or they can be part of the laundry room. Locating the sewing machine in the laundry area is sensible since most of the sewing done today is quick repairs.

And let's remember the other part of our family, our pets. They need spaces to sleep, eat, and even be groomed. We haven't forgotten them either, so look for a couple of spaces designed especially for them.

Back Hall Pantry

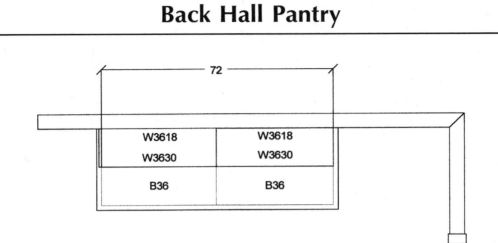

Cabinet List:

2 36″×30″ wall cabinets
2 36″×18″ wall cabinets
1 tall skin (split)
2 36″ base cabinets
2 base skins
1 8′-0″ base toe kick material
2 toe kick cap covers
2 8′-0″ crown molding
16 knobs or pulls
1 pint stain
1 putty stick

Additional Materials Needed:

• Miscellaneous fasteners and adhesives
• Countertop

Required:

• Skin the sides of the stacked wall cabinets to hide the joints and skin the sides of the base cabinets to match

Variation:

• Add rollout shelves to the base cabinets

An old-fashioned pantry cabinet will provide volumes of storage in the kitchen. Or place it near the garage door and unload groceries as you come in the door. Adding rollout shelves in the base cabinets will make stowing and retrieving stored items even easier.

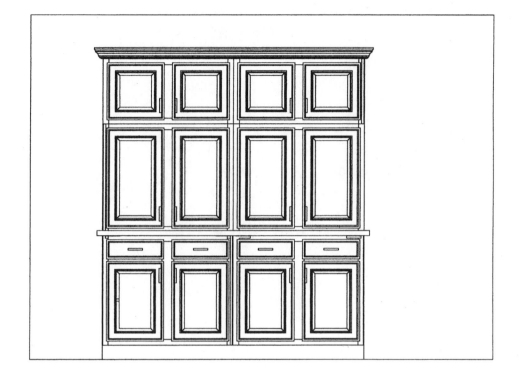

Basic Laundry

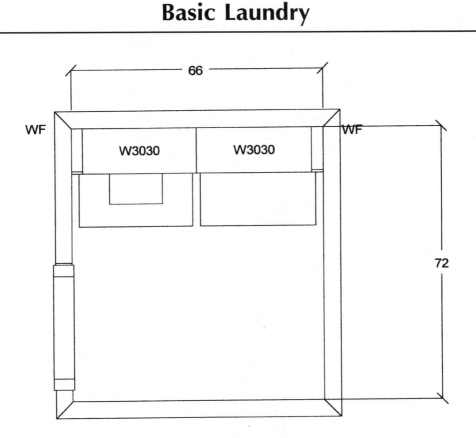

Cabinet List:

2 30″×30″ wall cabinets
2 wall fillers
1 8′-0″ crown molding
4 knobs or pulls
1 pint stain
1 putty stick

Additional Materials Needed:

• Miscellaneous fasteners and adhesives

Required:

• Minimum 1″ filler at the walls
• Check appliance specifications

Variations:

• Add undercabinet lighting below the wall cabinets
• Adjust width to fit appliances and job-site conditions
• Shorten one cabinet and install a closet rod

Basic storage for a basic laundry room includes wall cabinet storage above a traditional washer and dryer. Closed cabinets are preferable to open shelving to hide clutter. By shortening one of the two wall cabinets and installing a closet rod, garments can be hung right from the dryer.

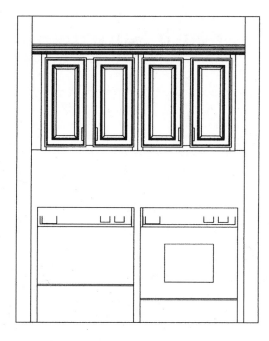

Bench Surround

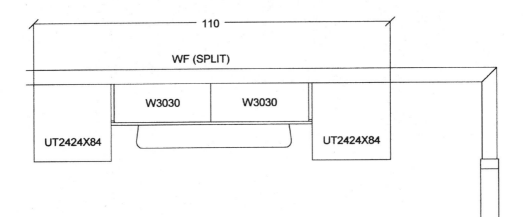

Cabinet List:

2 24″×24″×84″ utility cabinets
9 utility shelves
2 30″×30″ wall cabinets
1 wall filler (split)
1 8′-0″ base toe kick material
4 toe kick cap covers
2 8′-0″ crown molding
12 knobs or pulls
1 pint stain
1 putty stick

Additional Materials Needed:

- Miscellaneous fasteners and adhesives
- Clothing rod
- Dimensional lumber to block clothing rod in place

Required:

- Minimum 1″ filler where wall cabinets join tall cabinets for ease of door opening

- Install clothing rod in one utility cabinet and three shelves in upper section
- Second utility cabinet receives six shelves

Variations:

- Adjust cabinets to fit job-site conditions and size of bench
- Add a shelf to finish off the bottom of the wall cabinets

When there is not a closet at the rear entry of your home, this bench surround can meet that need and even provide additional storage. Built around a bench that is perfect for putting on and taking off shoes and boots, one tall cabinet can be fitted with a clothing rod and the other can be fitted with shelves for other types of storage.

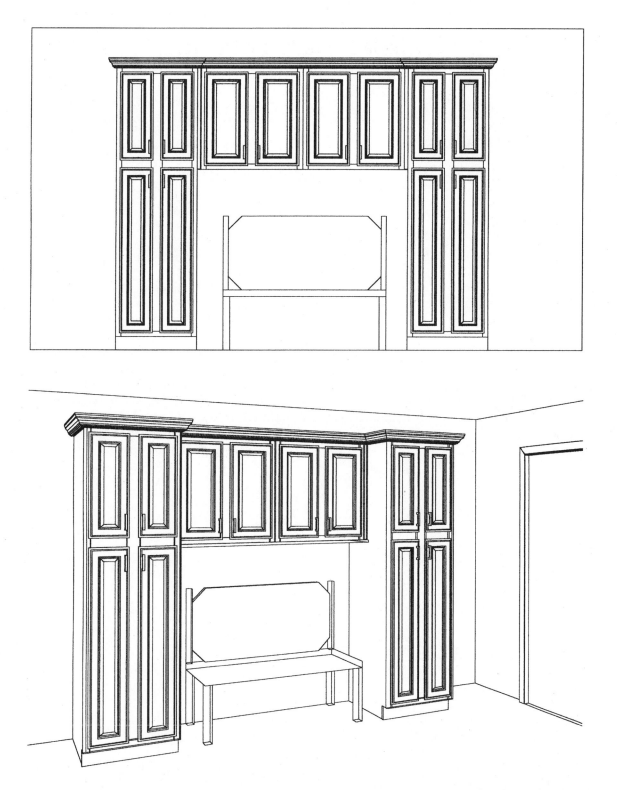

Compact Laundry Room

Cabinet List:

1 tall filler
1 18"×24"×90" utility cabinet
6 utility shelves
1 30"×15" wall cabinet
1 36"×36" wall cabinet
1 36" wall filler
1 36" base cabinet
1 base filler
1 8'-0" base toe kick material
2 8'-0" crown molding
2 8'-0"×6" tall fillers
2 8'-0" scribe molding
10 knobs or pulls
1 pint stain
1 putty stick

Additional Materials Needed:

• Miscellaneous fasteners and adhesives
• Stackable washer/dryer
• Dimensional lumber

• Two countertop sections
• Corbels to support folding counter

Required:

• Minimum 1" filler at the walls
• Check appliance specifications
• Block W3015 forward to 24"

Variations:

• Add undercabinet lighting below the wall cabinets
• Adjust width to fit appliances and job-site conditions
• Adjust molding detail to fit ceiling height

Even a small laundry area can have generous storage and work surfaces. A narrow folding counter can be left open for a feeling of spaciousness or shallow cabinets can be installed below. Ninety-inch tall cabinets and a molding treatment that goes up to the ceiling give a streamlined look.

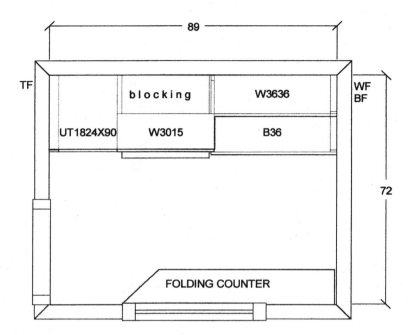

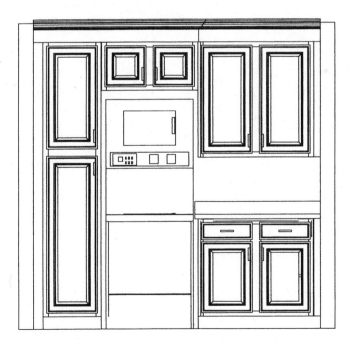

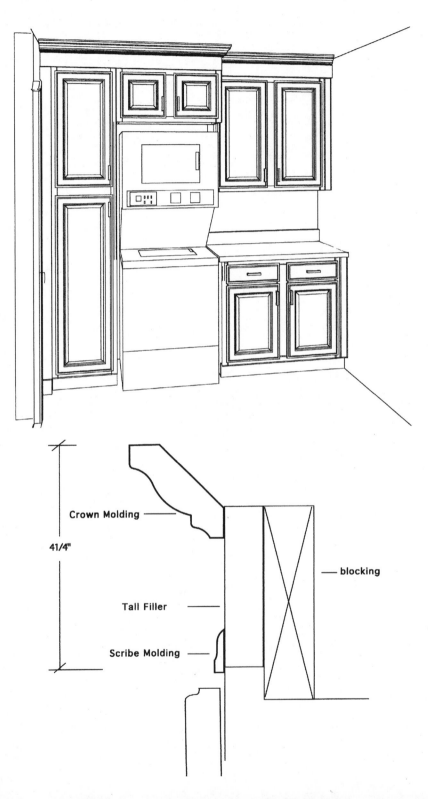

Crown Molding

41/4"

Tall Filler

Scribe Molding

blocking

Family Lockers

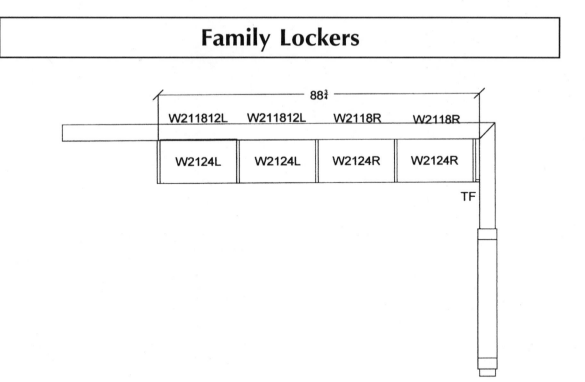

Cabinet List:

4 21″×18″ wall cabinets
4 21″×24″ wall cabinets
3 84″×24″×3/4″ tall panels (split)
1 3″×8′-0″ tall filler
1 8′-0″ base toe kick material
2 8′-0″ crown molding
8 knobs or pulls
1 pint stain
1 putty stick

Additional Materials Needed:

- Miscellaneous fasteners and adhesives
- Dimensional lumber
- 4 small countertop sections
- 4 hooks

Required:

- Build a 4″ high by 9″ deep platform
- Minimum 1″ filler at the wall

- Cut each 3/4″ panel in half to form two vertical dividers

Variations:

- Add or delete sections to accommodate the size of the family
- Cover the bottom of the upper cabinets with finished shelving if desired
- Panel the rear walls or paint them each a different color

These individual storage units organize family members with individual spaces to hang a jacket or a book bag. They also provide a landing area, as well as closed storage spaces. The small countertop sections are a great place to put lunches and outbound items such as dry cleaning and mail for an organized morning departure.

Gift Wrap Center

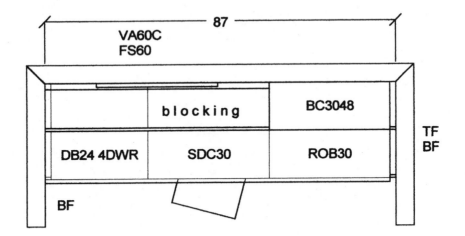

Cabinet List:

1 30″×48″ bookcase unit
1 30″ base cabinet with 2 full-width rollout trays
1 60″ arched valance
1 60″ finished self as soffit board
1 30″ spice drawer unit with matching wood knobs
1 24″ four-drawer base
1 8′-0″ base toe kick material
2 toe kick cap covers
1 tall filler
1 base filler (split)
1 8′-0″ crown molding
8 knobs or pulls
1 pint stain
1 putty stick

Additional Materials Needed:

- Miscellaneous fasteners and adhesives
- Dimensional lumber
- Strip lighting
- Bulletin board
- 2–3 gift wrap rolls with paper cutters
- Countertop

Required:

- Minimum 1″ filler at the walls
- Pull spice drawers forward 12″ and block
- Install strip lighting behind valance

Variations:

- Adjust width to fit job-site conditions

This family gift wrap center can be placed in a laundry or craft room, or in an area all by itself. The spice drawers hold tape, scissors, gift tags, and other small items. Commercially available gift-wrap roll holders, with paper cutters installed in the bookcase, hold department store-size rolls of all purpose paper. A bulletin board over the countertop is a great place to post a calendar and party invitations.

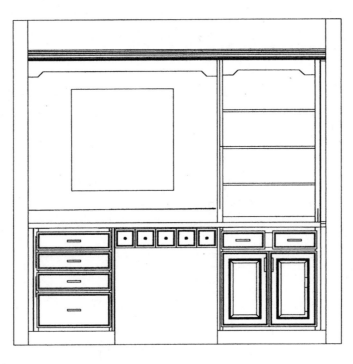

Laundry/Hobby Room Combination

Cabinet List:

1 30″×24″×90″ utility cabinet
1 96″ tall filler
2 utility shelves
4 utility rollout shelves
1 48″ straight valance (trimmed)
2 wall fillers (split)
1 36″×36″ wall cabinet
1 30″×24″ wall cabinet
1 30″ spice drawer cabinet with matching wood knobs
1 3/4″ tall end panel
1 24″×18″ wall cabinet
1 36″ trimmable kneehole drawer
1 36″ base cabinet
1 36″ drawer base
1 base filler (split)
3 8′-0″ crown molding
3 3″×96″ tall fillers as molding treatment
3 scribe molding
21 knobs or pulls
1 pint stain
1 putty stick

Additional Materials Needed:

- Miscellaneous fasteners and adhesives
- Dimensional lumber

- 2 countertops
- 1 closet rod
- Stackable washer/dryer

Required:

- Minimum 1″ filler at each wall
- Specific washer/dryer dimensions
- Pull cabinet over the washer/dryer forward 12″ and block
- Stack tall fillers, scribe molding, and crown molding as top molding treatment to the ceiling

Variations:

- Adjust cabinets to fit job-site conditions and appliance dimensions
- Adjust cabinet and molding heights to fit ceiling height

Today's utility rooms often need to serve multiple needs. When space allows, a sit-down work area can function as a place to do hobbies or to fold laundry. The closet rod is a handy place to hang clothing right out of the dryer.

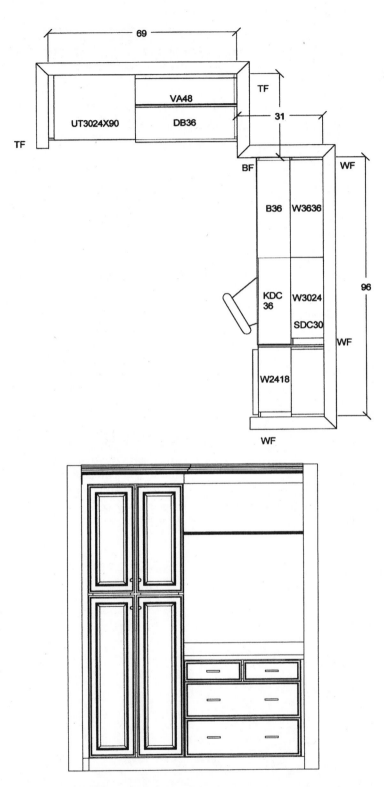

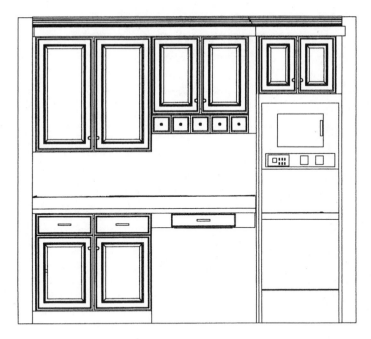

Laundry in a Closet

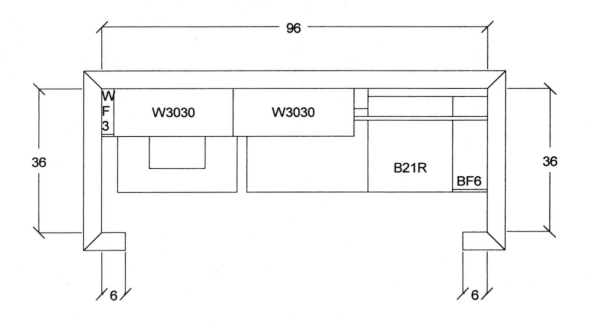

Cabinet List:

2 30"×30" wall cabinets
1 wall filler
1 21" base cabinet
1 6" base filler
1 8'-0" base toe kick material
6 knobs or pulls
1 pint stain
1 putty stick

Additional Materials Needed:

• Miscellaneous fasteners and adhesives
• Extra deep countertop
• Closet rod
• Washer and dryer

Required:

• 3" wall cabinet filler at the wall
• Wide base filler to allow for closet door clearance

• Minimum 36" deep closet space
• Pull base cabinet forward to the depth of the laundry equipment to maximize folding space

Variations:

• Crown molding can be added to the top of the wall cabinets
• Add undercabinet lighting below the wall cabinets

A compact laundry area that is usually found behind bi-fold doors still has ample storage for laundry necessities. A closet rod is added to the right of the wall cabinets to provide a place to hang clothing as it is taken from the dryer. Be sure to include adequate lighting in the closet area.

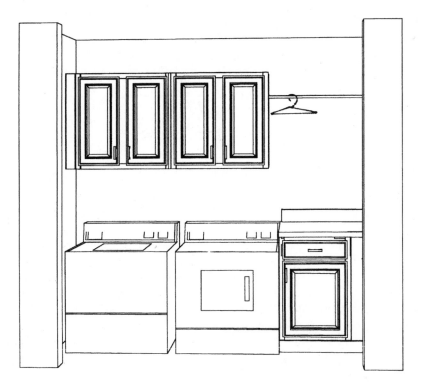

Laundry Niche

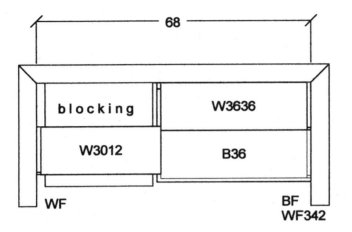

Cabinet List:

1 30″×12″ wall cabinet
1 36″×36″ wall cabinet
1 36″ wall filler (split)
1 36″ base cabinet
1 base filler
1 8′-0″ base toe kick material
1 8′-0″ crown molding
1 8′-0″ filler
1 8′-0″ scribe molding
8 knobs or pulls
1 pint stain
1 putty stick

Additional Materials Needed:

- Miscellaneous fasteners and adhesives
- Dimensional lumber
- Countertop
- Stack washer and dryer

Required:

- Minimum 1″ filler at each wall

- Check manufacturer's specifications to determine exact washer/dryer dimensions
- Pull the cabinet over the washer/dryer forward 11″ and block

Variations:

- Adjust size to fit job-site conditions and appliance specifications
- Adjust top molding to fit ceiling height
- Finish the bottom of the 12″ high wall cabinet

Perfect for a vacation home, this compact laundry niche is designed for a recess without a traditional jamb and door installation. Rollup blinds or shutters can be used to conceal the area. The molding treatment goes all the way to the ceiling to eliminate cleaning on top of the cabinets. In even the simplest laundry area, providing a place to fold laundry is a priority.

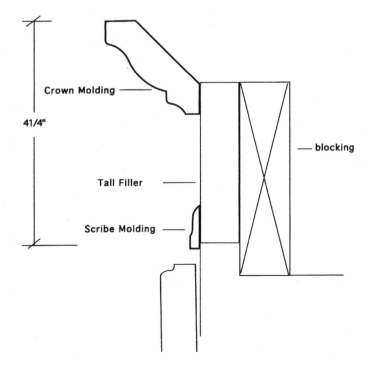

Crown Molding

41/4"

Tall Filler

Scribe Molding

blocking

Laundry Potting Area Combination

Cabinet List:

4 base fillers
1 9″ base cabinet
1 36″ lazy susan
1 30″ sink base
1 45″/48″ blind base cabinet
1 45″ base cabinet
1 tall filler
1 30″×12″ wall cabinet
1 30″×48″ bookcase
3 42″ wall fillers
2 33″×42″ wall cabinets
3 30″×42″ wall cabinets
3 8′-0″ base toe kick material
3 8′-0″ crown molding
24 knobs or pulls
1 pint stain
1 putty stick

Additional Materials Needed:

- Miscellaneous fasteners and adhesives
- Single-bowl sink and faucet
- Undercounter washer/dryer

Required:

- Minimum 1″ filler at walls
- Pull blind base cabinet per manufacturer's recommendations
- Stack bookcase over W3012
- Appliance specifications
- Leave additional space around the laundry equipment for easy removal for service
- Trim tall filler and install to the left of the stacked wall cabinets

Variations:

- Adjust cabinets to fit job-site and appliance conditions
- Skin the side of the bookcase stack to conceal the joint
- Add fluted fillers as filler overlays on either side of the sink

Laundry and gardening can be combined so that storage, counterspace, and a sink can serve dual duty. The bookcase is a wonderful place to store gardening books and vases for flower arranging. Undercounter laundry equipment gives a sleek look and increases counterspace.

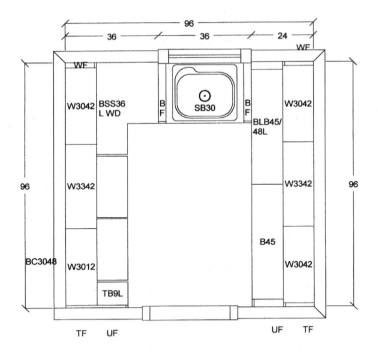

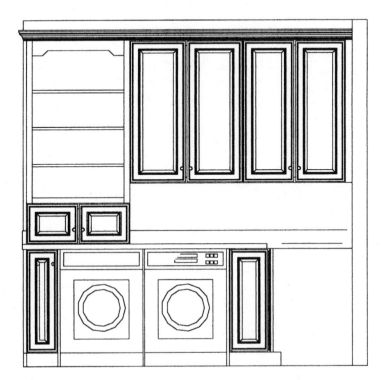

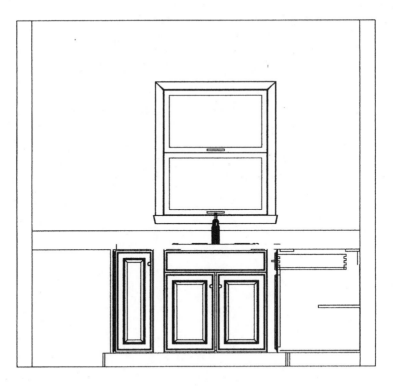

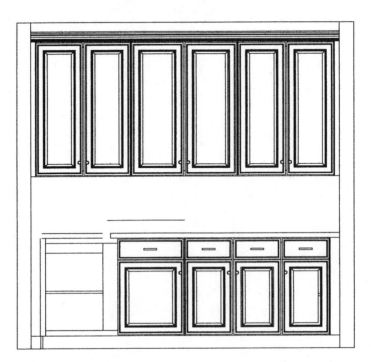

Laundry Room with Pet Niche

Cabinet List:

2 30"×30" wall cabinets
3 33"×30" wall cabinets
1 24" corner wall cabinet
2 wall fillers
2 base fillers
1 24" drawer base
2 15" base cabinets
1 30"×12" wall cabinet
1 blind base cabinet 45"/48"
1 30" sink base
1 48"×34 1/2" paneling
1 8'-0" outside corner molding
2 8'-0" base toe kick material
3 8'-0" crown molding
24 knobs or pulls
1 pint stain
1 putty stick

Additional Materials Needed:

- Miscellaneous fasteners and adhesives
- Dimensional lumber
- Pet bed
- Washer/dryer
- Built-in ironing board
- Single-bowl sink and faucet

Required:

- Minimum 1" filler at the walls
- Check appliance specifications
- Build a 4" high platform for W3012 and cover with paneling
- Finish edge of niche platform with outside corner molding
- Block W3012 forward 12"

Variations:

- Add undercabinet lighting below the wall cabinets
- Adjust width to fit appliances and job-site conditions
- Shorten one cabinet and install a closet rod
- Adjust niche to fit the size of the pet

Pets are a big part of many families. This laundry room incorporates a niche for a pet bed. Additionally, there is plenty of wall cabinet storage and counterspace for folding laundry or spreading out other projects. The built-in ironing board finishes off this well planned space.

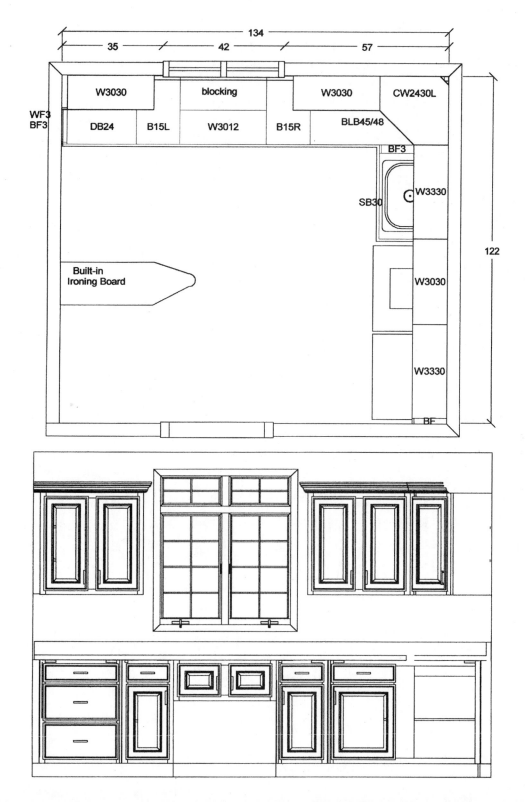

Laundry Room with Sewing Area

Cabinet List:

1 18″×18″ wall cabinet
1 18″×36″ wall cabinet
1 tall filler trimmed for stacked wall cabinets
1 45″×30″ wall cabinet
1 wall cabinet skin
1 24″ corner wall cabinet pulled to 27″
2 tall skins (split)
3 30″×30″ wall cabinets
1 wall filler
1 base filler
2 18″ file base cabinets
2 18″ drawer base
1 36″ easy-reach corner cabinet
1 8′-0″ base toe kick material
2 toe kick cap covers
3 8′-0″ crown molding
23 knobs or pulls
1 pint stain
1 putty stick

Additional Materials Needed:

- Miscellaneous fasteners and adhesives
- Dimensional lumber for blocking
- Washer and dryer
- Countertop

Required:

- Minimum 1″ filler at each wall
- Pull corner wall cabinet forward 3″ and block
- Stack 18″ wall cabinets and install on counter
- Trim tall skin to finish sides of pulled corner wall cabinet and stack of cabinets

Variations:

- Adjust design to fit job-site conditions

Combining the sewing and laundry areas in one space is a sensible idea. Clothing repairs can be easily taken care of and this design provides adequate space for the sewing hobbyist, too. Pulling the corner wall cabinet forward adds design interest and makes the molding installation easier because the molding butts cleanly into the side of the deeper cabinet.

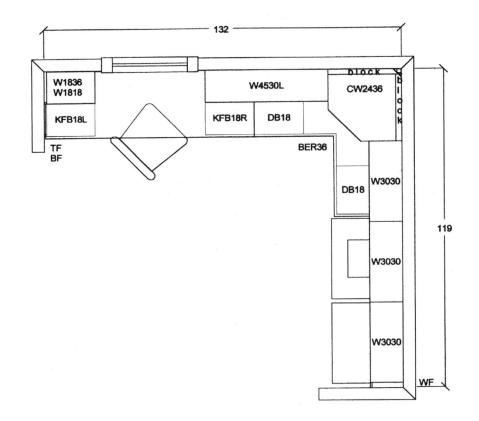

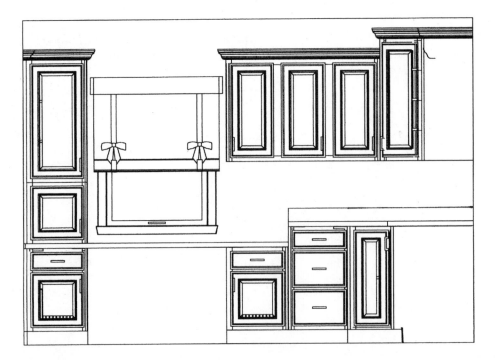

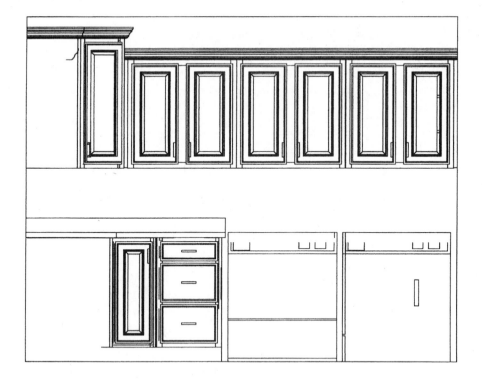

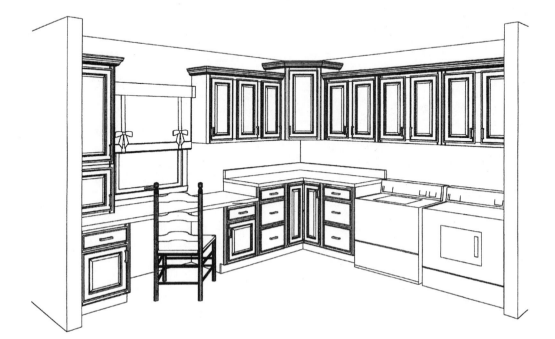

Linen Storage

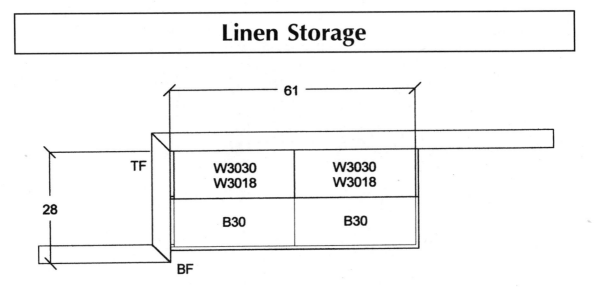

Cabinet List:

2 30"×30" wall cabinets
2 30"×18" wall cabinets
1 tall skin (split)
1 tall filler trimmed in height
2 30" base cabinets
1 base skin
1 base filler
1 8'-0" base toe kick material
1 toe kick cap cover
1 8'-0" crown molding
16 knobs or pulls
1 pint stain
1 putty stick

Additional Materials Needed:

- Miscellaneous fasteners and adhesives
- Countertop

Required:

- Minimum 1" filler at the wall
- Minimum of 27" wall depth for cabinets
- Skin the sides of the stacked cabinets to cover joint and skin exposed side of base cabinet to match

Variations:

- Adjust size to fit job-site conditions
- Add rollout tray to the base cabinets
- Increase the height of the upper wall cabinets for homes with higher ceilings

Many homes don't have nearly enough linen storage. But if there is room in a wide hallway in the bedroom wing, a built-in linen closet can solve this problem. With nearly fifty cubic feet of storage, this unit holds not only linens but extra toiletries as well.

Pet Grooming Station

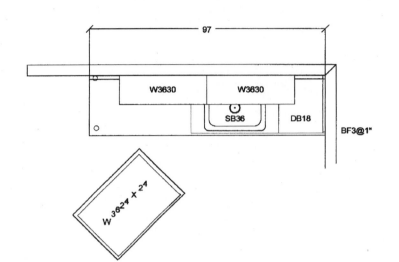

Cabinet List:

2 36″×30″ wall cabinets
2 36″ shelf undercabinet units
1 36″×24″×24″ deep wall cabinet
1 piece paneling 36″×25″
1 8′-0″ outside corner molding
1 base filler
1 18″ drawer base
1 36″ sink base cabinet
1 8′-0″ base toe kick material
1 toe kick cap cover
2 8′-0″ crown molding
11 knobs or pulls
1 pint stain
1 putty stick

Additional Materials Needed:

- Miscellaneous fasteners and adhesives
- Dimensional lumber for blocking castors
- Substrate material
- 1 countertop with backsplash
- 1 flat deck countertop with all four edges finished for mobile unit
- 4 castors
- 2 support legs
- Deep single-bowl sink and faucet with spray

Required:

- Minimum 1″ base filler at the wall
- Finish the back of the mobile cabinet with substrate, paneling and outside corner molding
- The combined height of the workstation including castors and countertop must be less than 34″ so that it easily rolls under the extended countertop.

Variations:

- Delete the shelf undercabinet units and add undercabinet lighting
- Add handles to the mobile cabinet to make it easier to roll

A long workspace counter and ample storage for grooming supplies creates the perfect area to care for any small pet. By adding castors to a 24″ deep wall cabinet it is transformed into a mobile grooming workstation that can be moved into the center of the room.

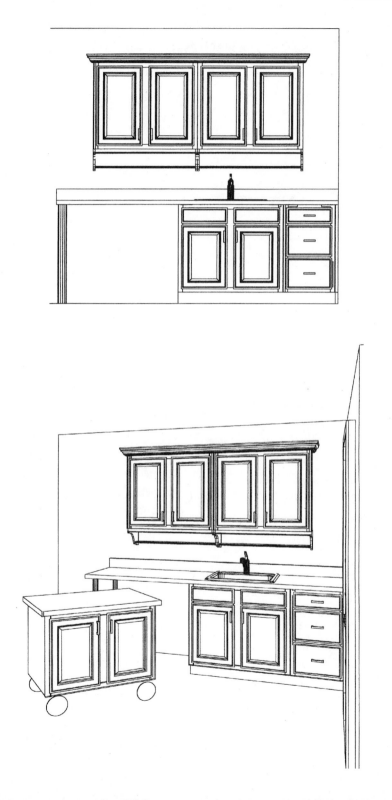

Pie Safe

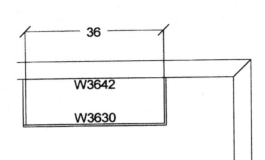

Cabinet List:

1 36″×30″ wall cabinet
1 36″×42″ wall cabinet
1 tall skin (split)
1 6″×84″ tall filler
1 8′-0″ inside corner molding
4 knobs or pulls
1 pint stain
1 putty stick

Additional Materials Needed:

• Miscellaneous fasteners and adhesives
• Dimensional lumber to build the platform

Required:

• Build a 4″ high platform to support cabinetry

• Trim with filler material and inside corner molding as base toe treatment
• Skin the sides of the cabinet to cover joints

Variations:

• Use a cathedral wall cabinet for the top section
• Order open-frame doors in both cabinets and install wire mesh inserts

This slim cabinet, inspired by an American antique, would be a welcome addition to nearly any room in the home. In the laundry room, it adds storage for detergents and cleaning supplies.

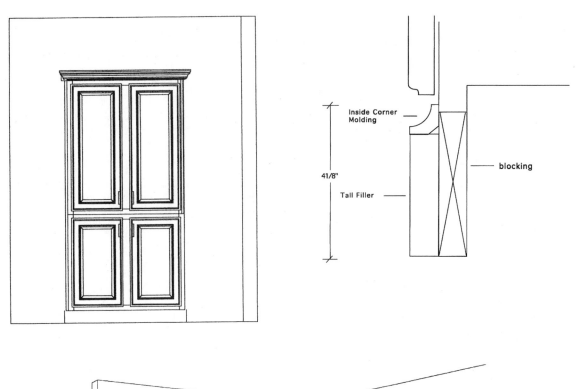

Inside Corner
Molding

41/8"

Tall Filler

blocking

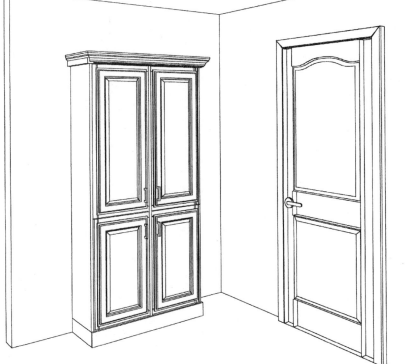

Raised Undercounter Washer and Dryer

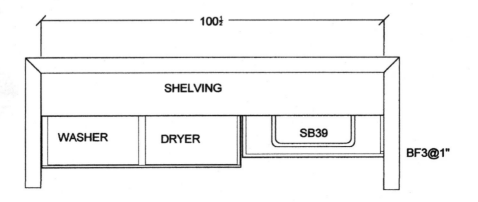

Cabinet List:

1 36″ sink base
1 3″ base filler
2 knobs or pulls
1 pint stain
1 putty stick

Additional Materials Needed:

- Miscellaneous fasteners and adhesives
- Dimensional lumber to build a platform for laundry equipment
- Countertop on top of laundry equipment
- Countertop for sink base
- Wire shelves and supports
- Sink and faucet
- Undercounter washer and dryer

Required:

- Build a 9″ high platform for washer and dryer and cover with flooring material to match the rest of the room
- A drain in the platform is advisable
- Minimum 1″ filler at the base cabinet
- Check appliance specifications for dimensions and other requirements

Variations:

- Adjust cabinet width to accommodate job-site conditions

The raised front-loading laundry equipment is designed to reduce the amount of bending required during the laundry process. The height of the platform should be adjusted to suit the user. To determine the width of the platform, check manufacturers specifications for appliance width plus recommended clearance.

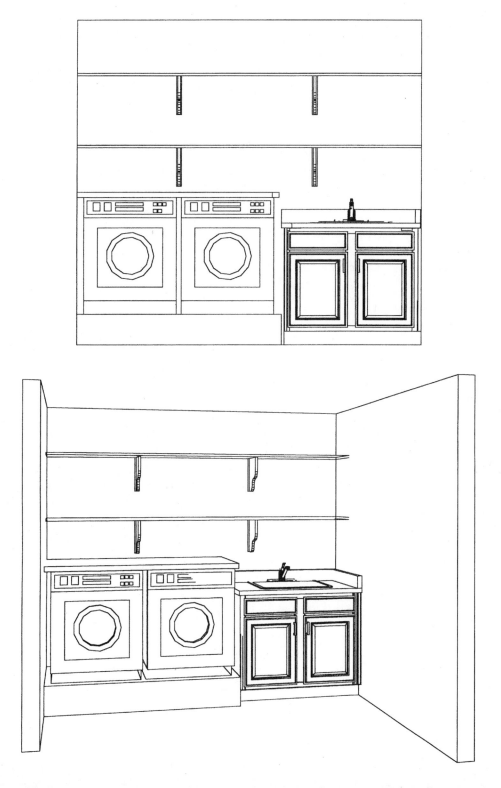

Recycling Center

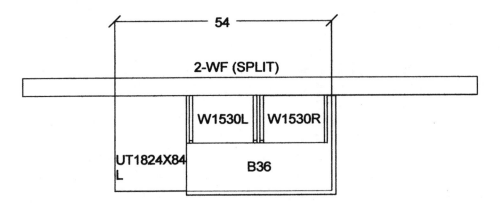

Cabinet List:

1 18"×84" utility cabinet
6 utility shelves
2 15"×30" wall cabinets
3 48" finished shelves as vertical dividers
2 wall fillers (split)
1 36" base cabinet
2 two-section recycling bin cabinet inserts
1 8'-0" base toe kick material
2 toe kick cap covers
2 8'-0" crown molding
8 knobs or pulls
1 pint stain
1 putty stick

Additional Materials Needed:

- Miscellaneous fasteners and adhesives
- Countertop

Required:

- Split fillers for each side of 15" wall cabinets

Variation:

- Adjust width to fit job-site conditions

Make recycling a breeze with this center designed specifically for that task. The wall cabinets hold supplies such as plastic bags and ties and the vertical dividers are sized to hold stacks of newspapers for recycling. Two double-bin units are housed in the base cabinet. The utility cabinet provides lots of extra storage for items needed near the garage.

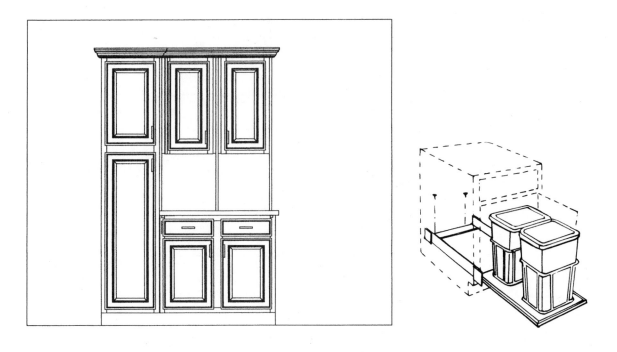

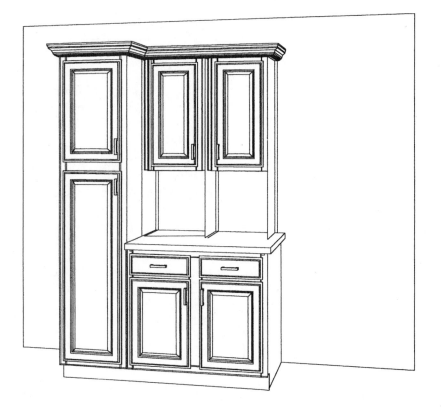

Sewing Closet

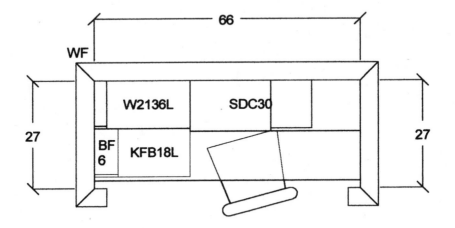

Cabinet List:

1 21″×36″ wall cabinet
1 36″ high wall filler
1 72″ finished shelf (trimmed)
1 48″ finished shelf (trimmed)
1 corbel
1 30″ spice drawer unit with matching wood knobs
1 18″ file base cabinet
1 6″ wide base filler
1 8′-0″ base toe kick material
1 toe kick cap cover
1 8′-0″ crown molding
1 8′-0″ light rail molding
3 knobs or pulls
1 pint stain
1 putty stick

Additional Materials Needed:

- Miscellaneous fasteners and adhesives
- Countertop
- Undercabinet light

Required:

- 3″ wall cabinet filler at the wall
- Install undercabinet light behind light rail
- Be sure that cabinet doors clear the bi-fold doors and header

Variations:

- Adjust to fit job-site conditions

An efficient sewing center tucked into standard bedroom closet features a cantilevered wall storage design. Staggered cabinets and shelving extensions create the look of contemporary practicality. A spice cabinet that holds sewing notions provides practical and attractive storage.

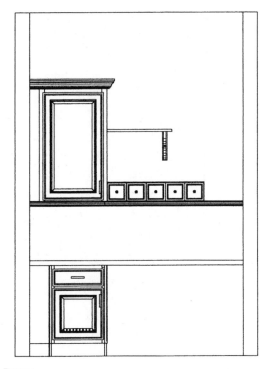

Storage Wall

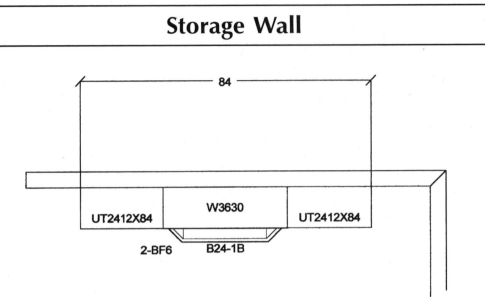

Cabinet List:

2 24″×84″×12″ utility cabinets
12 utility shelves
1 36″×30″ wall cabinet
1 24″ base cabinet reduced to 15″ depth
2 6″ base fillers
1 8′-0″ base toe kick material
2 toe kick cap covers
2 8′-0″ crown molding
13 knobs or pulls
1 pint stain
1 putty stick

Additional Materials Needed:

- Miscellaneous fasteners and adhesives
- Countertop

Required:

- Cut 6″ base fillers and install at 45° angle

Variations:

- Increase the depth of the unit to 24″ and use a standard base cabinet in the center section

This storage wall located near the garage entrance will provide a place to stow light bulbs, string, and other necessities that might be needed either in the garage or the main part of the house. The base cabinet is reduced to 15″ depth to keep the area slim, while still adding extra counterspace.

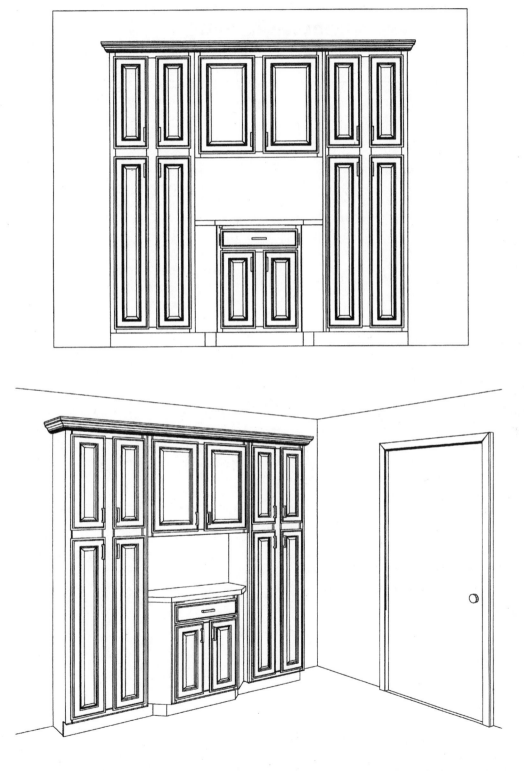

The Ultimate Laundry Room

Cabinet List:

5 36″×30″ wall cabinets
5 36″×18″ wall cabinets
2 18″×18″ wall cabinets
1 60″ finished shelf
1 18″×24″×84″ utility cabinet
6 utility shelves
1 84″ tall filler (split)
1 wall filler
2 base fillers
1 18″ drawer base
1 15″ base cabinet
1 30″ sink base
1 42″ base cabinet
1 30″ base cabinet with 2 double recycling bins
2 8′-0″ base toe kick material
3 8′-0″ crown molding
2 8′-0″ light rail molding
40 knobs or pulls
1 pint stain
1 putty stick

Additional Materials Needed:

- Miscellaneous fasteners and adhesives
- Dimensional lumber
- Strip lighting
- Clothing rod

- Single-bowl sink and faucet
- Ironing board insert for 18″ base cabinet
- 2 countertop sections
- Washer, dryer, and refrigerator

Required:

- Minimum 1″ filler at all walls
- Pull W3630 and W1818 forward 12″ and block
- Install strip lighting behind light rail molding
- Trim finished shelf and apply to the bottom of the cabinets over the washer and dryer
- Check specifications on all appliances

Variations:

- Adjust to fit job-site conditions

This laundry room with a 108″ ceiling height has it all. From stacked wall cabinets that hold out-of-season items in the upper cabinets to recycling and ironing board inserts. The clothing rod is an ideal place to hang garments right from the dryer and there is even room for a second refrigerator or an upright freezer.

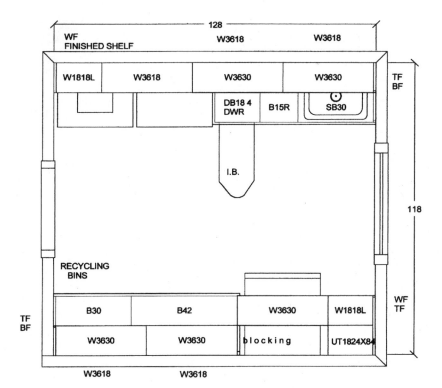

128

WF
FINISHED SHELF

W3618   W3618

W1818L   W3618   W3630   W3630   TF
BF

DB18 4
DWR   B15R   SB30

I.B.

118

RECYCLING
BINS

B30   B42   W3630   W1818L   WF
TF

TF
BF

W3630   W3630   blocking   UT1824X84

W3618   W3618

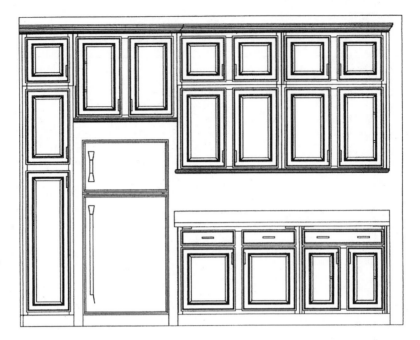

Victorian Bench

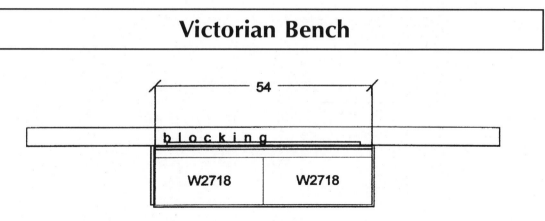

Cabinet List:

2 27″×18″ wall cabinets
4 3″×84″ tall fillers
1 48″×96″ beadboard paneling
1 8′-0″ countertop edge molding
1 8′-0″ crown molding
4 knobs or pulls
1 pint stain
1 putty stick

Additional Materials Needed:

• Miscellaneous fasteners and adhesives
• Dimensional lumber
• 1 piece plywood for bench top
• 4 coat hooks
• Cushion

Required:

• Trim paneling to 48″×60″ and frame with filler material
• Build up wall cabinets 3/4″ and edge with countertop edge molding
• Pull wall cabinets forward to 15″, block with dimensional lumber
• Use remaining beadboard paneling as end panels for cabinets

A bench with a high beadboard back has a Victorian feel and works well near the family entry. It provides a place to sit while putting on shoes and boots, a place to hang up jackets and hats, as well as providing storage below the seat. This bench adds charm and function to any entry area.

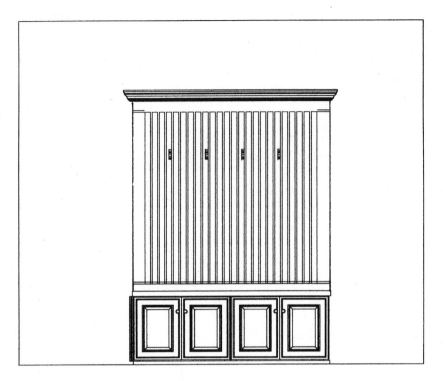

Wall Hutch

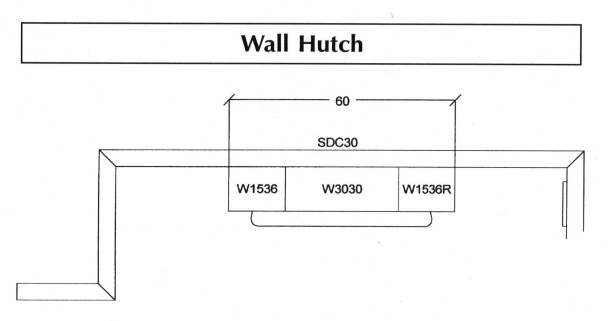

Cabinet List:

2 15″×36″ wall cabinets
1 30″×30″ wall cabinet
1 30″×6″ spice drawer unit with matching wood knobs
1 8′-0″ crown molding
4 knobs or pulls
1 pint stain
1 putty stick

Additional Materials Needed:

• Miscellaneous fasteners and adhesives

Required:

• Hang at a comfortable height for family members

Variation:

• Add skins and decorator matching doors to exposed ends of the cabinets

A wall hutch installed near the family entrance will provide storage for such things as hats and gloves. The spice drawers can each be assigned to family members and will hold lunch money, keys and other small personal items.

CHAPTER 8

Children's Rooms

One thing is certain, children change almost monthly. It makes sense to design the their spaces with great flexibility in mind. If you can't help yourself, go ahead, paint and furnish the nursery in pastels. But by the time a child is two or three years old, they begin to develop color preferences and interests that may call for special storage needs and the job may have to be done all over again.

A private retreat for a child, even if it is shared with a sibling, is important to their growth, development, and self-confidence. It is their place to be totally themselves and be surrounded with the things that matter to them. Computer games and surfing the Internet are among these interests, and while you might never think of putting a computer in the master bedroom, they are becoming more common in the children's bedrooms. It is important to note that if a child is very small, adjustments may be needed to the computer desk area to create an ergonomically correct workspace. One simple suggestion is to raise the seat of the chair and add a sturdy box as a footrest. This change will help to provide a correct seating position for the child.

Beyond computers and clothing storage, don't forget to make accommodations for audio-visual equipment, electronic games, and even a television. Today's children are technologically savvy and need the space to put their equipment.

Good general design rules to apply to children's spaces, with a few added considerations:

- Safety always come first, ease the corners of all countertops so that there are no sharp edges
- Be sure that all built-ins are fully secured to the wall
- Use sturdy materials for all surfaces
- Provide niches or open shelves for books, toys, and treasures

Bed Surround with Desk

Cabinet List:

1 tall filler
2 18"×24"×96" utility cabinets
12 utility shelves
1 30"×15" wall cabinet reduced to 10" deep
2 60" finished shelves trimmed to width and 10" deep
2 24"×18" wall cabinets
1 wall filler (split into three pieces)
1 60" arched valance trimmed to fit
1 36"×30" wall cabinet with mullion doors and matching interiors
2 tempered glass inserts
1 8'-0" light rail molding
1 18"×30" wall cabinet
1 18"×18" wall cabinet
1 18" file base cabinet
4 tall skins
2 48" skins
2 base skins
1 48" arched valance trimmed as knee space skirt
1 8'-0" base toe material
5 toe kick caps
3 8'-0" crown molding
16 knobs or pulls
1 pint stain

1 putty stick

Additional Materials Needed:

• Miscellaneous fasteners and adhesives
• Countertop

Required:

• Minimum 1" filler at the wall and where the wall cabinets join the tall cabinets
• Eased corners on all countertops for safety
• Skin all exposed cabinet sides

Variations:

• Panel wall above the open shelf area
• Add undercabinet lighting behind the valance over bed
• Add undercabinet light fixture over desk

A combination bed surround and desk area provides both storage and a study area. The addition of undercabinet lighting over the bed and above the desk encourages good bedtime reading and study habits. The repetition of the arch valance above the bed and as a desk skirt offers design unity.

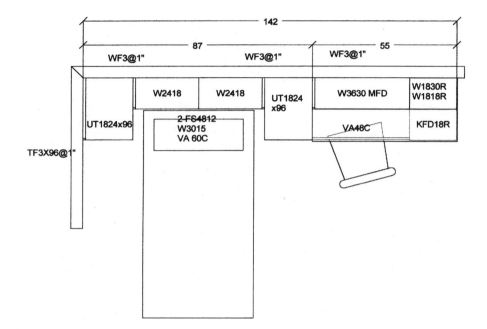

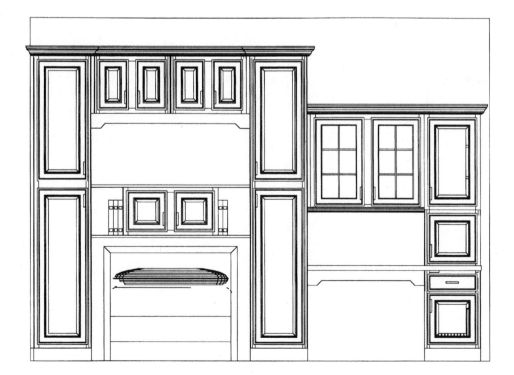

Changing Table

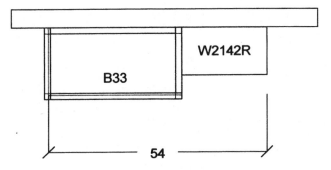

Cabinet List:

1 33″ base cabinet reduced to 17″ deep
1 21″×42″ high wall cabinet built on-toe
1 6″ tall filler (trim to height) as toe material
1 8′-0″ inside corner molding
5 knobs or pulls
1 pint stain
1 putty stick

Additional Materials Needed:

- Miscellaneous fasteners and adhesives
- Dimensional lumber for platform
- Countertop with guards in front and on the right
- Flat deck countertop for raised area
- Contoured changing pad with security strap

Required:

- Platform for W2142 to match toe height of base cabinet

- Eased corners on all countertops for safety
- Create furniture toe with tall filler and inside corner molding

Variations:

- Add a closet rod inside the taller cabinet to hold infant garments on hangers
- The unit can be made right or left-handed to suit the user

The contoured changing pad for this unit is available from the infant's department in most department stores. Check the size currently available before ordering cabinetry. Note the use of solid stock filler material to finish the toe space so that miters can be easily made at each corner. A built-in like this can be converted into regular storage, as the child becomes older, by removing the countertop guards.

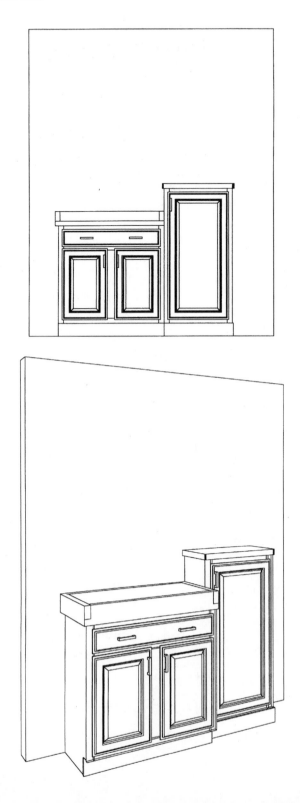

Chimney Cabinets

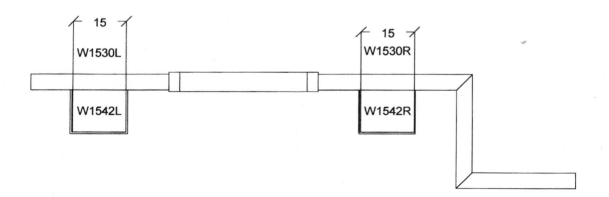

Cabinet List:

For each cabinet:
1 15″×30″ wall cabinet
1 15″×42″ wall cabinet
1 tall skin (split left and right)
1 42″×6″ wide filler
1 8′-0″ inside corner molding
2 knobs or pulls
1 pint stain
1 putty stick

Additional Materials Needed:

• Miscellaneous fasteners and adhesives
• Dimensional lumber for platform

Required:

• Platform for chimney cabinet
• Skins to conceal the joints of the combined cabinets

• Furniture toe treatment made from filler and inside corner molding

Variations:

• Use a cathedral door style for the upper cabinet
• Order the cabinets with open-frame doors and install wire mesh inserts

Used individually or as a pair these narrow cabinets hold a surprising amount of childhood treasures. Perfect for narrow spaces or to flank a door or window, these cabinets, like all other built-ins, must be secured to the wall with screws.

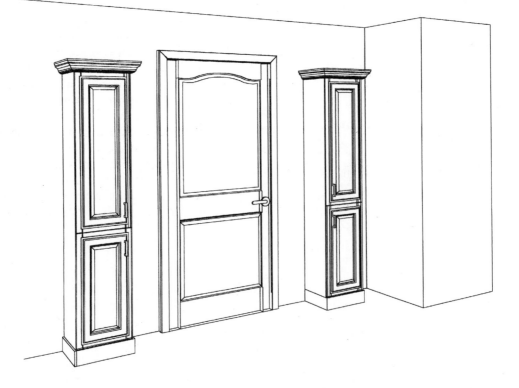

Computer Nook

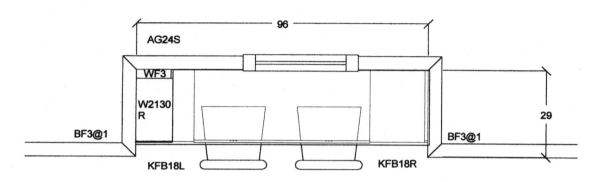

Cabinet List:

2 18″ wide×24″ deep file base cabinets
1 3″ base filler; use 1″ at each wall
1 3″ wide tall filler as apron
1 21″×30″ wall cabinet
1 3″ wall filler
1 24″ wide tambour unit
1 48″ high wall skin
1 8′-0″ base toe material
2 toe kick caps
1 8′-0″ crown molding
5 knobs or pulls
1 pint stain
1 putty stick

Additional Materials Needed:

- Miscellaneous fasteners and adhesives
- Countertop
- Laptop computer

Required:

- Minimum 1″ filler at each wall for the base cabinet
- 3″ filler at wall cabinet

Variations:

- Adjust width to fit job-site conditions
- Add a second stack of a tambour unit and a wall cabinet on the right side.
- If a full-size computer is to be used, delete the apron and add a keyboard tray
- Add decorator matching doors to the exposed end of the wall cabinet stack

This computer nook is designed for a parent and child to enjoy the Internet together using a laptop computer. The tambour unit can hide a slim printer or just conceal desk clutter. Placed in a hallway or a family room, everyone in the family will enjoy this spacious workspace.

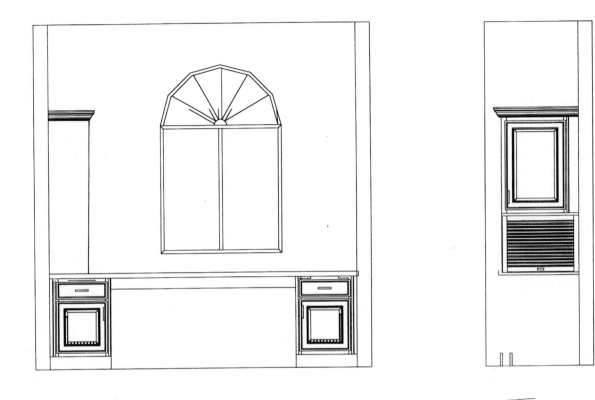

Corner Desk

Cabinet List:

1 30″ high corner wall cabinet
2 30″×24″ wall cabinets
2 30″ shelf undercabinet organizers
2 15″×24″ wall cabinets
1 48″ arched valance (trimmed to fit)
2 8′-0″ crown molding
1 8′-0″ piece of 6″ filler as toe material
1 8′-0″ piece inside corner molding
1 18″ piece of light rail molding
7 knobs or pulls
1 pint stain
1 putty stick

Additional Materials Needed:

- Miscellaneous fasteners and adhesives
- Dimensional lumber to build platforms
- Countertop

Required:

- Eased corners on all countertops for safety
- 4″ high platforms for the two wall cabinets used as base cabinets
- Create furniture base treatment with 6″ filler material topped with inside corner molding

Variation:

- Add decorator matching doors to the exposed end of the wall cabinet stack

This symmetrical corner desk can serve two children's needs. Each child can claim half of the storage as their own with common possessions fitting in the central corner wall cabinet. This unit might fit on a landing to the second-floor bedrooms or in the corner of family room.

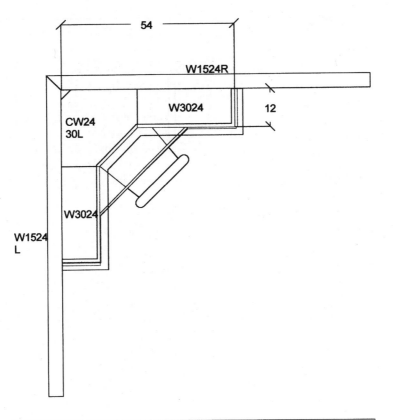

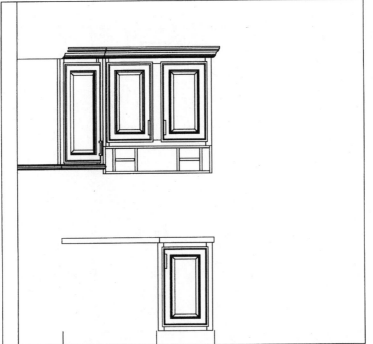

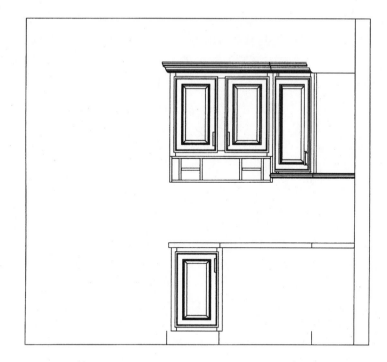

Corner Unit with Window Seat

Cabinet List:

1 24″ four-drawer base
1 36″×15″×24″ deep wall cabinet
2 15″ high fluted fillers
1 right-hand dishwasher return panel
1 3″ base filler
1 18″ base cabinet
1 36″ wide arched valance as kneehole skirt
1 18″ wide file base cabinet
2 24″×48″ bookcases
1 tall fluted filler trimmed to 48″ high
2 8′-0″ base toe material
4 toe kick cap covers
1 8′-0″ crown molding
1 countertop edge molding
10 knobs or pulls
1 pint stain
1 putty stick

Additional Materials Needed:

• Miscellaneous fasteners and adhesives
• Dimensional lumber to cleat corner countertop
• 3 countertop sections

• Cushion for window seat
• Chair and bulletin board

Required:

• Build a plywood top for the seating area and finish the leading edge with countertop edge molding
• Eased corners on all countertops for safety

Variations:

• Replace the arched valance with a keyboard tray
• Skin and apply decorator matching doors to all exposed ends

This corner unit provides storage for clothing in the drawers as well as open bookcases to display books and prized collections. A generous computer work area is part of this design for a child of any age. The 18″ base cabinet to the right of the knee space can even hide the computer's central processing unit (CPU) if proper ventilation is provided. Check with the computer manufacturer for requirements.

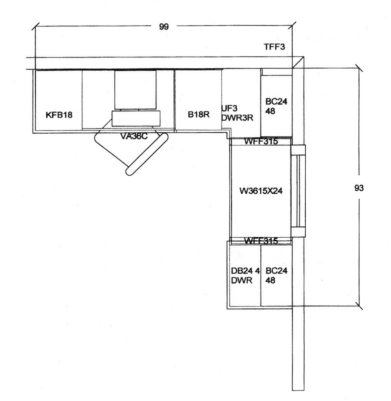

99

TFF3

KFB18

B18R

UF3
DWR3R

BC24
48

VA36C

WFF315

W3615X24

93

WFF315

DB24 4
DWR

BC24
48

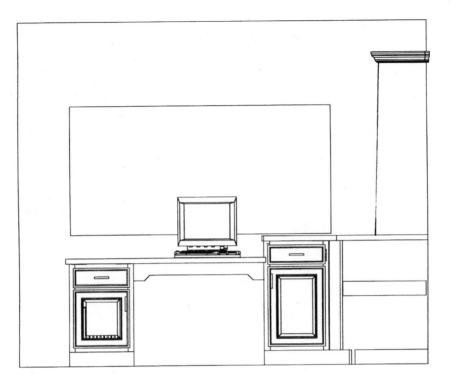

Double Twin Beds

Cabinet List:

4 39″×15″×12″ deep wall cabinets
1 filler cut to 1″ at each corner cube
1 piece 3/4″ paneling to cover both ends each bed
3 8′-0″ pieces of 6″ filler material trimmed as base treatment
3 8′-0″ pieces batten molding
8 knobs or pulls
1 pint stain
1 putty stick

Additional Materials Needed:

- Miscellaneous fasteners and adhesives
- Dimensional lumber to build recessed platform and corner cube
- Laminate or other material to cover corner cube
- Plywood for deck of bed
- 2 twin mattresses

Required:

- 4″ high platforms to support the wall cabinets

- Frame and block areas behind cabinets to support mattresses
- Construct one corner cube approximately 42″×42″×42″ high and cover with laminate or other material
- Minimum 1″ filler where cabinets meet the corner cube
- Create deck for bed, finish raw edge with batten molding

Variations:

- Add decorator matching doors to the exposed ends of the cabinets
- Build a platform for the entire bed area to create a raised Diaz

To maximize play and study areas in a shared bedroom, build in corner beds to free up floor space and provide a surface for bedroom paraphernalia. The 42″ cube acts as both headboards and landing space for alarm clocks. Raising the floor for the entire area creates a feeling of coziness and of entering an entirely different space.

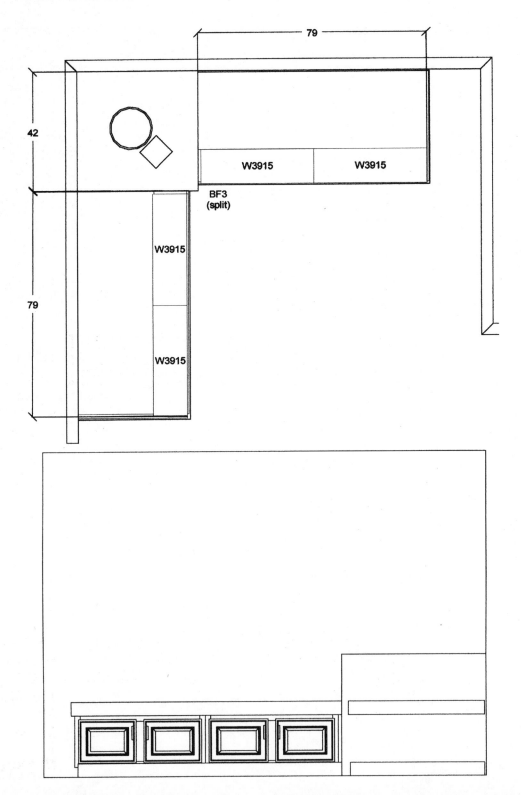

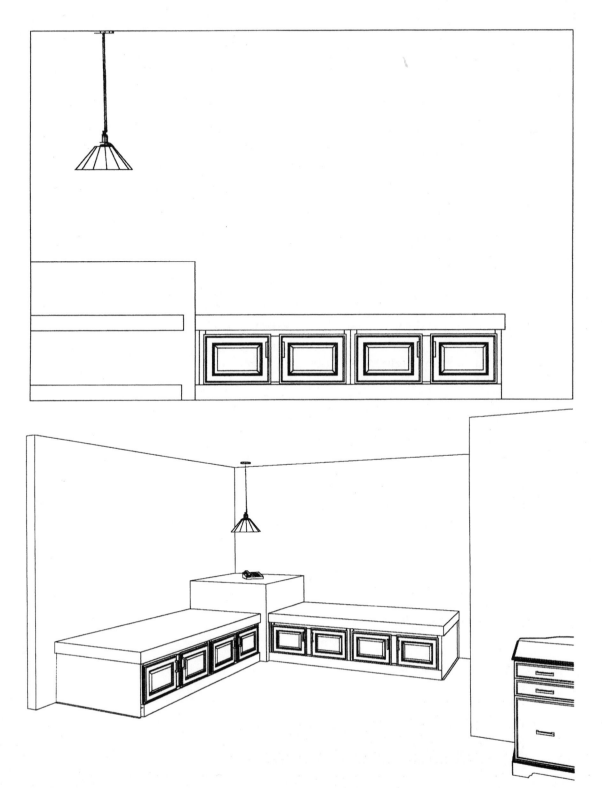

Floating Vanities

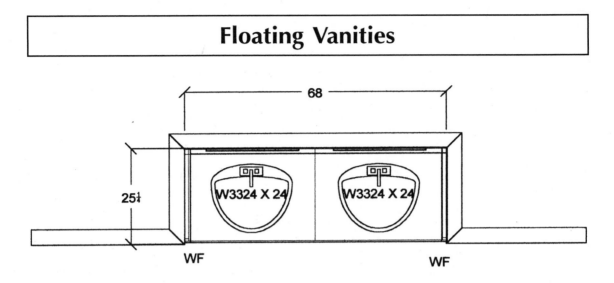

Cabinet List:

2 33″×24″×24″ deep wall cabinets
1 wall filler (split left and right)
4 knobs or pulls
1 pint stain
1 putty stick

Additional Materials Needed:

- Miscellaneous fasteners and adhesives
- Deep countertop with side and back splashes
- Two lavs with faucets
- Two mirrors

Required:

- Minimum 1″ filler at each wall
- Tops of the wall cabinets will have to be cut for lavs and plumbing installation
- Through-the-wall plumbing

Variations:

- Reduce depth of wall cabinets if a premade countertop is desired
- Vary height and width to suit job-site conditions
- Add lighting below the cabinets as a nightlight

Wall cabinets can be used as vanities if the cabinet tops are cut to accommodate the installation of the basins and plumbing. These cabinets can be placed at a child-appropriate height and installed at a higher height later if needed. Flexible supply and discharge lines will make this relatively easy.

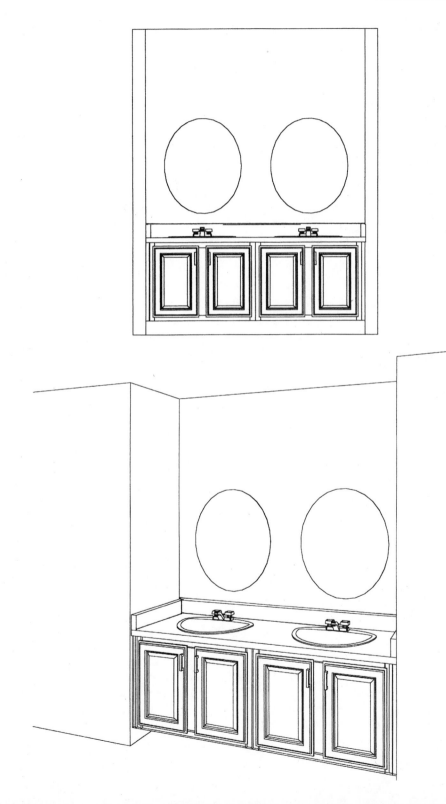

Girl's Makeup Area

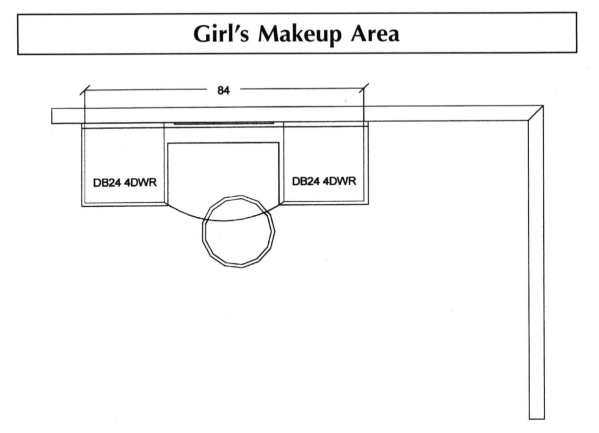

Cabinet List:

2 24″ four-drawer base cabinets
1 8′-0″ toe kick material
4 toe kick cap covers
8 knobs or pulls
1 pint stain
1 putty stick

Additional Materials Needed:

• Miscellaneous fasteners and adhesives
• Upper and lower countertops
• Mirror

Required:

• Eased edges on all countertops for safety
• Adjust space between cabinets to at least 30″ wide

Variations:

• If space is at a premium, make a lower countertop straight rather than curved
• Change drawer bases to standard base cabinets for cost savings
• Add skins and decorator matching doors to exposed ends

The lowered countertop extends to an arched shape, providing style and additional counterspace. Eight drawers provide space for makeup and hair accessories. Thoughtful placement of outlets for curling irons and blow dryers is a must.

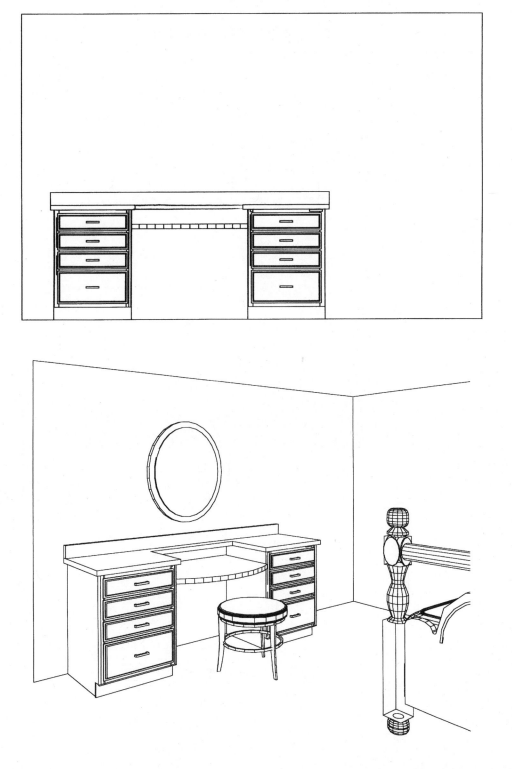

Imagination Room

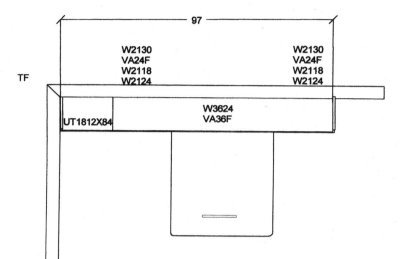

Cabinet List:

2 tall fillers
1 18″×12″×84″ utility cabinet
6 utility shelves
2 21″×30″ wall cabinets
2 24″ frieze valances
2 21″×18″ wall cabinets
2 21″×24″ wall cabinets
1 36″×24″ wall cabinets
1 36″ frieze valance
3 tall skins
1 72″ finished shelf (cut) as a soffit board and table leg
2 8′-0″ crown molding
2 6″ tall fillers
1 8′-0″ base toe material
10 knobs or pulls
1 pint stain
1 putty stick

Additional Materials Needed:

- Miscellaneous fasteners and adhesives
- Dimensional lumber
- Wood or metal stops to secure table leg
- Countertop

Required:

- Eased corners on all countertops for safety
- 4″ high recessed platforms for wall cabinets used as base cabinets
- Skin all exposed sides of cabinets
- Use toe material to back pierced area of frieze valances and stacked cabinets
- Fill difference between stack and utility cabinet with fillers trimmed to fit
- Trim and miter 6″ tall fillers as toe treatment on unit and around table leg

Variations:

- Add undercabinet lighting behind valance
- Panel rear wall or cover it with cork board

A place where crafts, games, homework, or science projects take shape is sure to inspire imagination in any child. The tall cabinet holds plenty of art supplies or games and the 36″×48″ table is a great place to spread out projects.

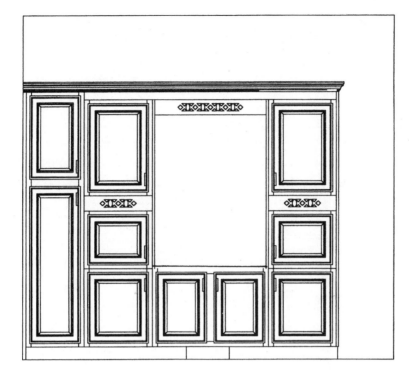

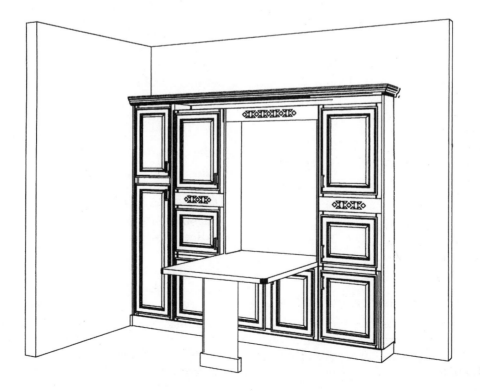

Loft Recreation Area

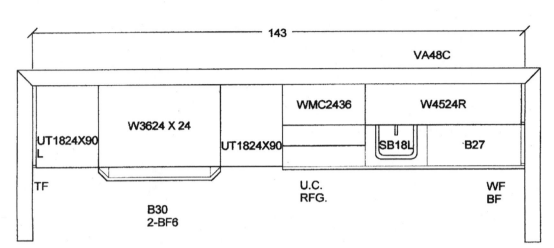

Cabinet List:

1 tall filler
2 18″×90″ utility cabinets
4 shelves for upper section of utility cabinets
8 18″ rollout shelves for lower section of utility cabinets
1 36″×24″×24″ deep wall cabinet
1 48″×34″ paneling
1 24″ microwave cabinet
1 45″×24″ wall cabinet
1 48″ arched valance
1 30″ wide base cabinet
2 6″ wide base fillers
1 18″ sink base
1 27″ base cabinet
1 wall filler
1 base filler
2 8′-0″ light rail molding
2 8′-0″ base toe material
20 knobs or pulls
1 pint stain
1 putty stick

Additional Materials Needed:

- Miscellaneous fasteners and adhesives
- 2 countertop sections
- 24″ undercounter refrigerator
- Microwave
- Television
- 15″×15″ beverage sink and faucet

Required:

- Minimum 1″ filler at each wall for tall, wall, and base cabinets
- Pull 30″ base cabinet forward 3″
- Cut 6″ fillers and install at 45° angle at the left and right of the B30
- Panel wall behind television
- Install light rail molding as top treatment and beneath wall cabinet over television

Variations:

- Add undercabinet lighting behind the valance
- Use beadboard paneling behind the television and above the backsplash
- Adjust design width to fit job-site conditions

Outfitted with a microwave, sink, an undercounter refrigerator, as well as a television, this area would work well in a bonus room, loft or finished basement. Be sure to carefully check the appliance and entertainment equipment specifications to make sure the cabinets accommodate their requirements.

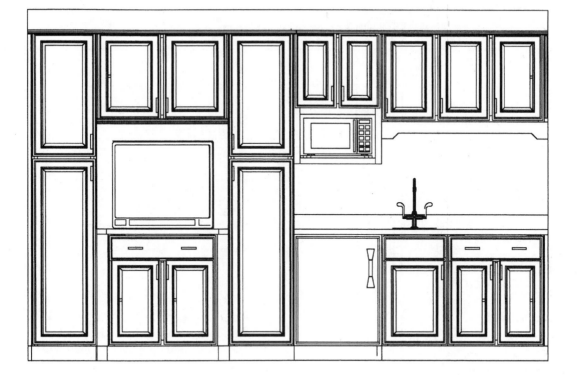

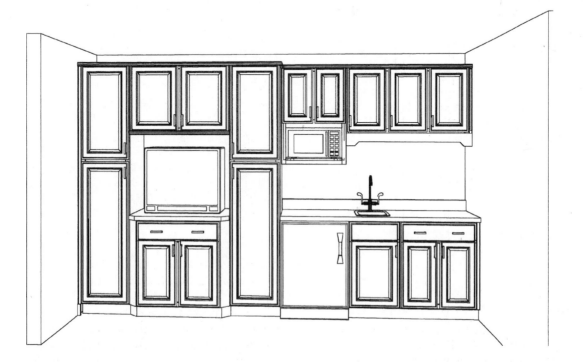

Sleeping Nook

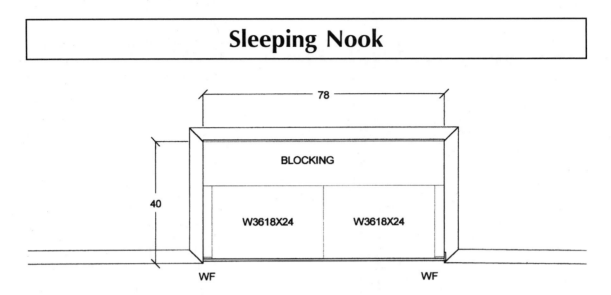

Cabinet List:

2 36"×18"×24" wall cabinets
2 wall fillers
2 8'-0" countertop edge molding
4 knobs or pulls
1 pint stain
1 putty stick

Additional Materials Needed:

- Miscellaneous fasteners and adhesives
- Plywood to create top for bed
- Dimensional lumber for blocking
- Twin size mattress

Required:

- Minimum 42" headroom
- Minimum 1" filler at each wall

- Pull the cabinets forward and block to accommodate a twin mattress
- Finish the edge of the plywood with the countertop edge molding
- Raise the cabinets 3/4" and fill void with countertop edge molding
- Twin mattress

Variations:

- Adjust depth of niche to accommodate a double mattress
- Add a recessed reading light

Many second-floor bedrooms back up to unused attic space, often with a sloped ceiling line. This sleeping nook can be recessed in to that space to create a wonderful sleepover space. The area can be concealed with shutters or curtains for a train berth effect.

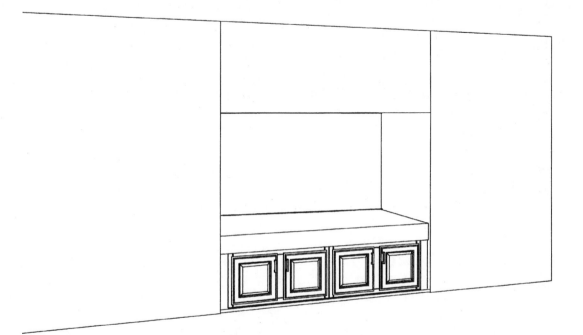

Storage and Craft Area

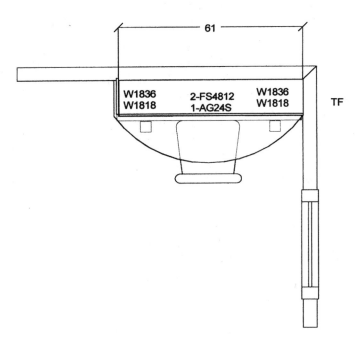

Cabinet List:

2 18"×18" wall cabinets
2 18"×36" wall cabinets
3 tall skins
2 3" wide tall fillers
2 48"×12" finished shelves (cut to three shelves and one soffit board)
1 24" wide tambour unit
1 piece 96"×34 1/2" paneling
1 8'-0" outside corner molding
1 8'-0" crown molding
4 knobs or pulls
1 pint stain
1 putty stick

Additional Materials Needed:

• Miscellaneous fasteners and adhesives
• Dimensional lumber
• 2 turned legs stained to match cabinetry
• Countertop
• Substrate material

Required:

• Minimum 1" filler at the wall
• Use remaining filler material first layer of top molding
• Support box, 28 1/2"×12", made from dimensional lumber and covered with substrate and finished paneling
• Trim skin and apply to exposed sides of stacked cabinets to hide joint

Variations:

• Delete tambour unit and add corkboard to wall below first shelf
• Panel or paint wall behind open shelves

In a little over 5' of wall space, a craft center can be created with a generous work area and storage. This area is perfect for building models, working on collections, or drawing. The tambour unit in the middle hides clutter and keeps the area neat.

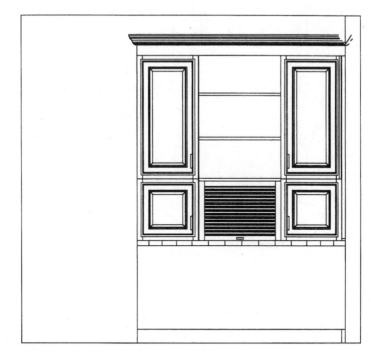

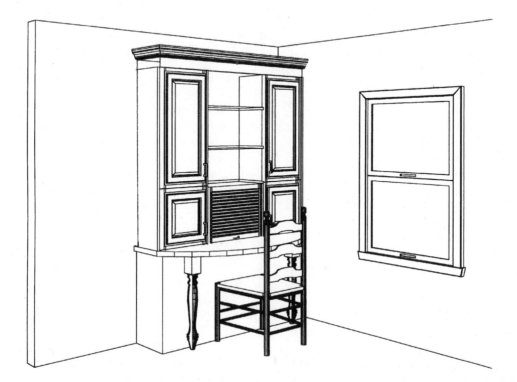

Study Hall

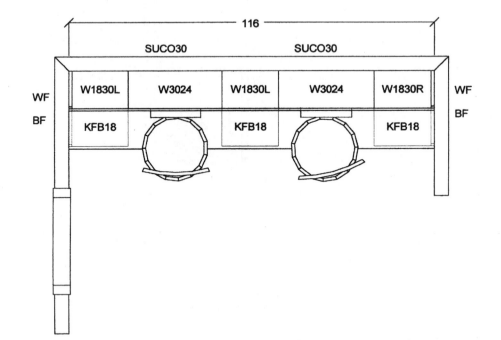

Cabinet List:

3 18″ wide file base cabinets
2 base fillers
2 wall fillers
3 18″×30″ wall cabinets
2 18″×24″ wall cabinets
2 undercabinet organizers
2 8′-0″ inside corner molding
1 8′-0″ base toe material
4 toe kick cap covers
13 knobs or pulls
1 pint stain
1 putty stick

Additional Materials Needed:

- Miscellaneous fasteners and adhesives
- 1 countertop
- 2 keyboard trays
- Dimensional lumber and drywall supplies to create a 14″ deep soffit

Required:

- Minimum for 1″ filler at each wall for wall and base cabinets
- Block wall cabinets 1/2″ below soffit and cover gap with inside corner molding
- Monitor and desktop CPU dimensions

Variations:

- Delete the soffit and trim the top of the wall cabinets with crown molding
- Adjust to fit computer equipment and job-site conditions

This study hall works well when placed between two children's bedrooms or in an adjacent common area. In well under 10′ of wall space, two computer workstations are created. The wall and base storage can accommodate hobby items as well as reference material for homework.

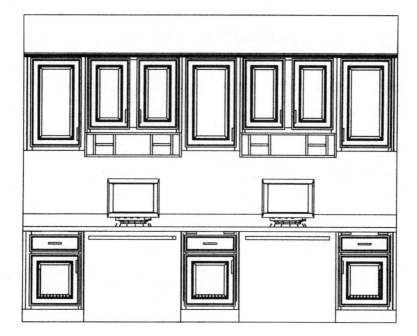

Teen Room Lounge

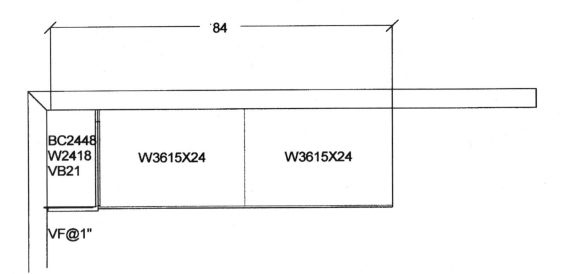

Cabinet List:

1 12″ wide vanity base
1 base skin
1 vanity filler trimmed to 1″
1 24″×15″ wall cabinet
1 24″×48″ bookcase
1 tall skin
2 36″×15″×24″ wall cabinets
1 base skin to cover exposed end of bench area
1 3/4″ thick tall end panel as bench top
1 6″ tall filler as base toe material
1 6″ base filler as base toe material
8 pieces knobs or pulls
1 pint stain
1 putty stick

Additional Materials Needed:

• Miscellaneous fasteners and adhesives
• Cushion

Required:

• Pull vanity cabinet to 24″ off wall
• Skin all exposed sides
• Trim and miter filler material as base toe treatment
• Minimum 1″ filler at the wall

Variations:

• Add decorator matching doors to exposed cabinet ends
• Unit can be reversed for a right-hand installation

A reading area tucked into the corner of a teenager's room serves many purposes. Adding soft pillows at the bookcase end makes it an excellent place to read or talk on the phone. The 24″ deep storage cabinets below the cushioned area will hold anything from additional bedding to shoes.

Television Cabinet with Pet Niche

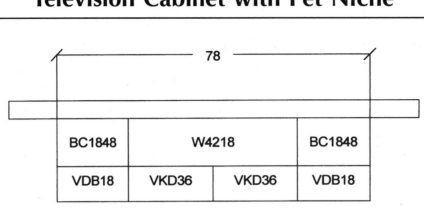

78

BC1848	W4218	BC1848
VDB18	VKD36	VKD36	VDB18

VA48C

Cabinet List:

2 18"×48" bookcase units
1 42"×18" wall cabinet
1 48" finished shelf
2 8'-0" crown molding
2 18" vanity drawer bases
2 kneehole drawers trimmed to 21" each
1 48" arched valance
1 piece paneling 42"×18"
1 8'-0" piece outside corner molding
1 8'-0" pieces of base toe material
2 toe kick cap covers
10 pieces knobs or pulls
1 pint stain
1 putty stick

Additional Materials Needed:

- Miscellaneous fasteners and adhesives
- Plywood or particleboard for substrate
- Dimensional lumber for platform
- Countertop
- Pet bed
- Television

Required:

- Platform to match toe recess of base cabinets
- Cover platform with matching paneling to create the floor of the pet niche
- Finish raw edge of the paneling with outside corner molding
- Eased corners on all countertops for safety
- Finish bottom of wall cabinet with finished shelf

Variation:

- Finish the two exposed back walls with matching paneling

Books, Bowser, and a television all in one spot. What pampered pet wouldn't love sleeping in his own private niche? Here, vanity cabinets are used as the base units for a more furniture-like proportion. To keep costs down, both exposed wall areas were left unpaneled.

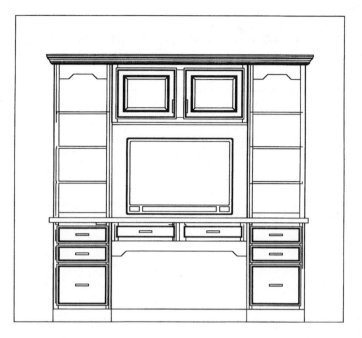

Twin Beds with Surround

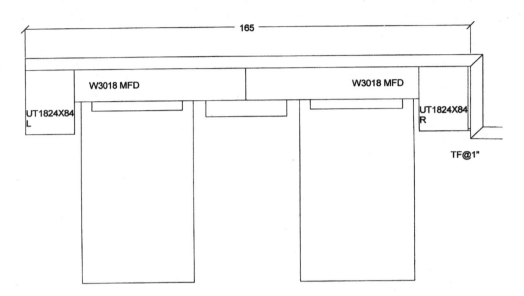

Cabinet List:

2 18″×24″×84″ utility cabinets
12 utility shelves
1 tall filler
2 30″×18″ wall cabinets with mullion doors and matching interiors
4 tempered glass inserts
4 72″ finished shelves
2 counter supports
3 8′-0″ crown molding
2 8′-0″ light rail molding
1 8′-0″ base toe material
3 toe kick cap covers
8 knobs or pulls
1 pint stain
1 putty stick

Additional Materials Needed:

• Miscellaneous fasteners and adhesives

Required:

• Install wall cabinets 4″ lower than utility cabinets
• Install finished shelves above and below wall cabinets
• Add light rail molding and counter supports on lower shelf
• Minimum 1″ filler at wall

Variations:

• Adjust cabinets to fit width of wall
• Add pull-out shelves or hamper baskets to lower section of utility cabinets
• Panel wall between mullion door cabinets
• Add undercabinet lighting behind light ray

A long narrow room might be the perfect place for this wall of built-ins surrounding two single beds. The utility cabinets offer many opportunities for customization of the interior storage. Adding lighting behind the light rail, and conveniently placed wall switches adds wonderful reading lights.

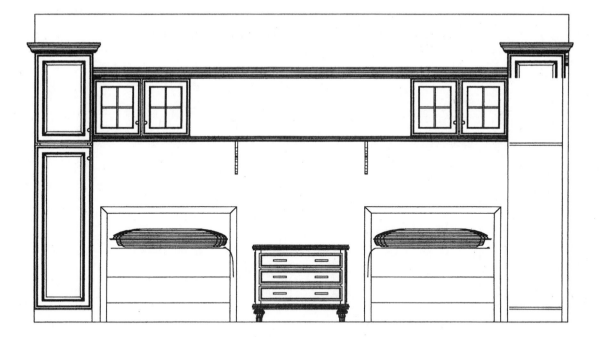

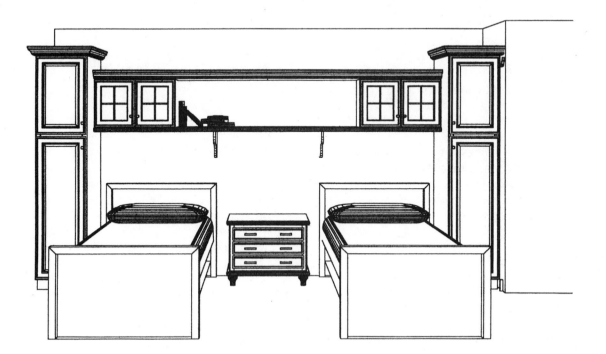

Vanity with Lowered Side Cabinets

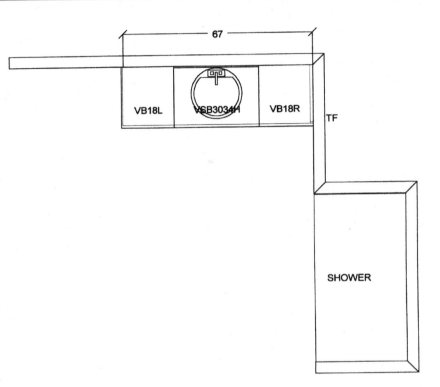

Cabinet List:

1 34″ high×30″ wide vanity sink base
2 31″ high×18″ wide vanity bases
1 vanity filler
1 8′-0″ base toe material
1 toe kick cap cover
6 knobs or pulls
1 pint stain
1 putty stick

Additional Materials Needed:

- Miscellaneous fasteners and adhesives
- 2 lower and 1 upper countertop
- One vanity sink with faucet
- Ceramic tile backsplash
- Mirror

Required:

- Minimum 1″ filler at the wall

Variations:

- Add decorator matching door to exposed cabinet end
- Vary width to suit job-site conditions

This dual height vanity will help transition growing children to the 34 1/2″ vanity height that has become standard today. The lower cabinets provide counterspace at a more comfortable height for children. A tile backsplash works best when there are multiple cabinet heights.

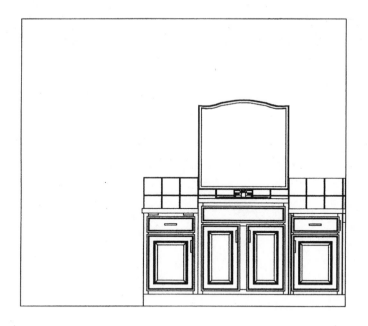

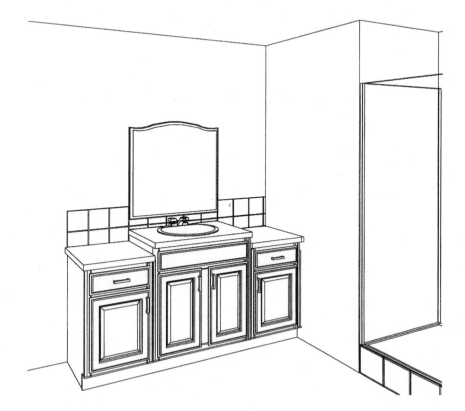

Wall Hung Cubbyholes

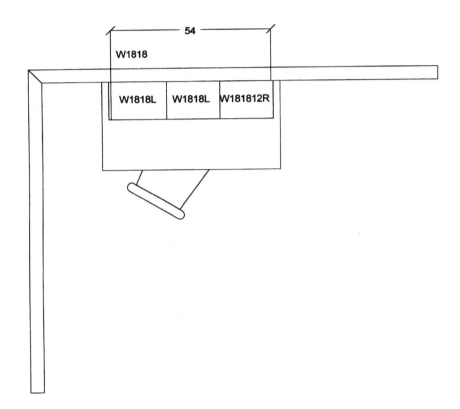

Cabinet List:

4 18″×18″ wall cabinets
4 60″ finished shelves
4 knobs or pulls
1 pint stain
1 putty stick

Additional Materials Needed:

• Miscellaneous fasteners and adhesives

Required:

• Trim and install finished shelving between each layer and add one piece on the left side to close in the end

Variations:

• Add light rail molding to the bottom of unit and install undercabinet lighting
• Reduce the depth of the cabinets and shelving as site conditions require
• Reverse the direction of the stagger
• Panel the wall of the two open cubbyholes or paint them a bright color

These staggered cubbyholes can be placed over a desk, as shown, or over nearly any low piece of furniture. The open areas can display photos, books, or sports trophies. The closed areas hide childhood clutter and treasures.

Wall of Storage

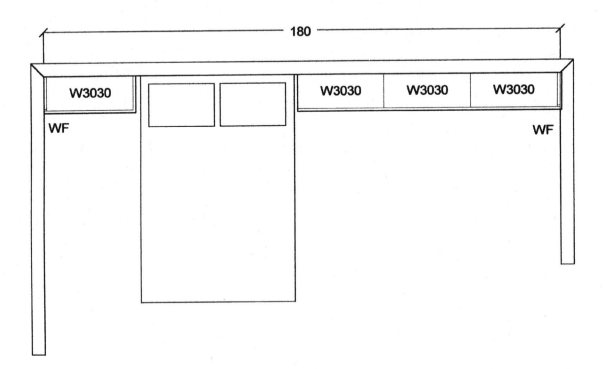

Cabinet List:

2 30″×30″ wall cabinets
2 30″×30″ wall cabinets with matching interiors; doors removed
2 fillers
2 8′-0″ beveled edge countertop molding
4 knobs or pulls
1 pint stain
1 putty stick

Additional Materials Needed:

- Miscellaneous fasteners and adhesives
- Dimensional lumber
- Countertop

Required:

- Eased corners on all countertops for safety
- Minimum 1″ filler at each wall
- Raise cabinets 3/4″ and trim with beveled edge countertop edge molding

Variation:

- Adjust cabinets to fit width of wall

No child's room ever has enough storage. These 12″ deep wall cabinets, used as base cabinets, provide both open and closed storage. Decorative baskets can be used to keep clutter under control on the open shelf areas. Lots of counterspace is a bonus for any child.

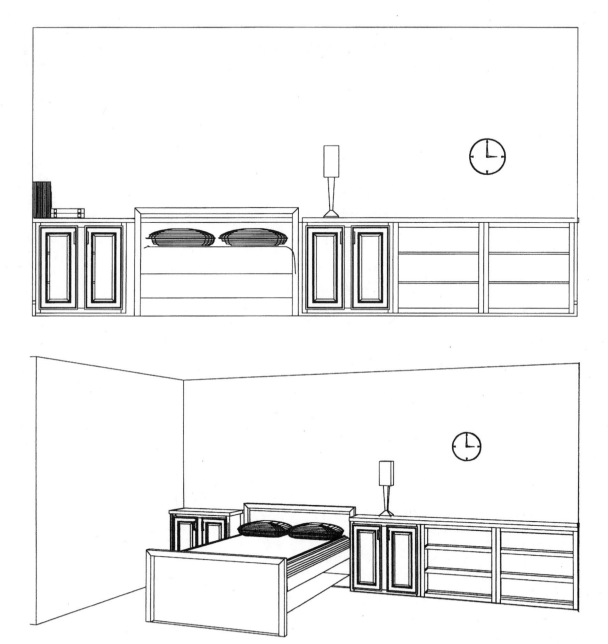

Window Seat

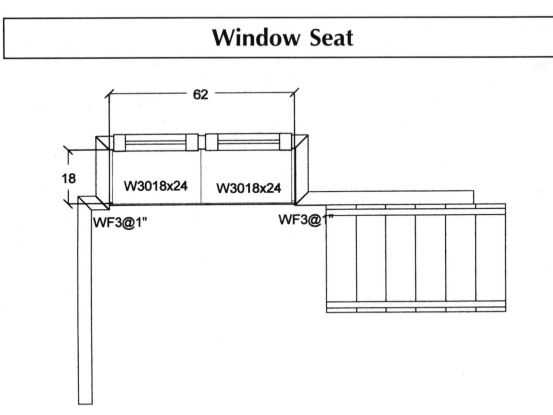

Cabinet List:

2 30″×18″×24″ deep wall cabinets reduced
   to 18″
1 wall filler (split left and right)
1 3/4″ thick tall end panel
4 knobs or pulls
1 pint stain
1 putty stick

Additional Materials Needed:

- Miscellaneous fasteners and adhesives
- Cushion

Required:

- Minimum 1″ filler at each wall
- Trim tall end panel as top of window seat

Variations:

- Adjust window seat to fit job-site conditions
- Raise cabinets if the door style is full overlay or if the flooring is thickly padded car-
  pet

This window seat tucked into a stair landing
is constructed from 24″ deep cabinets that
are typically used above a refrigerator. For
this application, they have been reduced to
18″ in depth. The seat top is made from a
trimmed 3/4″ tall end panel which can be
topped with an upholstered cushion.

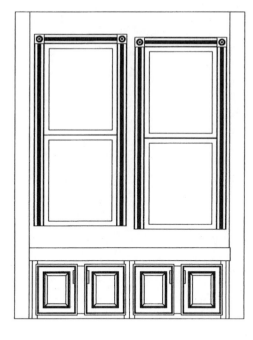

CHAPTER 9

Dining Areas

Today, when we talk about dining areas, we do not just mean a formal dining room. That room where we learned our manners and which was saved for special events. That room, while not totally obsolete, does mean that over two hundred square feet of our homes sits virtually empty much of the time. We just need various and multi-use areas to conduct the family meal gatherings.

Add to that, the informal lifestyles of the twenty-first century. Meals are often staggered to meet varying family schedules. Both parents often work full time and the children are engaged in many after school activities. Yet, eating together as a family has never been more important. Super-fast techno-ovens, the popularity of takeout and speed-scratch food, as well as the renewed interest in warming drawers, speak to this way of life. To make the family mealtime gathering happen, we need areas set aside for the dining experience. To support that need, homes require serving areas, a place to store our everyday and company dinnerware, and even casual plop-down, eat-a-meal spaces.

One of the most sought-after plop-down areas is a countertop extension at the kitchen island. That there is often an asso-ciated request for an attached snack bar, almost goes without saying. We'll look at three popular islands, as well as several peninsula designs, with space for eating casual meals. A word of caution here is good. Avoid placing cooktops or ranges in islands with attached eating areas. Cooking splatters or boil-overs could cause injury, particularly to the very young or elderly.

But if a formal dining room is the preferred choice, storage is the key. From recessed servers to hutches and breakfronts, we need places to store our tablecloths, placemats, dishes, and serving pieces. And if the dining room is one arm of an L-shaped kitchen, it is doubly important to match the hutch or server to the kitchen cabinetry.

Butlers' pantries are another opportunity to add storage in the dining areas. Butlers' pantries are those areas between the kitchen and dining rooms that hark back to our more formal dining roots. Still, they are great staging and storage spaces, often incorporating a secondary sink or even an undercounter refrigerator.

The bottom line is, dining areas are all about spending time with our loved ones, convenience, storage, and making our lives easier, no matter where we find the space.

Arts and Crafts Server

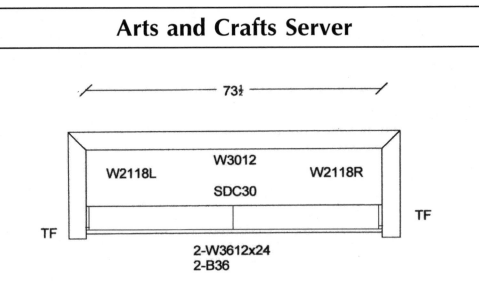

Cabinet List:

2 tall fillers (split)
2 36″ base cabinets reduced to 21″
2 36″×12″×24″ deep wall cabinets reduced to 21″
2 21″×18″ wall cabinets
1 30″×12″ wall cabinet
1 30″ spice drawer unit with matching wood knobs
1 8′-0″ crown molding
1 3/4″×84″ tall end panel
1 8′-0″ base toe kick material
2 48″ arched valances (trimmed)
16 knobs or pulls
1 pint stain
1 putty stick

Additional Materials Needed:

• Miscellaneous fasteners and adhesives
• Dimensional lumber
• Countertop

Required:

• Split tall fillers for upper and lower sections, allowing for a minimum 1″ at each wall
• Install crown molding on top layer of cabinets, block, and install 3/4″ tall end panel on top
• Install base toe material and then trimmed arch valances in toe space

Variations:

• Adjust cabinet width to accommodate job-site conditions
• Use a matching wood countertop

This built-in server has a base section that is reduced to 21″ to make the upper cabinets easier to reach. The heavy horizontal lines and base toe treatment give the unit an arts and crafts feel. The unit is approximately 64 1/2″ tall.

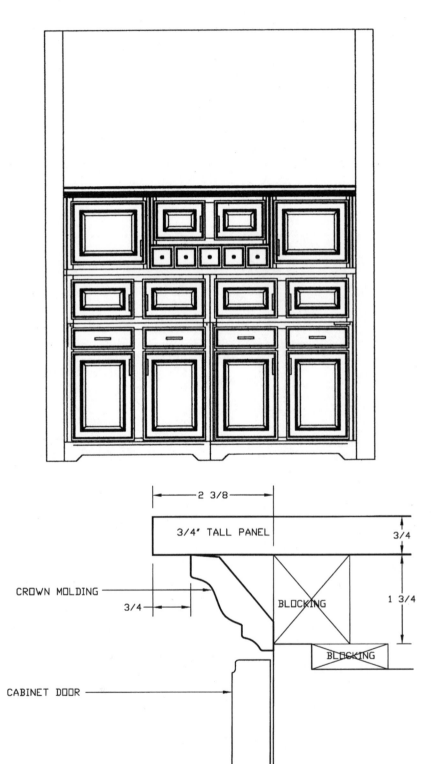

Basic Butlers' Pantry

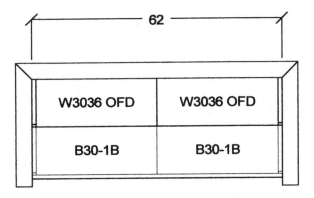

Cabinet List:

2 30"×36" wall cabinets with open-frame doors and matching interiors
4 clear glass inserts
2 30" base cabinets
2 36" wall fillers
2 base fillers
1 8'-0" classic crown molding
1 8'-0" dentil molding
1 8'-0"×6" wide tall filler
1 8'-0" scribe molding
1 8'-0" base toe kick material
12 knobs or pulls
1 pint stain
1 putty stick

Additional Materials Needed:

• Miscellaneous fasteners and adhesives
• Countertop with full-height tiled backsplash

Required:

• Finished opening of the wall should be 2" larger than the cabinets to allow for minimum 1" fillers at each wall

Variations:

• Adjust cabinet width to accommodate job-site conditions
• Change from open-frame to mullion door cabinets
• Add glass shelving and in-cabinet lighting
• Make one cabinet a sink base and add a small sink
• Add two full-width rollout trays to each base cabinet
• Add undercabinet lighting behind the light rail molding
• Add cutlery divider(s)

A butlers' pantry is often placed between the kitchen and dining room for staging to the dining room, and it also adds extra storage. Adding a small sink makes this butlers' pantry work even harder for the homeowner. This basic design is treated to a top molding build-up that goes to the ceiling.

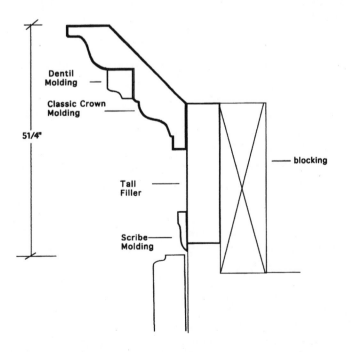

Dentil
Molding —

Classic Crown
Molding

51/4"

— blocking

Tall
Filler

Scribe—
Molding

Basic Peninsula with Raised Snack Bar

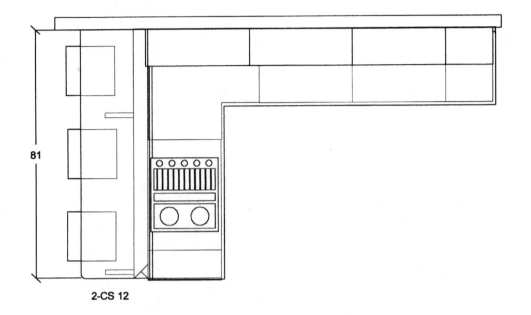

81

2-CS 12

Cabinet List:

Basic kitchen with peninsula
2 corbels
1 pint stain
1 putty stick

Additional Materials Needed:

- Miscellaneous fasteners and adhesives
- Dimensional lumber and drywall
- Countertop with eased corner for safety
- Stools with 30″ high seats

Required:

- Framed wall: 40 1/2″ high
- Minimum 24″ of counterspace per person
- Finish the bottom of the snack area countertop for strength and smooth appearance

- Allow a minimum of 36″ behind the countertop for easy passage

Variations:

- The 40 1/2″ high wall can be treated with paneling (plain or beadboard), tiled, or painted
- Adjust peninsula size to fit job-site conditions

Peninsulas are a convenient way to include a snack area in a kitchen or at a beverage bar. This 42″ high eating area requires stools with seats that are 30″ off the floor. The raised area is also perfect for hiding kitchen clutter from adjacent rooms or as a safety barrier when a cooktop is placed on the counter below.

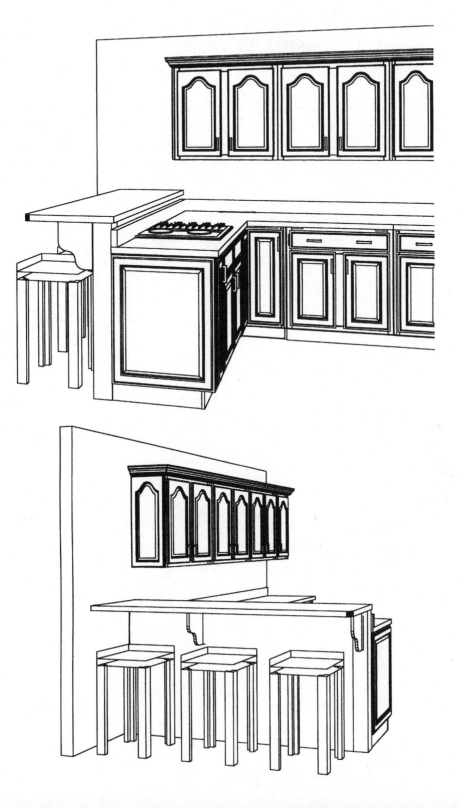

Block-Front Buffet

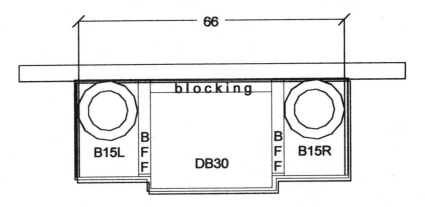

Cabinet List:

2 15″ base cabinets
1 30″ drawer base
2 base fluted fillers
4 base skins
2 base decorator matching doors
2 6″×96″ tall fillers
2 pieces inside corner molding
10 knobs or pulls
1 pint stain
1 putty stick

Additional Materials Needed:

- Miscellaneous fasteners and adhesives
- Dimensional lumber
- Countertop

Required:

- Pull center cabinet forward 3″ and block
- Skin all exposed ends of the cabinets

- Applying decorator matching doors to ends
- Create furniture base from filler material (trimmed to fit) topped with inside corner molding
- Outlets centered at 42″ A.F.F. for buffet lamps

Variations:

- Add cutlery dividers to drawer(s) for flatware storage
- Add rollout trays to base cabinet

This flexible buffet design provides storage for flatware and serving pieces in the dining room. The countertop can be made of wood (stained to match the cabinets), granite, or solid surface material. Artwork or a decorative mirror above the buffet would complete the look.

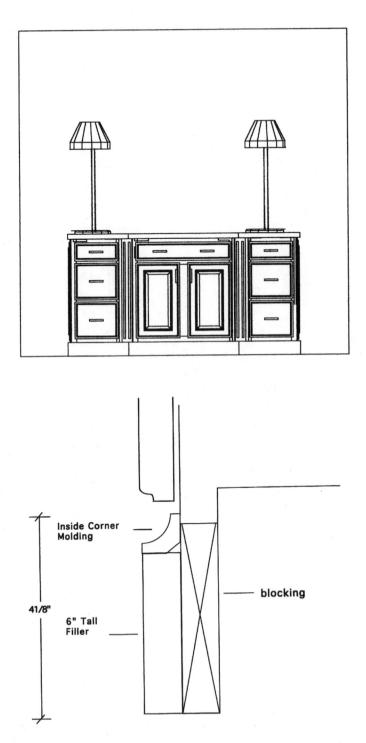

Inside Corner
Molding

blocking

41/8"

6" Tall
Filler

Breakfront

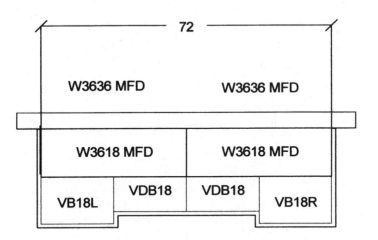

Cabinet List:

2 18″ vanity base cabinets
2 18″ vanity drawer base cabinets
2 36″×18″ mullion door cabinets with matching interiors
2 36″×36″ cathedral mullion door cabinets with matching interiors
2 8′-0″ crown molding
8 clear glass inserts for mullion doors
1 tall skin (trimmed and split)
4 base skins
2 8′-0″×6″ wide tall filler for toe material
2 8′-0″ inside corner molding
18 knobs or pulls
1 pint stain
1 putty stick

Additional Materials Needed:

- Miscellaneous fasteners and adhesives
- Matching wood countertop
- Dimensional lumber

Required:

- Pull the end cabinets forward 3″ and block
- Skin all exposed cabinet sides
- Create furniture base from filler material (trimmed to fit) topped with inside corner molding
- Order square cabinets for the lower wall cabinets in the stack and cathedral style for the top row

Variations:

- Change mullion doors to open-frame doors
- Add glass shelves and interior cabinet lights
- Add rollout trays to vanity base cabinets
- Add decorator matching doors to the exposed ends of the breakfront

This formal and elegant breakfront is packed with display space for dinnerware and collectibles. By adding glass shelving and interior cabinet lighting, the breakfront will add life to any dining room.

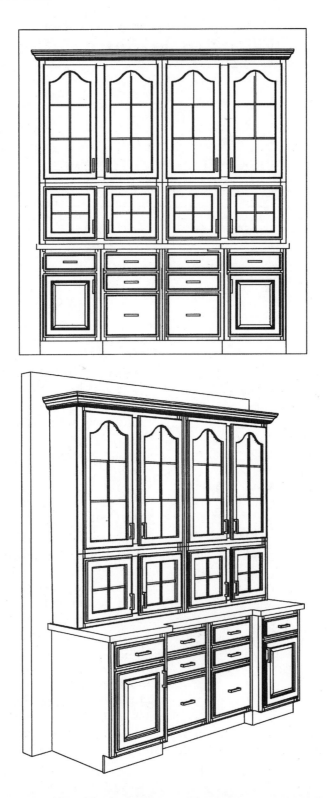

Butlers' Pantry with Plate Rack

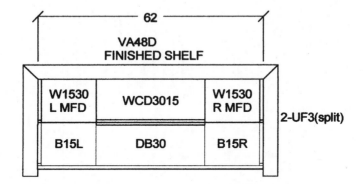

Cabinet List:

2 15″×30″ wall cabinets with mullion doors and matching interiors
2 clear glass inserts
1 30″×15″ plate rack cabinet
1 decorative valance
1 72″ finished shelf split for soffit board and top of plate rack
2 15″ base cabinets
1 30″ drawer base cabinet
1 piece finished paneling 30″×24″
1 wall fillers (split)
1 base fillers (split)
1 8′-0″ crown molding
1 8′-0″ base toe kick material
12 knobs or pulls
1 pint stain
1 putty stick

Additional Materials Needed:

• Miscellaneous fasteners and adhesives
• Countertop

Required:

• Finished opening of the wall should be 2″ larger than the cabinets to allow for minimum 1″ wall and base fillers at each wall

• Install plate rack 3″ lower than adjacent wall cabinets and top with finished shelf
• Trim and install remaining piece of finished shelving as soffit board behind the valance
• Finish the wall above the plate rack with paneling

Variations:

• Adjust width to accommodate job-site conditions
• Change from mullion door to open-frame cabinets
• Add glass shelving and in-cabinet lighting
• Make one cabinet a sink base and add an auxiliary sink
• Add light rail molding and undercabinet lighting
• Add cutlery divider(s)

A more countrified version of the basic butlers' pantry features a lowered plate rack. Lowering the plate rack adds design interest and provides more display space above. A light fixture installed in the soffit board behind the valance will highlight a favorite collectible. The wide drawers in the middle are a perfect place to store placemats and napkins.

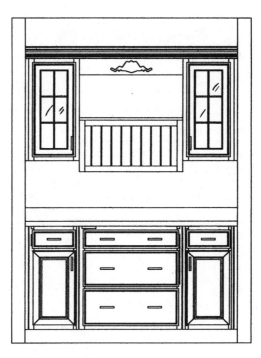

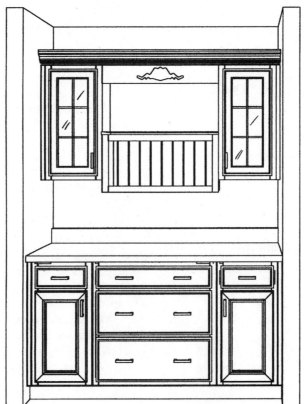

Corner Hutch

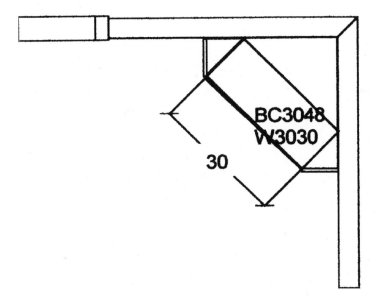

BC3048
W3030

30

Cabinet List:

1 30″×30″ wall cabinet
1 30″×48″ open bookcase
1 8′-0″ crown molding
1 6″ wide base filler
1 8′-0″ inside corner molding
2 corner angle moldings
1 tall panel 3/4″ thick (split)
2 knobs or pulls
1 pint stain
1 putty stick

Additional Materials Needed:

- Miscellaneous fasteners and adhesives
- Dimensional lumber

Required:

- Construct a 4″ high platform for wall cabinet used as base

- Create furniture toe treatment from 6″ filler topped with inside corner molding
- Cleats to secure returns made from split 3/4″ tall panel
- Corner angle molding makes the installation of the side panels a breeze

Variations:

- Vary top molding detail
- Panel rear of bookcase with beadboard paneling

A corner hutch with open and closed storage will fit into all but the tiniest dining areas. The open area is perfect for displaying serving pieces. The lower section is for tucking away other items. Consider placing two corner hutches in the dining room for symmetry and extra storage.

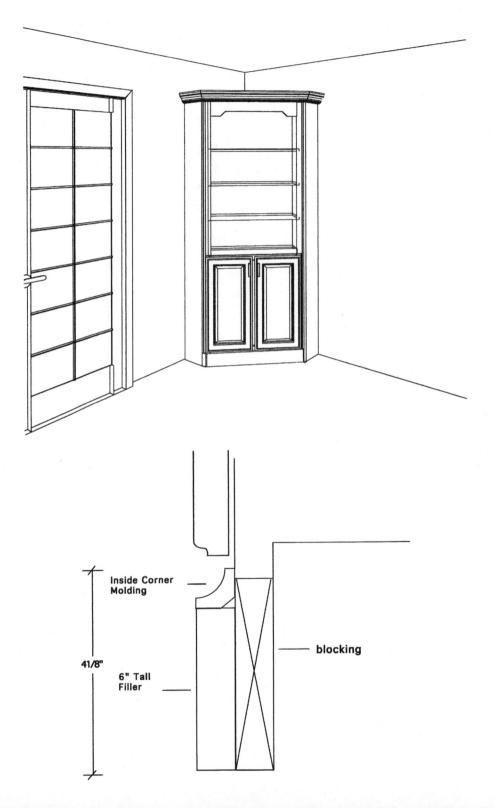

Inside Corner
Molding

blocking

41/8"

6" Tall
Filler

Cottage Hutch

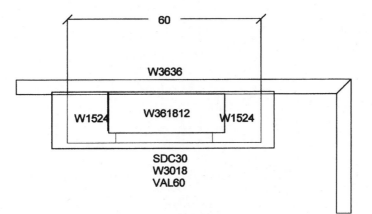

Cabinet List:

2 15″×24″ wall cabinets
1 30″×18″ wall cabinet
2 base skins
1 30″ spice drawer unit with matching wood knobs
1 36″×18″ wall cabinet
1 36″×36″ wall cabinet
1 tall skin (split)
1 8′-0″ crown molding
1 72″ scalloped valance
1 48″ straight valance as toe treatment returns
1 8′-0″ inside corner molding
8 knobs or pulls
1 pint stain
1 putty stick

Additional Materials Needed:

• Miscellaneous fasteners and adhesives
• Oversized countertop
• Dimensional lumber

Required:

• Pull base wall cabinets forward to 15″ and block
• Build a 4 1/2″ high by 10″ deep platform to support the base wall cabinets
• Cut and miter valances as the toe treatment and top with inside corner molding
• Skin all exposed sides

Variations:

• Make top cabinet in an arched style
• Make both upper cabinets in either mullion or open-frame doors, add glass inserts and matching interiors
• Add decorator matching doors to exposed ends

Made completely from wall cabinets, this charming hutch would look beautiful in a house by the sea or in nearly any kitchen or dining room. The extended countertop adds extra surface but also gives a unique proportion to the hutch.

Country Hutch

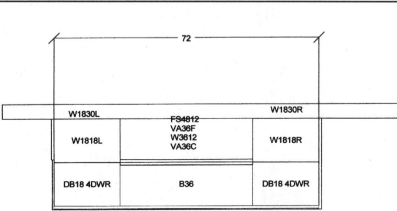

Cabinet List:

2 18″×30″ cathedral wall cabinets
2 18″×18″ square wall cabinets
1 36″×12″ square wall cabinet
1 48″ finished shelf as top for W3612
1 36″ pierced valance
1 36″ arched valance
1 48″ finished shelf as soffit board
2 18″ wide four-drawer cabinets
1 36″ wide base cabinet
2 tall skins (split and trimmed)
2 base skins
1 piece 48″×48″ paneling
1 72″ scalloped valance
1 60″ straight valance as base treatment returns
2 8′-0″ inside corner molding
2 8′-0″ crown molding
1 8′-0″ base toe material
18 knobs or pulls
1 pint stain
1 putty stick

Additional Materials Needed:

• Miscellaneous fasteners and adhesives
• Wood countertop to match the cabinets

Required:

• Use square door style cabinets on the bottom of the stack if you select cathedral cabinets for the top.
• Trim tall skins and apply to both sides of stacks to conceal cabinet joints
• Finish rear wall with matching paneling
• Install finished shelf on top of center wall cabinet
• Apply base toe material to toe space and then create scalloped toe detail. Use straight valances as returns. Top with inside corner molding

Variations:

• Change from solid doors to open-frame or mullion door cabinets with matching interiors
• Add cutlery divider(s) or other interior storage aids
• Reduced the depth of the 12″ high cabinet for design interest

This countrified hutch can easily go in the dining room or breakfast area with equal aplomb. The pierced valance can be changed to any style that you prefer, to create a different look. If the hutch is to be used in the kitchen, consider a more durable countertop made from laminate, solid surface, or stone.

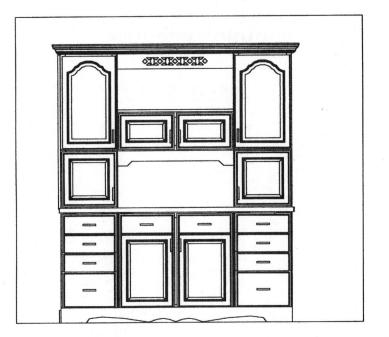

European Peninsula

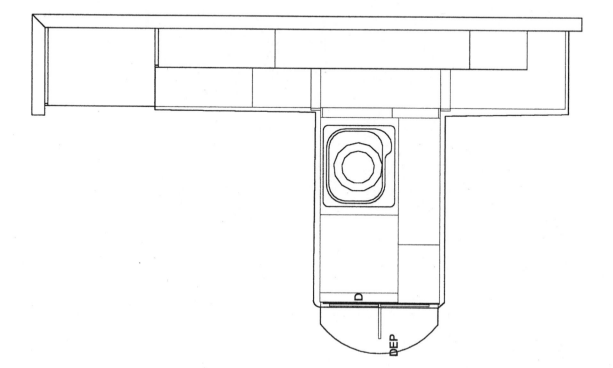

Cabinet List:

Basic island or peninsula cabinets
1 desk end panel trimmed to fit
1 filler as cleat

Additional Materials Needed:

- Miscellaneous fasteners and adhesives
- Countertop installed at 30″ A.F.F.
- Chairs with 18″ high seats

Required:

- Minimum of 36″ wide space for eating counter

- Cleat on cabinet to help support countertop

Variations:

- Make snack bar from a contrasting material
- Lowered eating area can be raised to counter height (36″)

A 30″ high eating area placed at the end of an island or peninsula has a definite European flair. Just big enough for coffee for two, this tiny eating area will fit where almost nothing else will.

Floating Server

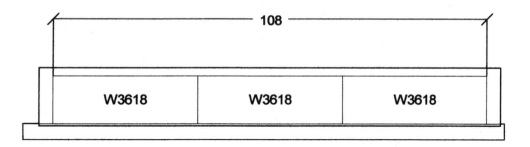

Cabinet List:

3 36″×18″ wall cabinets
2 crown molding
6 knobs or pulls
1 pint stain
1 putty stick

Additional Materials Needed:

• Miscellaneous fasteners and adhesives
• Countertop

Required:

• Install crown molding on top of cabinets
• Order a countertop large enough to allow for the extra width and depth created by the crown molding

Variations:

• Add light rail and undercabinet lighting
• Skin exposed ends and apply decorator matching doors
• Use mullion or open-frame doors and add interior lighting to create display cabinets
• Adjust width to fit job-site conditions
• Delete the crown molding trim

This floating server is made from 18″ high wall cabinets installed at 34 1/2″ off the floor. The top of the cabinets is trimmed with crown molding to add design detail and enlarge the counterspace. The floating server is a simple way to add storage and serving space to even the smallest eating area.

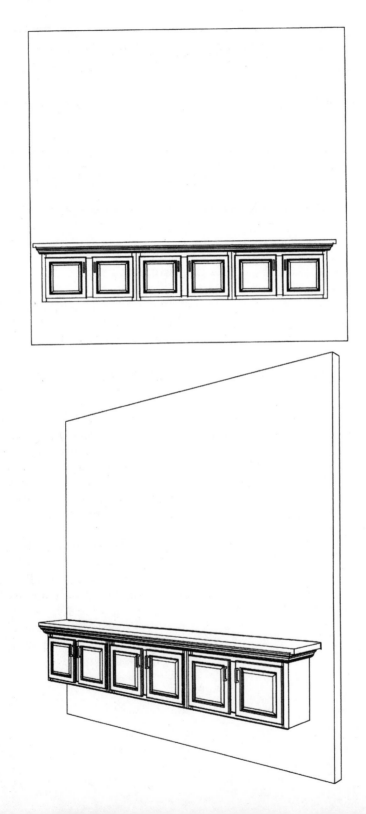

Frieze Valance Hutch

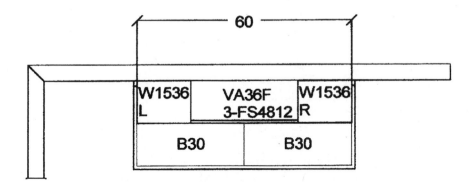

Cabinet List:

2 30″ base cabinets
2 15″×36″ wall cabinets
1 30″ frieze valance
1 48″ finished shelf as soffit board
1 piece paneling 36″×36″
1 60″ shelf split as two shelves
1 8′-0″ crown molding
3 shelf undercabinet units
1 8′-0″ toe kick material
2 toe kick cap covers
10 knobs or pulls

Additional Materials Needed:

• Miscellaneous fasteners and adhesives
• Countertop with backsplash

Required:

• Panel between cabinets before installing center shelf

• Set lower shelf flush with bottom of wall cabinets and attach shelf undercabinet unit

Variations:

• Use arched, straight, or other valance styles
• Skin exposed ends if desired and add decorator matching doors
• Change wall cabinets to mullion doors with matching interiors and add clear glass inserts
• Add cutlery dividers or rollout shelves to base units

This hutch features both open and closed storage space with small undercabinet shelving for spices or collectibles. The base can be fitted with a matching wood countertop or a more hard-working surface like tile or granite if placed in the kitchen. The decorative valance can be chosen to fit your personal decorating style.

Hoosier Cabinet

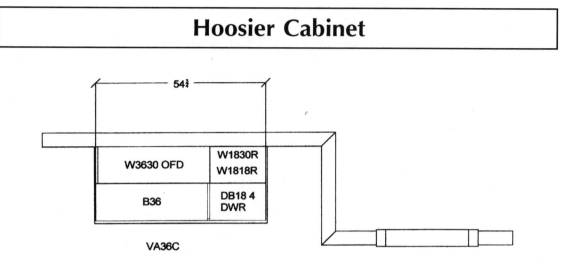

Cabinet List:

1 36″×30″ open-frame door wall cabinet with matching interior
2 clear glass inserts
1 18″×30″ wall cabinet
1 18″×18″ wall cabinet
1 36″×18″ piece paneling
1 48″ finished shelf used vertically as a side panel
1 tall skin (split)
2 base skins
1 36″ arched valance
1 base filler trimmed to 3/4″
1 36″ base cabinet
1 18″ four-drawer base
1 8′-0″ base toe kick materials
2 toe kick caps
1 8′-0″ crown molding
12 knobs or pulls
1 pint stain
1 putty stick

Additional Materials Needed:

• Miscellaneous fasteners and adhesives
• Flat-deck wood countertop to match cabinets

Required:

• Use a square door style on the W1818 even if a cathedral door style is selected for the upper wall cabinets
• 3/4″ base filler to accommodate the vertical finished shelf used as an end panel
• Panel the wall below W3630 OFD

Variations:

• Use opalescent or other glass inserts
• Select mullion doors instead of open-frame doors
• Use pierced, straight, or other valance styles
• Add halogen lights and clear glass shelves to open-frame door cabinet

Inspired by your great grandmother's first kitchen cabinet, this charming built-in is most comfortable in a country kitchen. Consider outfitting it with baking supplies and fit it with a marble countertop for the perfect bake center.

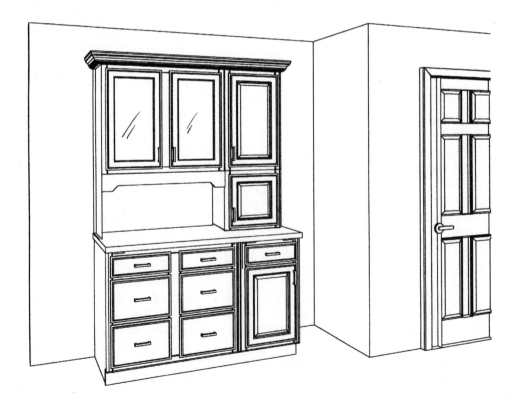

Island with 36″ High Snack Area for Two

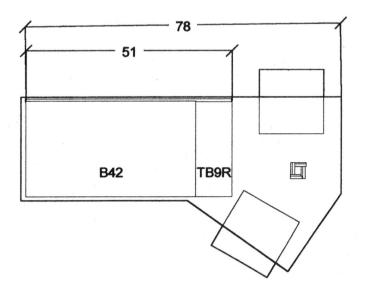

Cabinet List:

1 42″ base cabinet
1 9″ tray cabinet
1 tray divider
4 fluted base fillers to create post
1 piece 51″×34 1/2″ paneling
1 8′-0″ outside corner molding
1 8′-0″ base toe material
2 toe kick cap covers
5 knobs or pulls
1 pint stain
1 putty stick

Additional Materials Needed:

- Miscellaneous fasteners and adhesives
- Countertop
- 2 stools with 24″ high seats

Required:

- Countertop must be constructed to accommodate open span

- Adding a support plate on top of post to help support the countertop

Variations:

- The island can be made from any combination of base cabinets
- Substitute a turned post for the fluted filler column
- Back of the island can be enhanced with decorator matching doors or a wainscoting detail
- Add base skins and decorator matching doors to exposed ends

Even a moderately sized kitchen might accommodate this well-designed island with a counter height snack area. One advantage of the counter height eating surface is that it can serve many purposes. When not being used as a snack area, it can serve as additional counter workspace or even a place for paying bills and doing homework.

Island with Lowered Eating Area

Cabinet List:

1 24″×24″ base end angle cabinet
1 45″ base cabinet
1 30″ base cabinet
1 15″ sink base
1 front frame and doors for a 42″×24″ wall cabinet
1 48″ sink floor
1 finished paneling 96″×34 1/2″
1 8′-0″ outside corner molding
2 8′-0″ base toe kick material
2 toe kick end caps
15 knobs or pulls
1 pint stain
1 putty stick

Additional Materials Needed:

- Miscellaneous fasteners and adhesives
- 2 countertops (upper and lower)
- 12″×12″ bar sink and faucet
- 2 chairs with 18″ high seats
- Dimensional lumber to build a platform

Required:

- Cleats (stained to match) to support lower countertop

- Finish the bottom of the snack area for strength and smooth appearance
- Panel the back of the island and apply outside corner molding to cover raw edges
- Build a 4″ high platform for the angled storage area from dimensional lumber, cover with base toe material
- Trim sink floor to fit and install behind angled front frame and doors

Variations:

- Vary the countertop material on each level
- Delete sink
- Add base skins and decorator matching doors on exposed ends
- Add an extra shelf behind angled front frame and doors

The use of a lowered cabinet front frame and doors provides storage space, beneath the eating area, for out-of-season serving pieces or seldom-used items. The 30″ snack surface is perfect for standard chairs and is often preferred by older homeowners or those with children.

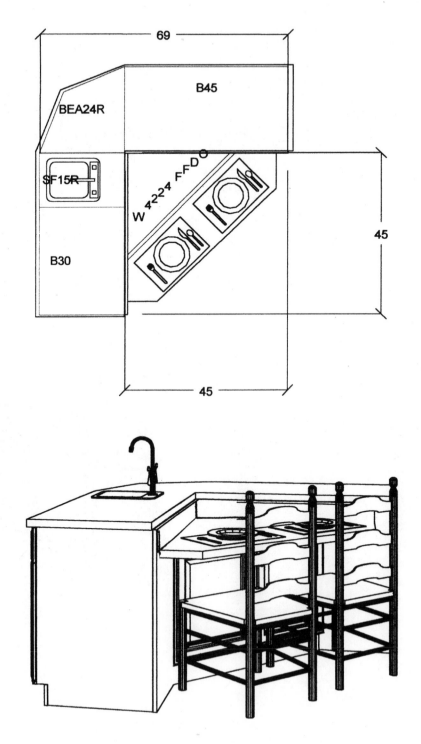

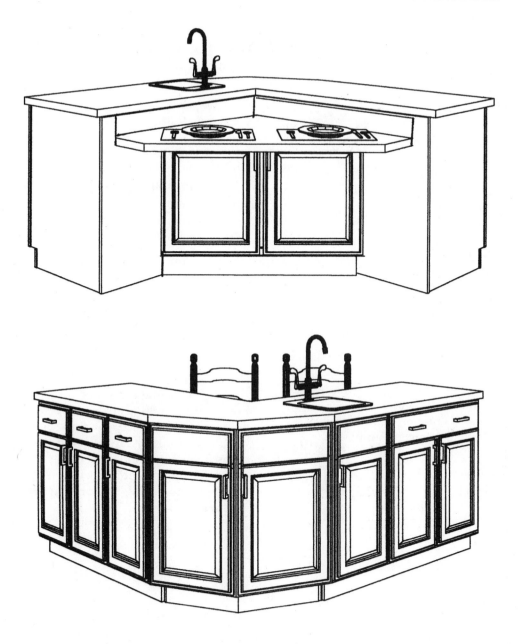

Island with Table Extension

Cabinet List:

1 30″ base
2 18″ drawer base cabinets
2 base skins
2 decorator matching doors
1 8′-0″ base toe kick material
2 toe kick end caps
1 piece paneling 66″×34 1/2″
1 8′-0″ outside corner molding
8 base fluted fillers
1 48″ frieze valances
2 36″ frieze valance
10 knobs or pulls
1 pint stain
1 putty stick

Additional Materials Needed:

- Miscellaneous fasteners and adhesives
- Upper and lower countertops
- Dimensional lumber to build pedestals
- Miscellaneous drywall supplies

Required:

- 2 framed and drywalled pedestals 9″×18″×28 1/2″ high

- Corner bracing for aprons
- Floor mounted stabilization bolts for columns
- Panel rear of cabinets and trim corners with outside corner molding
- Fabricate support columns from fluted fillers

Variations:

- Delete radius end on eating level
- Use plain valances or economical fillers as aprons
- Used turned post instead of fluted filler columns for table legs
- Texture pedestals or cover with ceramic tile

An elegant island combines pedestals, made from dimensional lumber and drywall, combined with cabinetry to form a two level work and dining island. While the countertop is ideal for solid surface material with a detailed edging, remember to support the open span according to manufacturer's specifications.

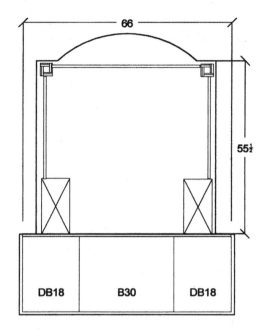

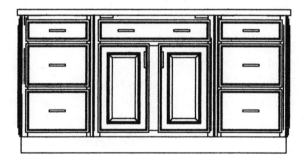

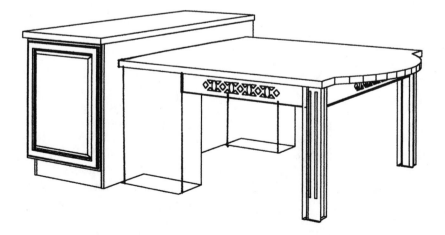

Kitchen Nook

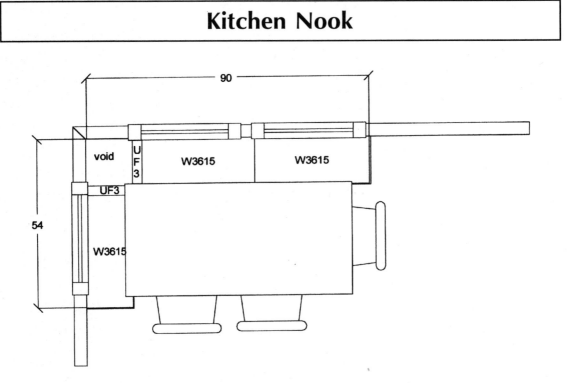

Cabinet List:

3 36″×15″×24″ wall cabinets reduced to 15″ deep
2 fillers
2 3/4″ thick tall end panels
2 8′-0″ scribe molding
6 decorative knobs or pulls
1 pint stain
1 putty stick

Additional Materials Needed:

- Miscellaneous fasteners and adhesives
- Upholstered cushions

Required:

- Install wall cabinets on the floor with fillers in the corner
- Trim 3/4″ thick tall end panels for top of seating area
- Trim cabinets with scribe molding at the floor

Variations:

- Adjust size of seating area to fit job-site conditions
- Add an angled back to the seating for even more comfort

The kitchen nook, also known as a banquette makes very effective use of space. That is why restaurants use them so often. The cabinets that form the seating provide storage for out-of-season items. The drawback of this type of built-in is having to shuffle around to let someone in or out. Still, this area will undoubtedly become a favorite spot for casual meals and conversation.

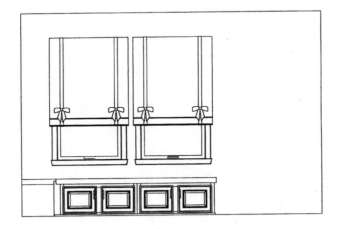

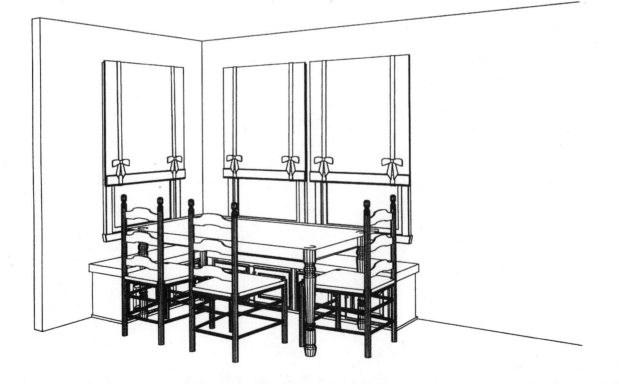

Mini Server

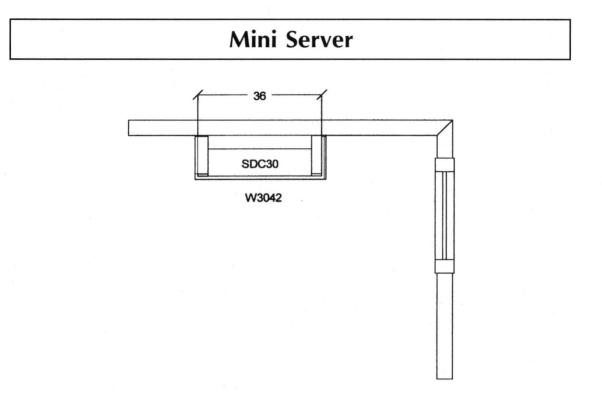

Cabinet List:

1 30″×42″ high wall cabinet
1 30″ wide spice drawer unit with matching wood knobs
2 3″×42″ fluted fillers
1 3″×15″ fluted filler cut to two 6″ pieces
2 60″×12 3/4″ finished shelves
1 6″×90″ filler
1 8′-0″ inside corner molding
2 knobs or pulls
1 pint stain
1 putty stick

Additional Materials Needed:

- Miscellaneous fasteners and adhesives
- Dimensional lumber
- 2 granite countertops, 3/4″ thick

Required:

- A 36″×4″ high platform made from dimensional lumber
- Finish platform with furniture toe treatment
- Trim finished shelves as returns for fluted fillers

Variations:

- Add mullion doors, matching interiors, and glass inserts to the bottom cabinet
- Use bunn feet instead of furniture base

Perfect as a small bar area or for extra storage in a dining area, this mini server is inspired by an antique occasional piece. Give it a two-tone look by keeping the upper and lower cabinets in a light wood and choosing the fluted fillers in a darker stain.

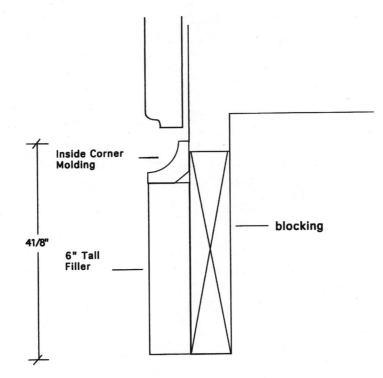

Inside Corner
Molding

blocking

41/8"

6" Tall
Filler

Multipurpose Attached Island

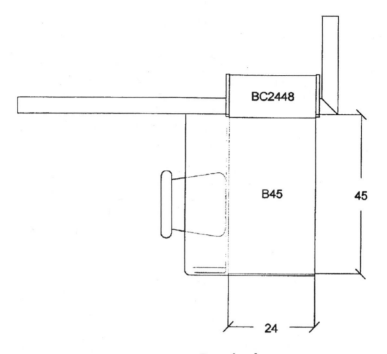

Cabinet List:

1 45″ base cabinet
1 piece 48″×34 1/2″ paneling
1 8′-0″ outside corner molding
1 24″×48″ bookcase
1 24″ wide straight appliance garage
1 tall filler (split)
1 8′-0″ toe kick material
1 toe kick cap cover
1 corbel
4 knobs or pulls
1 pint stain
1 putty stick

Additional Materials Needed:

- Miscellaneous fasteners and adhesives
- Substrate to reinforce paneling applied to back of island
- Flat-deck countertop with overhang
- Stool with 24″ high seat

Required:

- Recess in wall to accommodate bookcase and appliance garage
- Recess should be a minimum of 2″ wider than the cabinets to allow for 1″ fillers at each side
- Clip or round the corner of the countertop to soften the point

Variations:

- Add a base skin and a decorator matching door to the exposed end of the base cabinet

This island, attached to a kitchen wall, serves not only as a great bake center but also makes a snack bar for one. It can also serve as a convenient place for a child to do homework while the parent is preparing a meal. An area that serves so many purposes is a bargain!

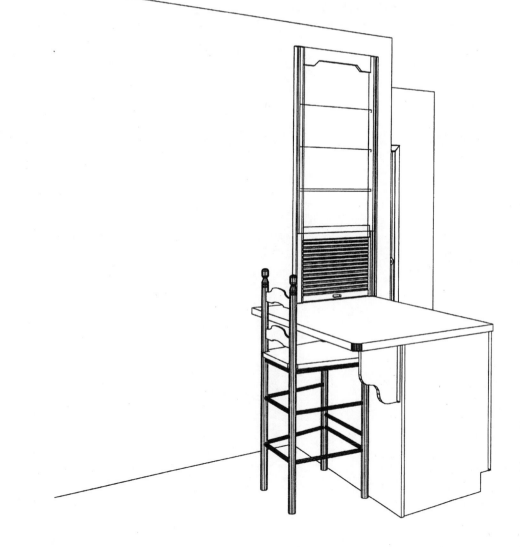

Old-Fashioned Butlers' Pantry

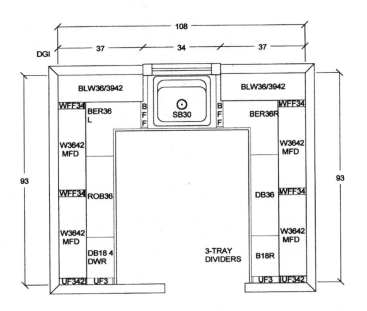

Cabinet List:

4 36″×42″ wall cabinets with mullion doors and matching interiors
2 36″/39″×42″ blind wall cabinets with mullion doors and matching interiors
2 42″ high wall fillers
12 clear glass inserts
4 42″ high fluted wall fillers
2 base fluted fillers
1 18″ wide four-drawer base
1 36″ wide base cabinet with rollout shelves
2 base corner cabinets (with or without lazy susans)
1 30″ sink base
1 36″ wide drawer base
1 18″ base cabinet
2 base fillers
4 8′-0″ pieces crown molding
3 8′-0″ pieces base toe kick material
32 knobs or pulls
1 pint stain
1 putty stick

Additional Materials Needed:

• Miscellaneous fasteners and adhesives
• Countertop
• Single-bowl sink and faucet

Required:

• Fillers at each wall and at the base of the U to allow for out-of-square conditions

Variations:

• Adjust to fit job-site conditions
• Change mullion doors to open-frame or solid doors
• A full-height backsplash is appropriate for this room but a standard 4″ height will work well, too

This old-fashioned butlers' pantry provides space to store food, dishes, and serving pieces. The sink makes a great place for flower arranging, too. By adding a microwave, warming drawer, a two-burner cooktop, and ventilation, this space turns into a perfect caterer's kitchen.

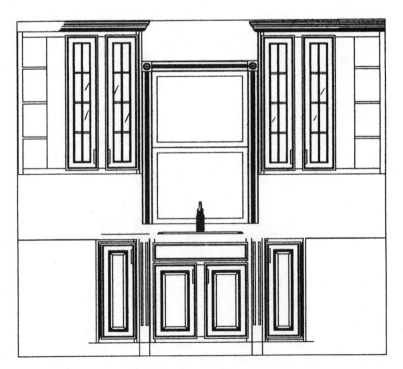

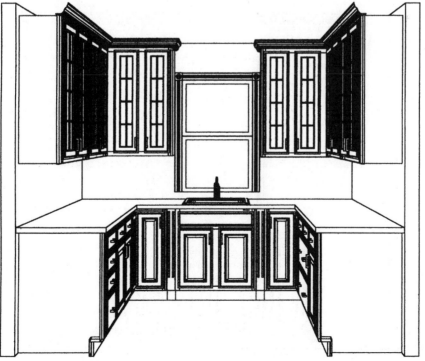

Open Hutch with Spice Drawers

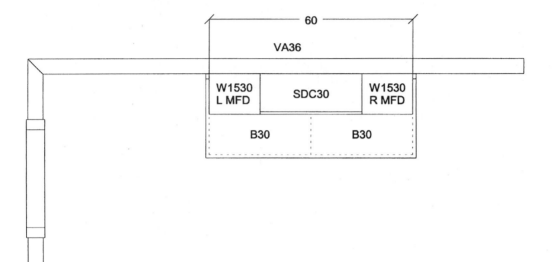

Cabinet List:

2 15″×30″ wall cabinets with mullion doors and matching interiors
1 48″ finished shelf (trimmed)
2 tempered glass inserts
1 36″ arched valance (trimmed)
1 30″ spice drawer unit with matching wood knobs
1 piece 30″×30″ paneling
2 30″ base cabinets
1 8′-0″ crown molding
1 8′-0″ base toe kick material
2 toe kick cap covers
10 knobs or pulls
1 pint stain
1 putty stick

Additional Materials Needed:

• Miscellaneous fasteners and adhesives
• Countertop

Required:

• Trim finished shelf as soffit board with arched valance in front
• Panel wall above spice drawers

Variations:

• Add decorator matching doors to exposed cabinet ends
• Use a matching wood countertop
• Use beadboard paneling in place of plain paneling
• Add in-cabinet lighting and glass shelves to mullion door cabinets

The open area of the upper section of the hutch provides display place for artwork or collectibles. A shelf can be added above the spice drawers, if desired. This hutch would add charm and extra storage to a kitchen or informal eating area.

Recessed Niches

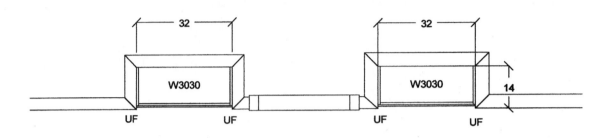

Cabinet List:

2 30″×30″ wall cabinets used as bases
1 8′-0″ beveled countertop edge molding
4 base fillers
2 arched valances
3 72″ finished shelves cut into six 32″ shelves
4 72″ shelves as vertical members
4 knobs or pulls
1 pint stain
1 putty stick

Additional Materials Needed:

- Miscellaneous fasteners and adhesives
- 2 flat-deck countertops 13″ deep
- Dimensional lumber to block up the cabinets 3/4″
- Shelf pins

Required:

- Finished opening must be 32″ wide to accommodate 1″ fillers at each lower wall cabinet

- Finished depth of niches should be a minimum of 14″ to allow for countertop overhang and ease of fit
- For door swing clearance, hold the cabinets up 3/4″ and finish with beveled countertop edge molding
- Drill vertical members to accept shelf pins

Variations:

- Finish the edge of the shelves with decorative molding
- Finish the rear wall with matching paneling or paint it a vibrant color
- Shelves can be glass or other material. Be sure to check with supplier for maximum width and stress loads

When space can be taken from an adjacent room, these recessed niches add a dramatic space to a dining room. This matching pair is made from wall cabinets used as base cabinets and finished shelving. Countertops can be made from either matching wood, solid surface, or even marble.

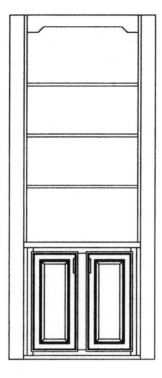

Recessed Server with Framed Mirror

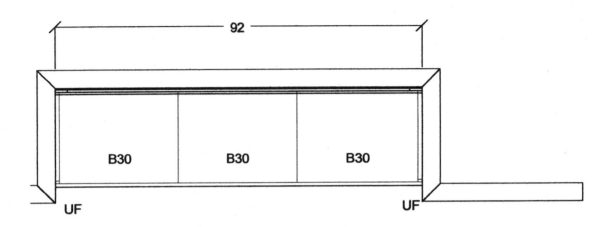

Cabinet List:

3 30" base cabinets
1 base filler (split left and right)
2 42" high fluted fillers
1 3" tall filler as top mirror trim
1 base toe kick material
12 knobs or pulls
1 pint stain
1 putty stick

Additional Materials Needed:

• Miscellaneous fasteners and adhesives
• Dimensional lumber and drywall to build soffit
• Countertop with backsplash to accommodate electrical outlets
• Mirror
• 2 recessed light fixtures

Required:

• Finished opening of the wall should be 2" larger than the cabinets to allow for minimum 1" fillers at each wall

• Soffit with recessed lights
• Recess that is a minimum of 27" deep
• Trim fillers to frame mirror

Variations:

• Adjust cabinet width to accommodate job-site conditions
• Add two full-width rollout trays to each base cabinet
• Add cutlery divider(s)

A recessed server with a deep, lighted soffit above provides dining area storage without taking up a lot of floor space. Best used in new construction where the recess can be incorporated into the overall house plan. A similar unit can also be surface-mounted for remodeling projects.

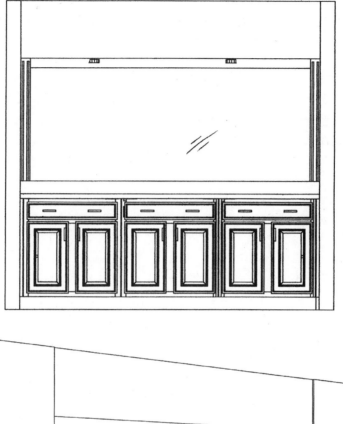

Room Dividers

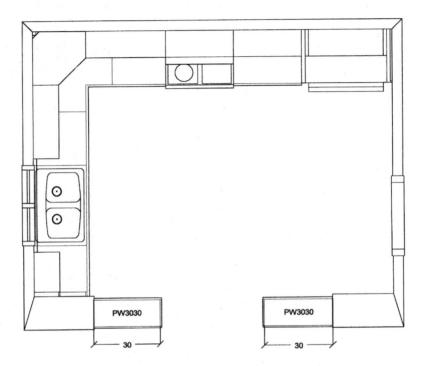

Cabinet List:

2 30"×30" peninsula wall cabinets
2 wall skins
2 decorator matching doors
2 6"×96" fillers
2 inside corner molding
4 knobs or pulls
1 pint stain
1 putty stick

Additional Materials Needed:

- Miscellaneous fasteners and adhesives
- 2 countertops
- Dimensional lumber to build platform

Required:

- 4" high platform to support the peninsula wall cabinets

- Furniture toe treatment fabricated from fillers and inside corner molding

Variations:

- Add columns on top of the countertop up to a header or ceiling for a traditional look
- Add mullion doors, matching interiors, and tempered glass inserts to create display cabinets

A pair of room dividers made from peninsula wall cabinets, that open from both sides, is a perfect arrangement for loading dishes from the kitchen side and unloading them in the adjacent breakfast area. If a caddy is added for flatware and napkins, even young children can set the table all by themselves.

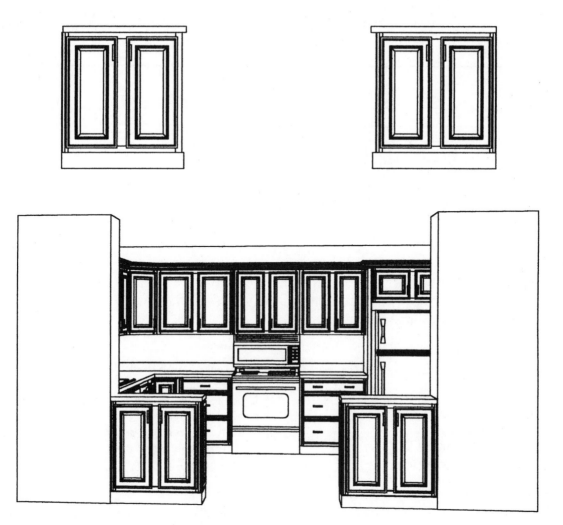

Rustic Hutch

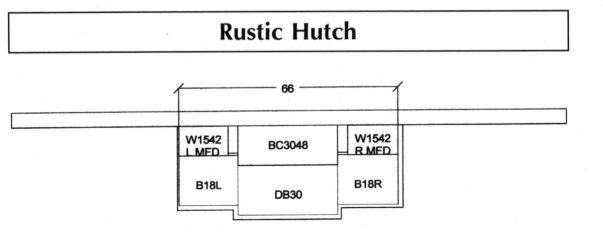

Cabinet List:

2 15″×42″ wall cabinets, reduced to 9″ deep, with mullion doors and matching interiors
2 tempered glass inserts
2 42″ fluted fillers
4 rosettes
1 30″×48″ bookcase unit
2 18″ base cabinets
1 30″ drawer base
1 8′-0″ crown molding
1 8′-0″ base toe material
4 toekick cap covers
12 knobs or pulls
1 pint stain
1 putty stick

Additional Materials Needed:

• Miscellaneous fasteners and adhesives
• Matching wood countertop

Required:

• Pull drawer base forward 3″

Variations:

• Add decorator matching doors to exposed ends
• Change from mullion door to open-frame cabinets
• Add glass shelving and in-cabinet lighting
• Panel rear of bookcase unit with beadboard paneling

Compact and charming, this rustic hutch would work well in hickory wood for a true country look. The center drawer base cabinet is pulled forward 3″ for design interest and additional countertop space. The reduced depth mullion door cabinets repeat the double depth theme of the base.

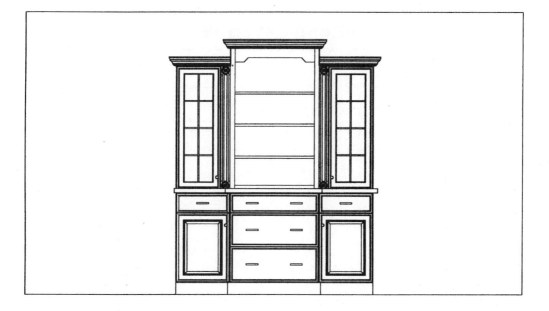

Shaker-Inspired Hutch

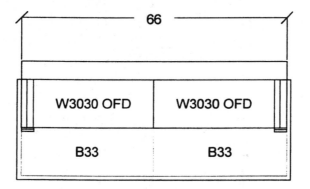

Cabinet List:

2 33″ base cabinets
2 30″×30″ wall cabinets with open-frame doors and matching interiors
2 shelf undercabinet organizers
4 tempered glass inserts
1 piece 60″×15″ paneling
2 96″ tall refrigerator returns
3 3″×96″ tall fillers
1 8′-0″ toe kick material
2 toe kick cap covers
12 knobs or pulls
1 pint stain
1 putty stick

Additional Materials Needed:

- Miscellaneous fasteners and adhesives
- Wood countertop to match hutch

Required:

- Trim refrigerator returns to 48″ high, install two together for overall width of 3″
- Cover refrigerator returns with tall fillers trimmed to fit
- Install remaining tall fillers as top molding treatment

Variations:

- Replace clear glass with shirred fabric mounted on sash rods attached to the inside of the door
- Use granite or other durable countertop material if the hutch is placed in the kitchen
- Use simple crown molding, in place of the filler, as the top molding treatment

Inspired by the simple functionality of Shaker design, this hutch adds charm to dining rooms, breakfast nooks, or the kitchen. The design incorporates undercabinet organizers, usually thought of as desk pigeonholes, to store spices and other small collectibles.

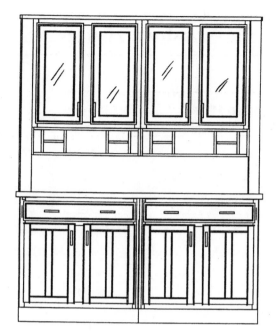

Shallow Hutch

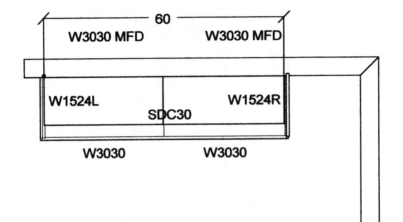

Cabinet List:

2 30″×30″ wall cabinets with mullion doors and matching interiors
4 tempered glass inserts
2 15″×24″ wall cabinets
1 30″ spice drawer cabinet with matching wood knobs
1 72″ scalloped valance trimmed to fit as base
1 48″ straight valance as base returns
1 8′-0″ base toe kick material
2 8′-0″ inside corner molding
1 8′-0″ crown molding
1 piece paneling 30″×24″
2 base skins
2 tall skins split and trimmed
10 knobs or pulls
1 pint stain
1 putty stick

Additional Materials Needed:

• Miscellaneous fasteners and adhesives
• Optional black paint
• Countertop
• Dimensional lumber

Required:

• Construct a 4″ high by 12″ deep platform for wall cabinets used as bases
• Cover base with base toe kick material or paint it black to make it disappear
• Pull and block base cabinets 3″ from wall and panel sides back to wall with base skins
• Create furniture toe treatment with valances topped with inside corner molding

Variations:

• Use reduced-depth base cabinets as the hutch base
• Select open-frame doors and shirred fabric or other inserts

When space is at a premium, this shallow hutch can be just the answer. The top portion can be any configuration desired, and the base can be made from economical wall cabinets pulled 3″ from the wall, as shown. Or choose reduced-depth base cabinets, but whichever is selected, finish off the toe with a furniture treatment made from valances and inside corner molding.

Snack Bar Peninsula

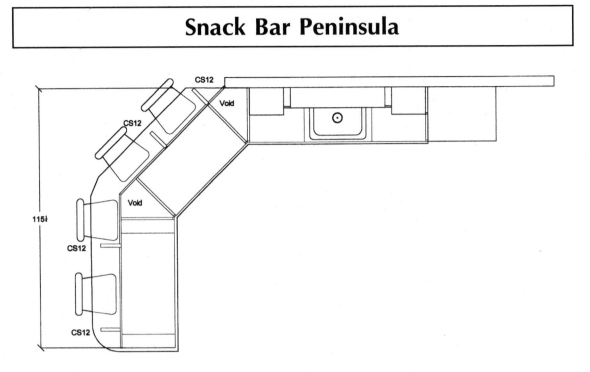

Cabinet List:

Peninsula cabinets in an angled configuration

4 corbels
2 pieces 96″×34 1/2″ paneling
1 outside corner molding
1 pint stain
1 putty stick

Additional Materials Needed:

- Miscellaneous fasteners and adhesives
- Countertop designed with an overhang
- Dimensional lumber
- Substrate to reinforce back of island behind finished paneling
- Stools with 24″ high seats

Required:

- Minimum 24″ per person of eating space
- Minimum of 12″ countertop overhang

Variations:

- Finish rear of peninsula with decorator matching doors or wainscoting detail
- Adjust size of peninsula to suit job-site conditions

The angle created by this peninsula eating area is more conducive to mealtime conversation than stools arranged in a perfectly straight line. Since the kitchen countertop and snack bar are both at the same level, the area feels more spacious. It easily accommodates all the serving pieces and condiments that comprise a typical family meal.

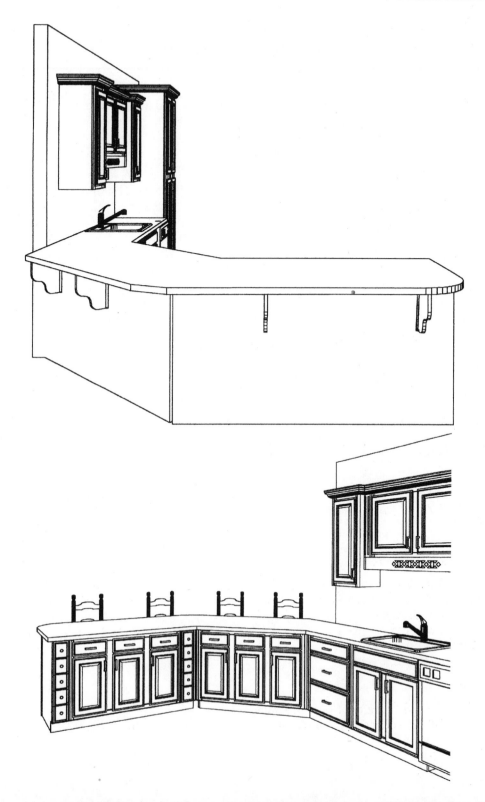

Table Surround

Cabinet List:

2 12″×24″×84″ utility cabinets
12 utility cabinet shelves
1 30″×30″ wall cabinet
1 15″×30″ wall cabinet
1 tall filler
2 8′-0″ crown molding
1 8′-0″ light rail
1 48″ finished shelf
1 base toe kick material
3 toe kick caps
11 knobs or pulls
1 pint stain
1 putty stick

Additional Materials Needed:

- Miscellaneous fasteners and adhesives
- Table and chairs

Required:

- Minimum 1″ filler at wall
- For chair clearance, allow at least 36″ between table and nearest wall

- Install finished shelf on bottom of wall cabinets

Variations:

- Mullion doors and matching interiors on center cabinets
- Panel or wainscot the entire wall between the tall cabinets
- Add decorator matching doors on the exposed cabinet end
- Adjust center cabinets to accommodate table width

Two 12″ deep pantries and additional wall cabinet storage would be welcome in almost any home. A side benefit of the surround is that even a small dining area will feel larger when the table is placed against a wall. If company comes, the table can be pulled out and an extra chair placed at each end.

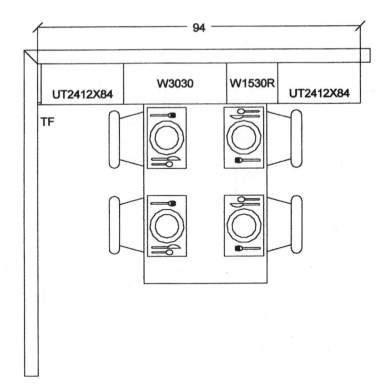

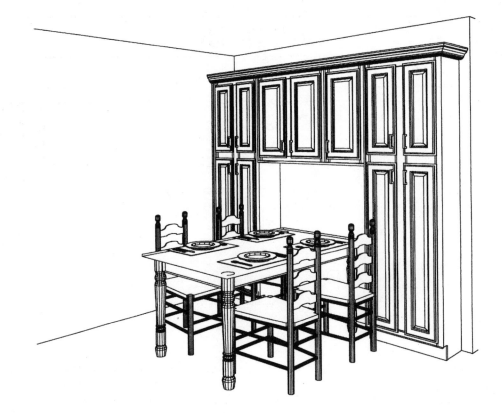

Tall Divider

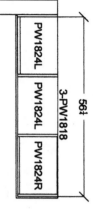

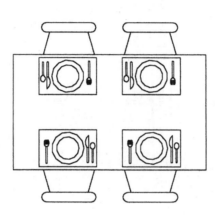

Cabinet List:

7 72″ finished shelves
3 18″×18″ peninsula wall cabinets
3 18″×24″ peninsula wall cabinets
2 8′-0″ crown molding
2 tall fillers
2 8′-0″ inside corner molding
12 knobs or pulls
1 pint stain
1 putty stick

Additional Materials Needed:

- Miscellaneous fasteners and adhesives
- Dimensional lumber

Required:

- Build a 4″ high platform for unit
- Cover platform with furniture toe of filler and inside corner molding

- Install four finished shelves as verticals
- Cut three finished shelves to cover tops and bottoms of the 18″ wall cabinets
- Attach to wall at side

Variations:

- 18″×18″ wall cabinets can be arranged in other configurations
- Add a soffit above the cabinets
- Add decorator matching doors to exposed end

Because peninsula cabinets open from both the front and back, this wall divider is identical on both sides. Open cubbyholes provide space to show off art objects or books. This unit is not recommended for freestanding installation.

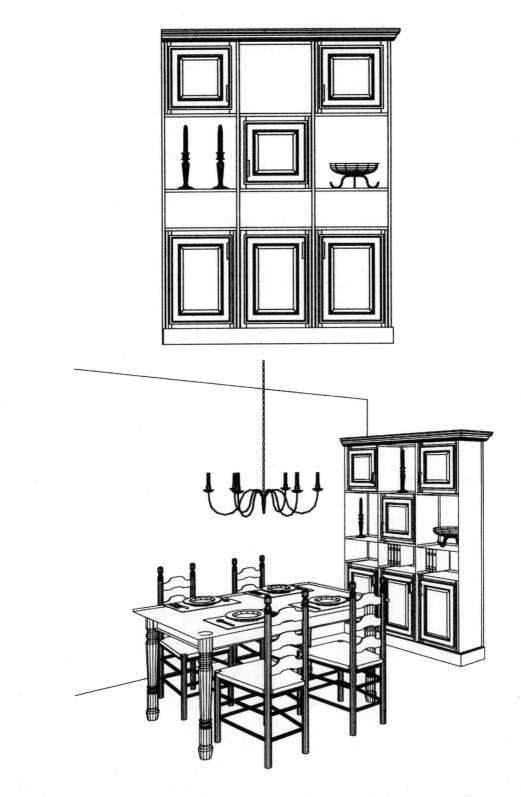

Traditional Hutch

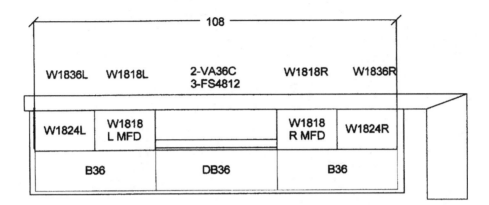

Cabinet List:

2 36″ base cabinet
2 base skins
1 36″ drawer base
2 18″×24″ wall cabinets
2 18″×36″ wall cabinets
2 tall skins (split)
2 42″ high skins (trimmed)
2 18″×18″ wall cabinets
2 18″×18″ wall cabinets with mullion doors and matching interiors
2 tempered glass inserts
2 36″ arched valances
1 36″ finished shelf trimmed to 9″
2 36″ finished shelves trimmed to 8 1/4″ deep
1 36″×34″ piece of paneling
1 72″×30″ piece of paneling
1 tall filler as backsplash
2 8′-0″ crown molding
2 8′-0″ base toe kick material
2 toe kick cap covers
22 knobs or pulls
1 pint stain
1 putty stick

Additional Materials Needed:

• Miscellaneous fasteners and adhesives
• Countertop

Required:

• Cover all exposed ends with skins
• Panel the wall behind the open shelves and above countertop
• Use tall filler as backsplash

Variations:

• Change from mullion to open-frame doors
• Add decorator matching doors to exposed cabinet ends
• Add two full-width rollout trays to each base cabinet
• Add cutlery divider(s)

This expansive hutch can be outfitted with rollout trays and cutlery dividers to customized the storage to meet individual needs. The use of stacked 18″ square cabinets instead of a single cabinet adds charm and just a hint of glass in this 9′ long super hutch.

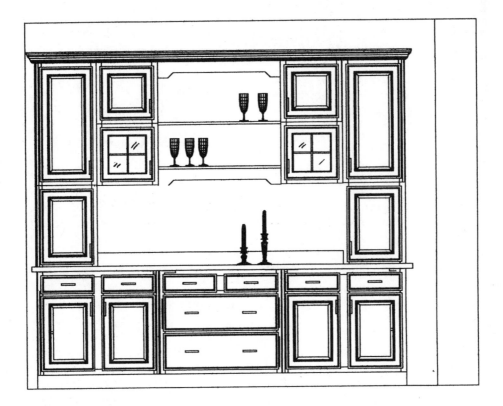

CHAPTER 10

Cabinetry for Every Purpose in Your Luxury Home

The kitchen has long been the heart of the home. It has even become control central for most families. From here we pay bills, oversee homework, and post the family schedules. But kitchen cabinets are no longer relegated to only that space. They have moved out into all areas of the home, giving more storage and adding more style than ever before.

Rooms designed with a specific purpose are not new. Laundry rooms, libraries, and game rooms have been around a long time. New homes are being designed with special spaces for extra storage, hobbies, or home offices. Unused bedrooms in existing homes are being converted to better uses. Garages are being organized to hold gardening supplies and auto care items. Rooms with well thought-out built-ins give any space the feeling of being organized, and the absence of clutter helps create a stress-free environment. The question is, what has caused this expansion of cabinetry throughout the home?

The buying public received the architect's introduction of the open floor plan with overwhelming approval. The concept fits our busy lifestyles and the move to less formal living environments. It is this change in housing that has driven the concept of built-ins made from cabinetry. When the kitchen is open to the family room, surrounding the television with cabinetry of the same wood and finish makes the two rooms flow seam-lessly together. It works the same way if the kitchen opens to the dining area. There, your choices are hutches, servers, and breakfronts all made from the same modular cabinetry that is in the kitchen.

Another key factor is the increased cabinet quality offered by many manufacturers. Stock cabinet manufacturers have stepped up to the plate, offering features and finishes that used to be considered custom. Dovetail drawers, rich moldings, and furniture-grade finishes are the accepted norm. Gone are the days of utilitarian boxes that had to be tucked away in the scullery. Cabinetry has evolved to keep pace with lifestyle changes, providing storage of every kind.

It is a given fact that no home ever has enough storage. The question is often where to put the CD collection or what to do with the newly purchased set of dinnerware? But storage, in and of itself, is not a sufficient reason to add built-ins to a home. They must also fit with the overall look and theme of the home. In part, that comes from the selection of the appropriate door style, finish, and decorative hardware. After that, built-ins can be customized by the selection of moldings or other decorative elements such as mullion doors and the overall the cabinet arrangement.

In this chapter, we will look at a beautiful 4,500-square foot luxury home with a dozen rooms of built-in cabinetry. And that does not include the kitchen. We will focus on seven of those rooms and take a quick look at the kitchen, too. The home office is just steps away from the kitchen and has its own private entry (see Fig. 10-1a). The spacious master bath hints at the spa lifestyle with separate his and hers vanities. Even the laundry is treated to some special features.

The second-floor of the home features a built-in linen storage. True to the lifestyles of today, an alcove in the upstairs hall is used for a computer station. Beyond the alcove are a loft library (see Fig. 10-1b) and an imagination room for young and old alike. Sprinkled throughout the rest of the home are bathroom vanities and a garden suite with nearly a full kitchen for a nanny, in-law, or bounce-back kid. This home shows how modular cabinetry can enhance nearly every room in the home and make it a better place to be.

Kitchen

Here stock cabinets in the kitchen provide a dramatic backdrop for contemporary lifestyle. Special features include the pulled forward sink base, with an arched toe detail and fluted fillers on either side. Stacked cabinets balance the tall ceiling height and are embellished with decorator matching doors on exposed ends.

Home Office

This corner workstation in cherry makes working at home a pleasure. Fluted fillers,

decorator matching doors, and stacked cabinetry lend a rich look. The wall behind the computer monitor is paneled with a wainscoting detail.

Master Bathroom

The resort-like feeling of this master bathroom is enhanced by the spacious his and her vanity areas. A special feature is the use of wall cabinets built up on platforms as storage for toiletries, instead of traditional medicine cabinets.

Laundry Room

Never before was doing laundry such an organized process and so much fun. The appliance garage conceals detergents and the spice drawers hold mending supplies and small gadgets. The niche below the counter

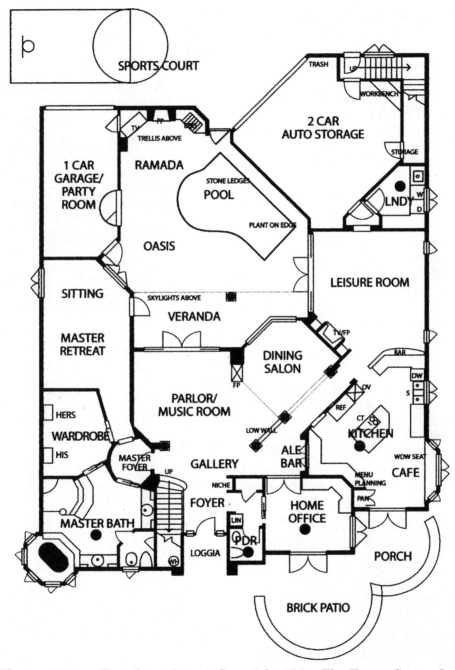

Figure 10-1a   First-floor plan. © Copyright 2000, The Evans Group, Inc.
All Rights Reserved.

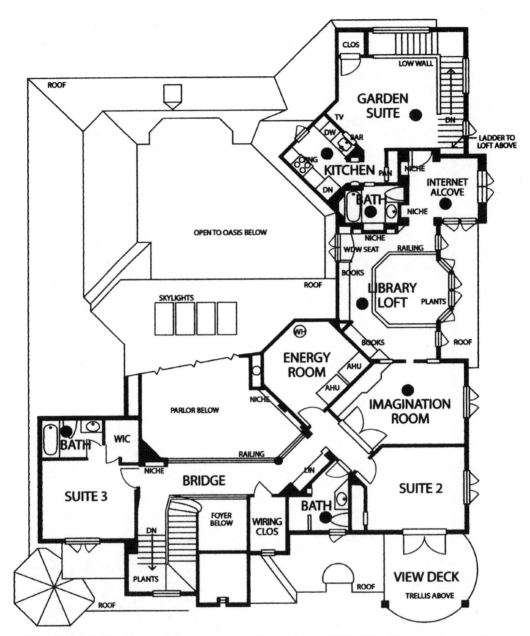

Figure 10-1*b*   Second-floor plan. © Copyright 2000, The Evans Group, Inc.
All Rights Reserved.

could even become a place to put the pet bed for the family puppy.

Library

An extra wide hallway was pressed into use as a library. Bookcases show off collectibles as well as books. The top row of cabinets feature mullion doors, matching interiors, and interior cabinet lighting for a warm glow. The base cabinetry is actually wall cabinets pulled forward and given a furniture toe treatment.

Linen Storage

A recessed niche in the upstairs hall was fitted with built-in cabinetry for extra linen storage. This additional storage makes it easy to stock up on sale items and for every member to have space of their own to store toiletries.

Imagination Room

In the fifties it used to be called the playroom, but this room takes the concept to a new level with a worktable and bookcases to hold finished craft projects. Ample storage conceals materials for school projects and crafts.

Internet Nook

True to today's lifestyles, even the upstairs hall can be transformed into a space for a computer. The knee space is extra wide to accommodate a parent and child surfing the Internet together. The tambour storage conceals paperwork and keeps the area tidy.

CHAPTER 11

Details, Details, Details

Good cabinetry design consists of a series of large and small details that make up the whole. Throughout this book examples of the larger components are illustrated: stacking, staggering, pulling, and reducing cabinet depth all add to the visual appeal of any built-in. We have also illustrated that one of the easiest ways to give interest to a cabinet arrangement is to add mullion or open-frame doors to one or two feature wall cabinets. While clear tempered glass is the standard insert for these cabinets, other choices are available that will produce a unique look. Among the possibilities are shirred fabric, textured or colored glass, and metal or wire mesh inserts. Stock manufacturers do not typically include such items in their standard offering. See the Appendix listing sources for inserts and other interesting components that will enhance any built-in.

In this chapter, we'll look at many of the smaller, yet critical, details that have a major impact on the success of any design. For example, well-crafted top molding treatments will take any group of cabinets from plain to knockout status. For simplicity's sake, the illustrations in this book show a simple layer of crown molding as the top embellishment. But moldings can be combined in many ways and this chapter will show you several combinations. Moldings are one of the easiest

ways to achieve a richly detailed look on even a simple built-in.

Some of the details in this chapter are simple, like layering fluted filler over standard filler. Others involve fairly complicated molding combinations. There are details that are purely for beauty and others, like light rail molding, also serve a function by concealing undercabinet lighting. Look for special base toe treatment details or consider adding wainscoting to the back of a desk for a men's-club look. No matter which, or how many you choose, interesting details all work their design magic.

One of the most important factors in the success of details is the quality of the installation. Nothing takes the place of a well-cut miter. Even after the perfect cut is achieved, all of the raw miter joints should be stained to insure that the joint remains unobtrusive even after normal expansion and contraction occurs.

Adding details does increase the project cost, but it is often in the details that the built-in really shines. It is these well-chosen touches that fill the owners with a sense of pride every time they see their entertainment center or other built-in. It is in the details where it often becomes difficult to tell the difference between custom and high-quality stock cabinets.

Top Molding Details

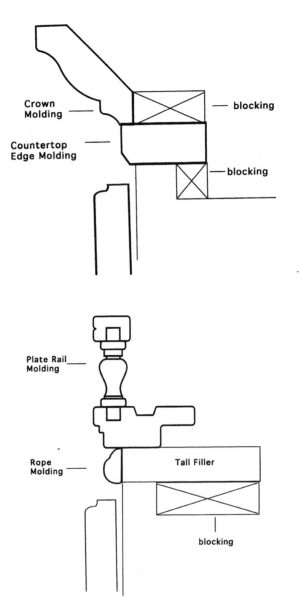

Crown
Molding

Countertop
Edge Molding

blocking

blocking

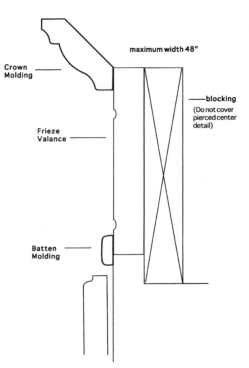

Crown
Molding

maximum width 48"

Frieze
Valance

Batten
Molding

blocking
(Do not cover
pierced center
detail)

Plate Rail
Molding

Rope
Molding

Tall Filler

blocking

Top Molding Treatment

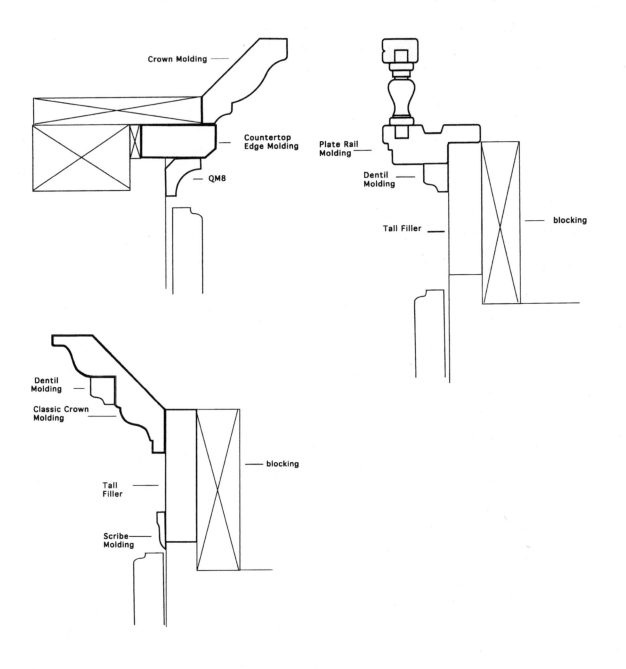

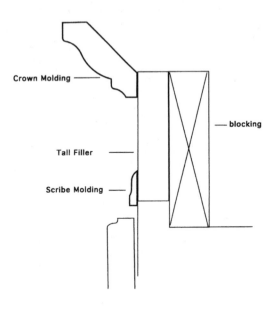

Crown Molding

blocking

Tall Filler

Scribe Molding

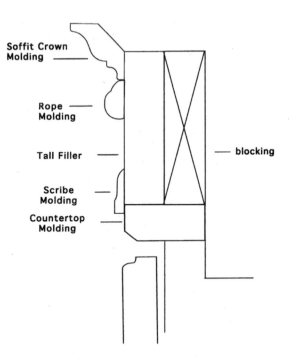

Soffit Crown Molding

Rope Molding

Tall Filler

blocking

Scribe Molding

Countertop Molding

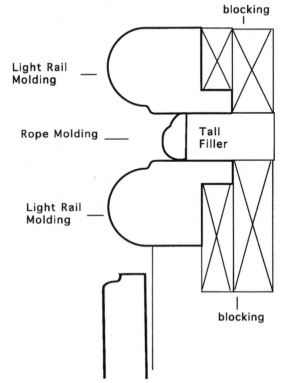

blocking

Light Rail Molding

Rope Molding

Tall Filler

Light Rail Molding

blocking

Light Rail Treatments

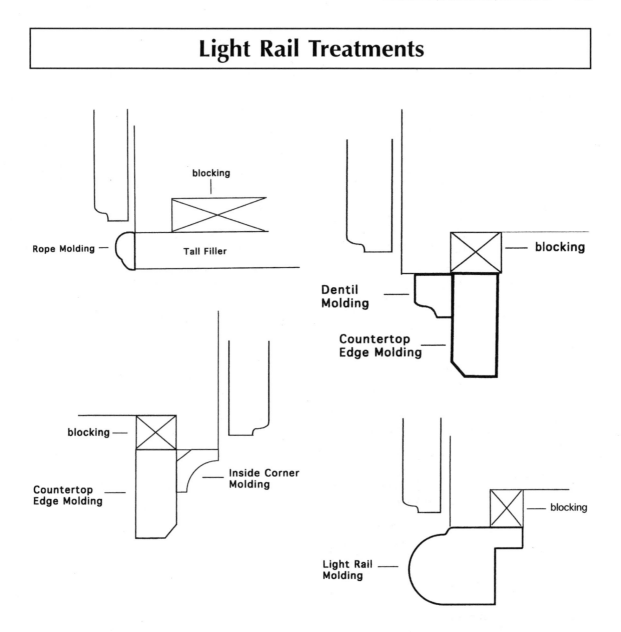

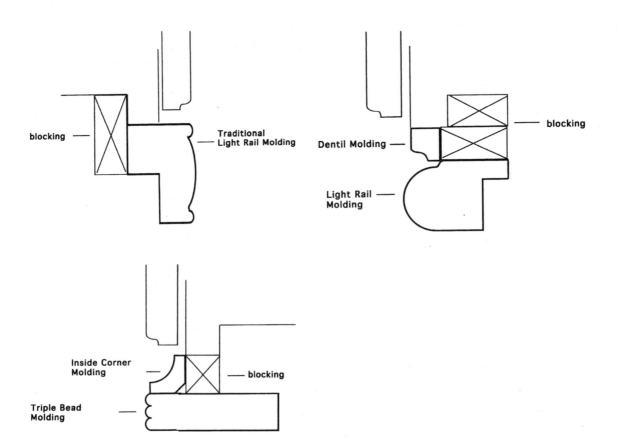

blocking — Traditional Light Rail Molding

Dentil Molding — blocking — Light Rail Molding

Inside Corner Molding — blocking — Triple Bead Molding

Base Treatments

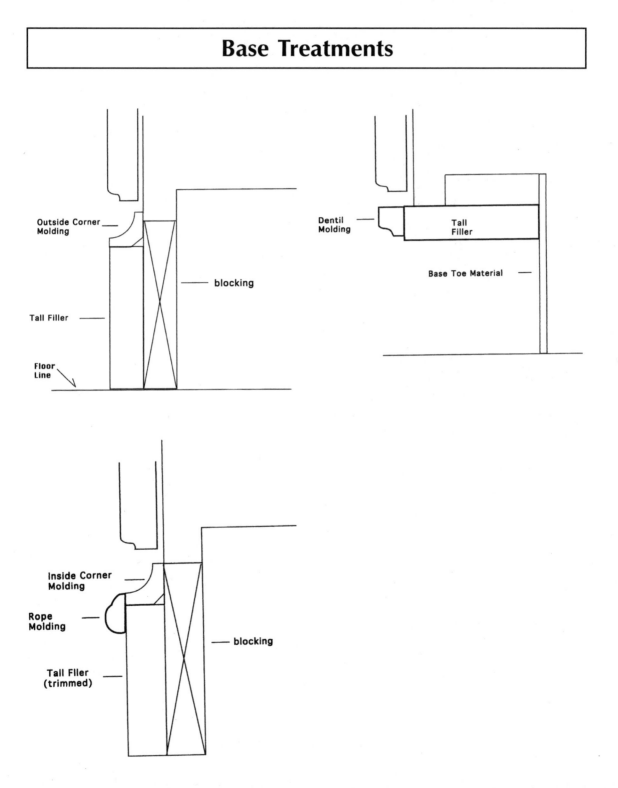

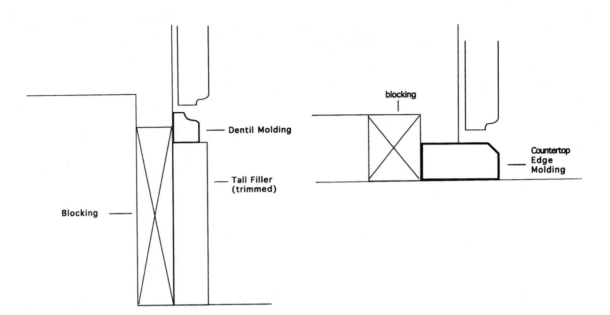

Dentil Molding

Tall Filler
(trimmed)

Blocking

blocking

Countertop
Edge
Molding

Other Details

Layered Fluted Filler

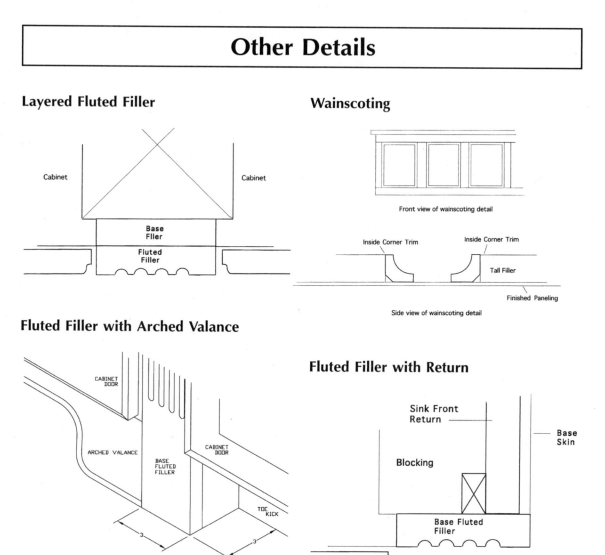

Cabinet

Cabinet

Base
Filler

Fluted
Filler

Wainscoting

Front view of wainscoting detail

Inside Corner Trim

Inside Corner Trim

Tall Filler

Finished Paneling

Side view of wainscoting detail

Fluted Filler with Arched Valance

CABINET
DOOR

ARCHED VALANCE

BASE
FLUTED
FILLER

CABINET
DOOR

TOE
KICK

3

3

Fluted Filler with Return

Sink Front
Return

Base
Skin

Blocking

Base Fluted
Filler

Wood Countertop

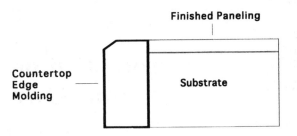

Finished Paneling

Countertop
Edge
Molding

Substrate

Wood Countertop with Rope Molding Edge

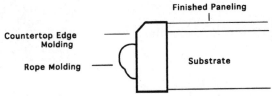

Finished Paneling

Countertop Edge
Molding

Rope Molding

Substrate

Wood Countertop with Crown Molding Detail

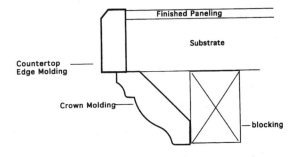

Finished Paneling

Substrate

Countertop
Edge Molding

Crown Molding

blocking

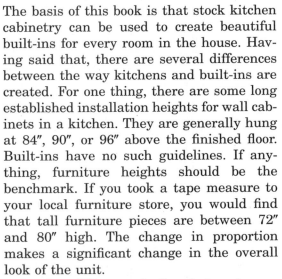

CHAPTER 12

Striking Out on Your Own

The basis of this book is that stock kitchen cabinetry can be used to create beautiful built-ins for every room in the house. Having said that, there are several differences between the way kitchens and built-ins are created. For one thing, there are some long established installation heights for wall cabinets in a kitchen. They are generally hung at 84″, 90″, or 96″ above the finished floor. Built-ins have no such guidelines. If anything, furniture heights should be the benchmark. If you took a tape measure to your local furniture store, you would find that tall furniture pieces are between 72″ and 80″ high. The change in proportion makes a significant change in the overall look of the unit.

Another difference is the choice of countertop materials. If the built-in is more decorative than functional, a matching wood countertop is the first choice. Most stock companies will not offer them. But they can be fabricated from substrate, countertop edge molding and finished paneling. See Chapter 11, *Details, Details, Details* for several ideas. If the built-in surface is subject to heavy use, select one of the beautiful solid surface countertop materials or a natural stone such as granite.

A third difference between built-in and kitchen installations is the overall proportion of the unit. Kitchen countertops are standard at 36″ high, but other-room furniture varies to suit the intended use. Entertainment centers often have the base cabinets significantly lower so that the television is at the eye-level of a seated viewer. Hutches may have base sections that are less than 36″, too, because no one is going to stand and work at them for extended periods of time.

Adapting Designs

Every design in this book can be varied to suit personal preference or job-site conditions. Some designs in this book are shown installed between walls. If the built-in is to be installed by itself on a longer wall, additional finished material for the sides will be required.

There are some basics that never change however:

- The dimensions and other requirements of the audio-visual equipment or appliances must be known before the design is even begun. Appliances and audio-visual equipment sizes, clearances and tolerances will actually drive the design and must be accounted for from the very beginning.
- Use a minimum of a 1″ filler at each wall for free movement of doors and drawers after installation. This also helps to compensate for out of square wall conditions.
- Always securely screw the units together and to the wall.
- For simplicity, most of the designs are shown in a square raised panel design, but they can be adapted to nearly any door style. If you are creating a built-in with a stacked cathedral style wall combination, order the bottom cabinet in a square style. It gives a grounded, more stable look that is pleasing to the eye.

Finding Inspiration

The homeowner or end user is the single biggest (and best) source for inspiration. Their requirements will dictate the final design. You may begin with a design from this book and then find that their needs cause the design to go in another direction. That is what good built-in design is all about, tailoring a project to a specific need or desire.

Other sources of ideas are antiques. They were the inspiration for the Hoosier Hutch and the Barrister Bookcase shown in this book. And finally, most cabinet suppliers can provide you with plans for built-ins that they have created in the past.

Stacking

Many interesting cabinet combinations can be created by artistically arranging the standard components in a stock cabinet line. Two methods are stacking and staggering the cabinetry. Usually, this is more commonly used in wall cabinet arrangements, but they can be useful techniques in base cabinet designs too. Figure 12-1 shows how to create a tall bookcase by combining a wall cabinet and a bookcase unit. They are shown installed on a platform with an arched valance toe detail.

When stacking cabinets, it is best to vary the heights of the combined cabinets. Figure 12-2 illustrates a short over long combination. Figure 12-3 depicts a long over short arrangement. The cabinets shown in both drawings are 18″ and 30″ tall. These sizes create a 3:5 ratio, which is a visually appealing combination.

Changing the façade of just one section can eliminate the monotony of a long, straight run of cabinets. Figure 12-4 shows how a spice drawer unit can be incorporated into a stacked arrangement breaking up a

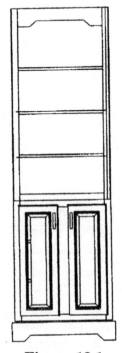

Figure 12-1

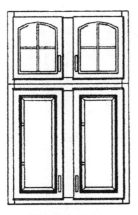

Figure 12-2

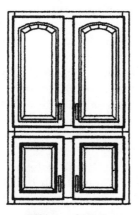

Figure 12-3

Figure 12-4

Figure 12-5

cabinets that mathematically add up to the correct height.

When the stacked cabinets are on the end of a cabinet run they require a skin be applied to the exposed side. This conceals the joint. Even though stock cabinets come with finished ends, once a side is skinned, skin all exposed sides for continuity. Adding decorator matching doors gives additional richness to the design.

Staggering

Varying cabinet heights is another way to add visual appeal. The upper section of an entertainment center is shown in Fig. 12-6. The center section is raised approximately 4″ above the adjacent cabinets. The trick here is to make the taller cabinet deeper, too. That allows the molding from the lower cabinets to butt neatly into the side of the taller cabinet. If the molding treatment is a build-up of several layers, the difference in cabinet height must exceed the total molding height.

Pulling

Sometimes base cabinets are pulled to create an interesting layout. Other times, they are pulled forward to accommodate the depth of a television. When a base cabinet is pulled forward, it is often referred to as a coastline.

straight cabinet line. Figure 12-5 illustrates a 12″ high wall cabinet combined with a 30″ high mullion door cabinet. On either side are 42″ high cabinets. The secret is selecting

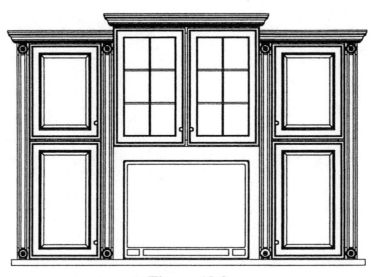

Figure 12-6

A wall cabinet may be pulled for function or to create the desired look. Pulled wall cabinets will require blocking behind them to help support the cabinet. The sides must also be covered, by finished panels or skins, to conceal the blocking. Finishing the bottom of an extended wall cabinet is often a good idea, too.

Finishing Touches

Once the basic layout has been done, enhance the built-in by choosing the right decorative hardware, adding fluted fillers or a creative molding treatment. A variety of sources exist that offer everything from interesting materials for open-frame doors to swivel shelves for entertainment centers. Your choices are almost limitless.

One Final Tip

If you are using white cabinetry, keep the design simple. Molding build-ups should be no more than two layers and avoid very complicated designs. White shows every less-than-perfect installation detail. Natural or stained wood seems to be far more forgiving in this area and should be considered when a large or highly detailed design is selected.

Glossary

A.F.F.: Abbreviation for above finished floor, usually having to do with measurements such as placing electrical outlets centered 42″ A.F.F.

Apron: Extension below a window or countertop, often provides support.

Asymmetrical: Unequal but balanced design arrangement.

BF: Abbreviation for a base filler

Blind cabinet: Base or wall corner cabinets that are partially concealed by its adjacent cabinet. A filler is required to provide proper door and drawer clearance.

Built-ins: Cabinets designed to be permanently installed.

Bun feet: Low turned legs, usually 3″ to 7″ high.

Butt joint: A plain square joint between two members.

Coastline: Bumping out cabinetry to create a staggered front profile.

Corbels: Decorative supports or brackets usually made of wood.

Custom cabinetry: Factory or shop-built cabinetry made to exact specifications.

Decorator matching doors: Doors applied to the exposed ends of cabinets for a paneled look. A wood veneer skin is usually required for cabinets with frame extensions. *See* Skins and End panels.

Dimensional lumber: Pre-cut lumber in standard sizes.

Dovetail drawers: A construction technique that joins the corners of the drawer box by interlocking wedge-shaped joints. The term is often associated with very high quality construction.

End panels (wall, tall, and base): Veneer paneling applied to the exposed ends of cabinets. Decorator matching doors are often applied on top of the end panels. *See also* Skins.

Ergonomics: Coordinating the relationship between the human body and work surfaces, furniture, and equipment allowing minimum fatigue.

Flat deck countertop: A countertop made without a backsplash.

Framed cabinets: Cabinets made with a face frame attached to the sides of the cabinet. Doors are installed on the frame.

Frame extensions: Recess created on framed cabinet sides where the side is set back approximately 1/4″ from the front frame. Also called reveals.

Frameless cabinetry: Cabinets with doors hung directly to the sides of the case.

Full overlay: Cabinet style that features a door that nearly covers the frame. It is considered sleeker and more contemporary.

Light rail: Molding usually applied beneath wall cabinets to conceal undercabinet lighting or to add a decorative look.

Mullion doors: Cabinet doors with slender vertical and horizontal dividing bars and usually backed with glass inserts.

Other-room furniture: A term used to describe built-ins throughout the house that are fabricated from kitchen cabinetry.

Open floor plan: House plans with minimal wall structures, creating rooms that flow from one to another. Kitchens are usually open to an adjacent room, often the family public area.

Open frame doors: Cabinet doors made without a center panel for decorative inserts.

Scale: Drawn or built according to a fixed ratio. Architects draw to 1/4″ = 1′-0″ scale and the cabinet industry generally works in 1/2″ = 1′-0″ scale.

Scarf joint: An angled, lapped joint used when joining lengths of molding.

Semi-custom cabinets: Factory-made cabinets with a variety of options, sizes, and accessories.

Skins: Veneer paneling applied to the exposed ends of cabinets. Decorator matching doors are often applied on top of the skins.

Soffit board: A flat, finished board placed behind a valance to close in the space.

Solid surface material: Homogeneous material often used for countertops. It is a composite, often made from acrylic or polyester materials.

Split: Indicates that paneling or filler is cut (not always equally) and used is more than one place.

Standard overlay: Cabinet style that features a door smaller than the cabinet frame. It is considered more traditional in style.

Staging area: Area set aside to assemble items for a project. When the term refers to the kitchen, it generally means the area designated for either meal preparation or serving.

Stock cabinetry: Moderately priced, modular cabinetry made to standard dimensions.

Symmetrical: Designs that are exactly the same on either side of an imaginary centerline.

TF: Abbreviation for tall filler. Tall fillers vary in height from 80″ to 96″.

Thermofoil: A synthetic material used to sheathe cabinet doors. It is most often used on white cabinetry and produces a seamless finish.

Toe kick cap covers: Wood caps applied to the end of the cabinet toe kick for a finished look.

Substrate: Material used as a backer to provide support for a more decorative material. Substrate is usually plywood or particleboard.

VF: Abbreviation for a vanity filler.

WF: Abbreviation for a wall filler.

Wainscoting: Wooden paneling treatment used on the backs of desks, islands, or on wall areas.

Appendix

The following list represents manufacturers, wholesalers and retail companies. Some manufacturers may require large minimum orders, but most can refer you to distributors that can meet smaller needs.

Built-in Ironing Boards

Woodworker's Supply

CD Storage

Amerock Industries
FM Plastics
Rockler Woodworking and Hardware
Woodworker's Supply

Cabinet Locks

Ilco Unican
Woodworker's Supply

Cane Door Insets

Rockler Woodworking and Hardware

Castors

C.H. Briggs
Doug Mockett & Co., Inc.
Hafele
Outwater Plastics Industries
Rockler Woodworking and Hardware
Van Dyke's Restorers
Woodworker's Supply

Corbels

Van Dyke's Restorers
Hafele

Decorative Hardware

Amerock
C.H. Briggs
Berenson Decorative Hardware
Outwater Plastics Industries
Restoration Hardware
Rockler Woodworking and Hardware
Van Dyke's Restorers
Woodworker's Supply

Door Inserts

Hafele
Outwater Plastics Industries

Gift Wrap Holder/Cutters

Elman Labels

Hoosier Accessories

Van Dyke's Restorers

Keyboard Trays

C.H. Briggs
Hafele
Rockler Woodworking and Hardware
Woodworker's Supply

Library Ladders

Rockler Woodworking and Hardware

Lighting

C.H. Briggs
Outwater Plastics Industries
Hafele
Rockler Woodworking and Hardware
Van Dyke's Restorers
Woodworker's Supply

Table Legs/Wood Turnings

Adams Wood Products
Doug Mockett & Co., Inc.
Osborne Wood Products
Van Dyke's Restorers
Woodworker's Supply

TV Lifts

Inca Corp.

TV Swivels

C.H. Briggs
Hafele

Wire Management Grommets

Alliance Plastics
Hardware Concepts Inc.
Outwater Plastics Industries

Wood Appliqués

Hafele
Outwater Plastics Industries
Rockler Woodworking and Hardware
Van Dyke's Restorers
White River Hardwoods
Woodworker's Supply

Wood Moldings

Hafele
Klise Mfg. Co.
Rockler Woodworking and Hardware
Outwater Plastics Industries

Directory of Suppliers

Adams Wood Products
P.O. 728
Morristown, TN 37815-0728
Phone: 423/587-2942
FAX: 423/586-2188
www.adamswoodproducts.com

Alliance Plastics
10024 Romandel Avenue
Santa Fe, CA 90670
Toll Free: 888/867-3737
FAX: 562/944-6852
www.finishingproducts.com

Amerock Industries
4000 Auburn Street
P.O. Box 7018
Rockford, IL 61125
Phone: 815/969-6308
FAX: 815/969-6138
www.amerock.com

Berenson Decorative Hardware
2495 Main Street, Suite 222
Buffalo, NY 14214-2152
Phone: 716/833-3100
FAX: 716/833-2402
www.berensonhardware.com

C.H. Briggs
2047 Kutztown Road
Reading, PA 19612
Toll Free: 800/355-1000
FAX: 800/355-3131
www.chbriggs.com

Doug Mockett & Co., Inc.
Box 3333
Manhattan Beach, CA 90266
Toll Free: 800/523-1269
FAX: 800/235-77443
www.mockett.com

Elman Labels
9301 Gaither Road
Gaithersburg, MD 20877
Toll Free: 800/442-2247
FAX: 301/417-9310

FM Plastics
9950 Marconi Drive, Suite 105
San Diego, CA 92154
Phone: 619/661-5929
FAX: 619/661-5977
www.fm-plastics.com

Hafele America
P.O. Box 4000
Archdale, NC 27263
Toll Free: 800/423-3531
FAX: 336/431-3831
www.hafeleonline.com

Hardware Concepts
4780 NW 128th St. Rd.
Opa Locka, FL 33054
Phone: 305/685-1101
FAX: 305/685-1505
www.hardwareconcepts.com

Ilco Unican
2941 Indiana Avenue
Winston Salem, NC 27105
Phone: 336/725-1331
Toll Free FAX: 800/346-9640
www.ilcounican.com

Inca Corp.
13030 Cerise Avenue
Hawthorne, CA 90250
Phone: 310/676-0070
FAX: 310/676-0339

Klise Mfg. Co.
601 Maryland Avenue NE
Grand Rapids, MI 49505
Phone: 616/459-4283
FAX: 616/459-4062
www.klisemfg.com

Osborne Wood Products
8116 Highway 123
Toccoa, GA 30577
Toll Free: 800/849-8875
FAX: 706/886-8526
www.osbornewood.com

Outwater Plastics Industries
22 Passaic Street
P.O. Box 347
Wood-Ridge, NJ 07075
Toll Free: 800/835-4400
FAX: 800/835-4403
www.outwater.com

Restoration Hardware
104 Challenger Drive
Portland, TN 37148-1703
Toll Free: 800/762-1005
FAX: 615/325-1398
www.restorationhardware.com

Rockler Woodworking and Hardware
4365 Willow Drive
Medina, MN 55340
Toll Free: 800/279-4441
FAX:800/865-1229
www.rockler.com

Van Dyke's Restorers
39771 SD HWY 34 E.
P.O. Box 278
Woonsocket, SD 57385
Toll Free: 800/558-1234
Phone: 605/796-4425
FAX: 605/796-4085
www.vandykes.com

White River Hardwoods
1197 Happy Hollow Road
Fayetteville, AR 72701
Toll Free: 800/558-0119
FAX: 501/442-0257
www.mouldings.com

Woodworker's Supply
1108 North Glenn Road
Casper, WY 82601
Toll Free: 800/645-9292
FAX: 800/853-9663

Note: Every effort was made to verify the accuracy of this list at the time of printing. However, suppliers may change phone numbers and web sites without notice.

Index

About the Author

Connie Edwards, CKD, CBD (certified kitchen and bath designer) has been involved with the cabinet industry for more than twenty-five years. She is an Allied Member of ASID and a chairholder in the Color Marketing Group.

Ms. Edwards' design work and articles of the trade appear nationally. As director of design for American Woodmark Corporation, she is involved in showroom display design as well as trade show management, design training, and showhouse design. She is a member of the Board of Trustees for The National Council of Housing Industry, a council of the National Home Builders' Association. She is also chairman of the manufacturers council of NKBA (National Kitchen and Bath Association).

Being well known in the industry, Ms. Edwards has appeared on *HGTV* as well as on *Good Morning America*. She frequently speaks nationally at trade shows, such as the Kitchen and Bath Industry Show and the International Builders Show, on topics such as trends, project management, and design.